DATE DUE

DEC 0 6 2017

CANON
FODDER

CANON
FODDER

HISTORICAL
WOMEN
POLITICAL
THINKERS

PENNY A. WEISS

THE PENNSYLVANIA STATE UNIVERSITY PRESS
UNIVERSITY PARK, PENNSYLVANIA

LIBRARY OF CONGRESS CATALOGING-IN-PUBLICATION DATA

Weiss, Penny A.
    Canon fodder : historical women political thinkers /
Penny A. Weiss.
            p.   cm.
Includes bibliographical references and index.
Summary: "A discussion of women thinkers in political
philosophy, and the nature of political inquiry" — Provided
by publisher.
ISBN 978-0-271-03519-2 (cloth : alk. paper)
ISBN 978-0-271-03520-8 (ppk : alk. paper)
1. Women political scientists.
2. Women political scientists — History.
3. Feminism — Political aspects.
I. Title.

JA92.W45   2009
320.092'2 — dc22
2009000981

To BERENICE CARROLL,
whose light has inspired many.
With love, admiration, and gratitude.

CONTENTS

PREFACE

As a senior in college, finally and reluctantly taking the dreaded theory class required of all political science majors, I fell in love with political theory. Unlike the law classes I repeatedly and eagerly enrolled in, theory, I assumed, would be politically irrelevant and mysteriously difficult. Nonetheless, practically from the moment I cracked the covers of Plato's *Republic* and Aristotle's *Politics* I loved the questions that were being asked, the debates about the answers, the styles of writing, and the connections between ideas and practices that testify to theory's importance.

However, even as I was falling in love with theory, I was also wrestling with what was being said about women, trying to overlook it, correct it, or explain it away. I was embarrassed for myself and the authors, unaccepting of what they had to say, and certainly not elevated or enlightened by it. In *The Book of the City of Ladies* (1405), Christine de Pizan introduces Christine, a character who has "great love . . . for inquiring into the truth of things through long and continuous study" (Pizan 1997, 123). Not despite but because of her study, Christine "despised [her]self and the entire feminine sex" (120). As Pizan knew, any woman accepting philosophy's verdicts about women would be filled with self-hatred and disdain for her sex. "I cannot understand this hostility," she confessed (120). Lady Reason suggests that Christine stop "think[ing] that all the words of the philosophers," despite their status, "are articles of faith and that they cannot be wrong" (122). Indeed! We should also start reading some different philosophers. Questioning what the canon has to say about women only begins to tap into what constitutes its patriarchal assumptions and approaches.

Even in graduate school, I never read political philosophy written by a woman. Ever since then, however, I have been trying to fix that. As I look back on the syllabus of the first course I taught in the history of feminist theory, in 1988, I see that about half of it was feminist analysis of male thinkers. But I had begun my quest, for also on the syllabus were Emma Goldman, Mary Wollstonecraft, and Simone de Beauvoir. I never would have guessed, as I opened up the *Republic,* where the journey would take me. From the moment I discovered this other history, this is the book I have wanted to write, or pretty darn close to it, which is so exciting and amazing to me. I feel as though I have been working on it for about twenty years; it has been a lengthy reeducation. I am a little anxious about cutting the cord, continually tempted as I am to tinker and embolden, but I am definitely ready for some new projects, too. "Here goes everything," is kind of how letting go of this one feels, as though it is the last child leaving home (what a coincidence).

Discovering historical women political thinkers is what has sustained me in academia, a world that has never really felt like home. Whether because of my working-class background, my politics, or my personality, the university and I have long been a little uncomfortable with one another. I am grateful to Purdue University especially for the opportunity to teach what I want (usually) how I want to teach it (always) and for an office in which to work, with my beloved books all around me. Purdue has also given me some cherished colleagues, as well as a small grant that enabled me to visit Howard University, home of Anna Julia Cooper's papers. The first woman to earn tenure in the political science department, I have had my fair share of struggles there, too. As I finish this book I am also closing things up at Purdue, frustrated by low pay and credibility. Choosing not to live with so much resentment, and offered greener pastures, I look eagerly forward to what comes next, as I move on to become the director of women's studies at St. Louis University. Thanks especially, and best wishes, to the women and the theorists in the department.

My largest debt is to my students. For twenty years they have been on this road with me. I learn from their questions, responses, and papers and feed off their intellectual and political energy. Since I wrote this book without major grants or leaves, nearly everything in it emerged from my classroom. I have tried out all the ideas in this book in the classroom first. We read texts no one else was reading, and they wrote about them in ways that sometimes gave me goose bumps, for they took the authors and their essays as seriously as they took any canonical thinker, not always knowing how remarkable that was. I'm never sure how serious other academics are when they talk about learning from their students, but I have certainly learned *with* mine, and this book would not exist without them.

My deepest intellectual debt is to Berenice Carroll and Hilda Smith. They were two of the organizers of a 1991 National Endowment for the Humanities Summer Seminar, "Integrating Women into the Undergraduate

Curriculum," where I first encountered some of the women I write about here, and both continue to support and inspire me personally and through their work.

In the end, the challenge to political theory presented here is a broad and deep one, touching on who we read, what questions we ask, and how we talk about core issues. It doesn't take balls to question the legitimacy of philosophy's canon, or the necessity of a canon at all. In fact, given that men are celebrated by the canon as, variously, more rational, more political, more courageous, more virtuous, and decidedly more influential, they may get in the way. Perhaps it takes ovaries to deliver.

Chapter 3, "The Politics of Form," is a modestly revised version of "Sei Shōnagon and the Politics of Form," published in *Journal of Political Philosophy* (2008) despite the fact that the editor said I should assume that no reader had ever heard of Sei Shōnagon. I thank that editor for taking the chance. Chapter 6, "Childhood: Emma Goldman," was written for *Feminist Interpretations of Emma Goldman* (Pennsylvania State University Press, 2007), a lovely collection I coedited with Loretta Kensinger and urge you all to read, as it is the first book to treat Goldman as a political thinker. Chapter 7, "Power: Mary Astell," appeared in *Hypatia: A Journal of Feminist Philosophy* (2004) as "Including Women's Voices in Political Thought." It went through many revisions to please their always demanding but encouraging editors and readers. I thank these presses for permission to reprint my work.

INTRODUCTION: SEARCH AND RECOVER

I was once shocked to discover that feminist theorists actually existed as far back as we have records of political writings. As traditionally trained as possible, with a Ph.D. from Notre Dame (the fighting Yiddish?),[1] I was introduced as a student to only those exalted male figures who to this day continue with astonishing perseverance to dominate every textbook, syllabus, journal, and conference in political theory. It was simply understood that there *were* no women political philosophers (a few of my peers and teachers thought that unfortunate). Well, not only is that familiar understanding completely without merit, it is not even true that there is a "*relative* absence of texts in the history of political thought . . . by women," or that "female (let alone feminist) texts in political thought [a]re an anomaly" (Springborg 1995, 621; emphasis added). What we are faced with is not the absence of writings—they exist in gratifying abundance. The seemingly intractable problems include, instead, failure to keep works by women theorists in print, paucity of academic commentary on the texts, an unmistakable pattern of underestimation and careless analysis in the few judgments on those texts that scholars have rendered (Carroll 1990), and omission of women philosophers in standard college courses.

After the shock of discovery wore off came anger. Thinking back, I was mildly infuriated, for example, that I had to sit through a "Medieval Political Thought" class studying what for me were the nearly unbearable texts of Augustine and Aquinas, when I could have at least also been reading, to name just a few from those same centuries, Hildegard of Bingen; or Saint Catherine of Siena; or Theresa of Avila; or Christine de Pizan; or even, taking a more global approach, Sei Shōnagon or Murasaki Shikibu. I was incensed that liberalism was taught without reference to women such as

---

1. I learned this from Roz Saz, a dear friend in my years at Notre Dame.

Mary Wollstonecraft or Harriet Taylor, that anarchism was written about without mention of women like Emma Goldman or Voltairine de Cleyre, that one could read collections on "the Enlightenment" or "democratic theory" and never learn about a single woman who contributed masterfully to such eras or bodies of thought. In fact, whether the approach of teachers and texts was based on concepts or periods of time or schools of thought, women vanished from reading lists in a remarkable political process of erasure. To this day hefty tomes with unabashedly bold and sweeping titles such as *Readings in Classical Political Thought* (Steinberger 2000) and *Classics of Moral and Political Theory* (M. Morgan 2006) include not a single female thinker.[2] Even today, in what is supposed to be "postfeminism," publishers persist in regularly reissuing nearly identical selections from the all-male roster of noteworthy thinkers, and it remains ridiculously rare to find more than token inclusion of women thinkers—at the tail end of the book, speaking only on the subject of feminism. A few female figures are beginning to make repeated appearances—most notably Wollstonecraft, Hannah Arendt, and Simone de Beauvoir—often because editors can link them easily, though not always correctly, to canonized male writers or established schools of thought. But we have barely begun to tap the lengthy list of women thinkers that some date back to Enheduanna (around 2300 B.C.E.), to read them on the wide range of topics they addressed, to understand the diverse theoretical frameworks they used in their work, and to reflect on the contributions they can make to our thinking about and living in various political communities.[3]

As more and more women thinkers throughout the history of political thought are brought to light, I am no longer surprised, though I am occasionally still frustrated by those who both continue to act as if these thinkers did not exist and nonetheless exert much influence in the field. Ultimately, though, I find myself absolutely delighted by the amount of material they produced and the depths and integrity of its intellectual challenges. My goal in this book is to urge inclusion of a broad array of female theorists in the conversations that constitute the history of political ideas (Weiss 1998, 1). To accomplish this I show a favored set of them both working with and contesting traditional categories and concepts of political thought and offer

2. With these works at more than six hundred and twelve hundred pages, respectively, lack of space would be a tough justification. The latter is even in its fourth edition, and still no women.

3. Carroll writes that Enheduanna's writings constitute "the earliest significant body of literary-political works by a named author, male or female, that have survived to the present" (Smith and Carroll 2000, 3).

comparisons of them with more familiar political thinkers. Throughout, I also use the ideas and examples of a larger troupe of theorists to give a small sense of the still-growing roster from which we can all draw. I hope I convey some of the reasons for my own intellectual and political enthusiasm for their writings.

THE TITLE

cannon fodder: *n:* soldiers subject to the risk of being wounded or killed by artillery fire

Individuals might choose to be involved in a particular war, but no one wants to be cannon fodder, with all it implies about being exposed to attacks from all sides (and protected by none), finding oneself in the thick of every fight, and being treated as expendable. In my referring to historical women philosophers as "canon fodder," the primary image I have in mind is of women thinkers as needless and unjustifiable casualties of various culture wars, those enduring arguments about what art and literature and philosophy should be studied for its quality and influence.

The "Western canon" is a body of literature and art said to define either Western civilization or the educated person within it. The same widespread consensus that supposedly determines who shall live forever, in books enshrined on the shelves of every respectable library and educated person (who can afford them), also decides what losses are acceptable and who shall be sacrificial lambs to what cultural gods. Remote and academic as they sometimes appear, debates about what to include in the canon ultimately touch almost everyone: students handed texts from lists of "great books" to guide them, for example; members of groups whose history and literature is more or less available or widely known; and citizens whose governments justify their actions with ideas from political texts deemed classic.

While there is an element of joyful wordplay involved in the title, ultimately analogies are useful in life, law, and literature because of their power to help us see something from a new angle. *Cannon fodder* is a political expression. It reveals and criticizes how some group is being treated, usually by the government or the military, and details the losses that mistreatment entails. The implication is that avoidable injuries and deaths are not being avoided, or are even being purposely inflicted, to serve some other end or supposedly greater good.

In calling historical women political theorists canon fodder, I am also using the phrase as part of a political critique. The works of these thinkers have been deemed by the gatekeepers of the canon as dispensable, relatively worthless, despite the fact that the texts have often not even been read by them, much less seriously studied, and that the standards used to mark them as inferior are, as I show in the following chapter, both questionable and inconsistently applied. All sides seem to come together in this: antifeminism provides rare common ground between socialist, liberal, and conservative political theorists, between individualists and communitarians, statists and anarchists. Women in general and women political thinkers in particular are, variously, ignored, underestimated, plagiarized, and ridiculed. They are canon fodder: attacked from all sides, their ideas are silenced, their protest punished, and their visions erased or mocked, for the sake of maintaining the beauty and purity of a canon that has no interest in the pleasure of their company. Their often nontraditional personal lives get the attention their ideas deserve, and are unimaginatively and disingenuously used against them, while every flaw in their work is considered potentially fatal, giving them responsibility for their own demise.

The realms of action and thought depend upon each other; they are neither always easily distinguishable nor independent. I take women's erasure from the history of ideas to be part of what many refer to as a broader "war against women"; thus, rediscovering and reconsidering them is, potentially, literally vitally important. The significance of parallels and connections between *cannon fodder* and *canon fodder* outweighs my reservations about using military terms, especially during the current "war on terror" when their renewed popularity seems evidence that they effectively function to normalize and justify violence.

FRAMEWORK FOR THIS BOOK

My work on historical women political thinkers can be placed in the larger context of feminist and political theory in a number of different ways. First, it contributes most obviously to the study of individual figures such as Anna Julia Cooper, Christine de Pizan, Mary Wollstonecraft, Sei Shōnaganon, Emma Goldman, Mary Astell, and Elizabeth Cady Stanton. Second, it adds to the study of important concepts in political thought, such as revolution and community, knowledge and power, childhood and equality. Third, though to a lesser extent, it speaks to contemporary debates about different feminist theories, especially the liberal-radical divide. Finally, this work contributes to the history of political thought generally, introducing neglected figures or incorporating them back into the world of ideas in which they played or could play such important parts, perhaps even inviting reconsideration of political theory's main actors and philosophical divides.

In Part 1, I use a range of thinkers from the history of feminist theory to discuss political inquiry itself. Here political theory and epistemology overlap. In Chapter 1, "The Politics of the Canon: Gatekeepers and Gate-Crashers," I confront a number of arguments used to explain or defend women's absence from the canon. To make the conversation as grounded as possible, I look in political theory and philosophy textbooks for editors' justifications for including and excluding specific philosophers and use the irrefutably impressive accomplishments of historical women political thinkers to challenge the editors. While these textbooks use criteria that are not wholly irrational, as judges like to say, neither are they truly receptive to consideration of many great works or consistently applied. Even a criterion that sounds simple, uncontroversial, and innocuous, such as being "influential," is tough to measure: influence how, on whom, and as evidenced by what, for example? What about unacknowledged indebtedness? Indirect influence? Influence measured by pains taken to discount someone's work? Potential influence? Finally, I examine the grounds for inclusion offered by editors of feminist theory collections and consider what consequences they are likely to have on whom and what we read.

In Chapter 2, "The Politics of Ignorance: Christine de Pizan," I shift the focus from women's exclusion from the canon in general to forms of exclusion that persist even in contemporary feminist theory. While I conclude that there are differences in feminist and antifeminist practices, both result in perpetuating an all-male history of political theory. I look to Christine de Pizan to provide both the theoretical framework for this examination (the politics of ignorance), and the style of argument (confrontational conversation). Again I use numerous historical women political thinkers to support my claims and to argue for their importance. Patterns of ignorance can be political phenomena that, Pizan argues, need urgently to be remedied.

Next, Chapter 3, "The Politics of Form: Sei Shōnagon," is also about what we read and confronts the argument that women have written in forms that do not constitute or are incompatible with political thinking. I use Sei Shōnagon as a fascinating case study—an author who used forms of writing that were associated with both the feminine and the nonphilosophical. Focusing on her use of lists, in particular, I question in what forms and genres political theory might be found. I even use some of her style from *The Pillow Book* to make the argument.

The use of historical women figures themselves in Part 1 to make the arguments about the history of political theory is perhaps the most unique feature of this text. I am true to the spirit of my own work by not only studying the ideas of these thinkers, but also using them. Each chapter becomes a demonstration of the power of their thought, and their work itself becomes part of a larger argument, genuine applications that add to the explication of them. After all, for example, Sei Shōnagon's style of writing in the tenth century can itself be used to argue for openness to variety of form in political thought. Not only can Pizan's fifteenth-century argument about the literary misrepresentation of women help us to understand feminist misrepresentation of our feminist foremothers such as Pizan herself, her style can be imitated as a useful form of friendly political confrontation.

In Part 2, I examine political thought in a more traditional manner, through explication of texts, though I treat neglected subjects, works, and theorists. Chapter 4, "Community: Mary Wollstonecraft and Anna Julia Cooper," focuses on the two figures of Wollstonecraft and Cooper. In it, I challenge some annoyingly persistent interpretations of Wollstonecraft that do not do justice to her politics, and I introduce a very beloved Anna Julia Cooper into my work, and into political theory, where she has rarely been studied at all and never on this particular subject. Together, I argue, they suggest a politics of community distinct from that usually associated with communitarian political thought.

Chapter 5, "Revolution: Declaration of Sentiments at Seneca Falls" is the first serious study of the politics expressed in the Declaration of Sentiments, the neglect of which sits oddly next to assertions of the 1848 document's groundbreaking importance. My argument is that *Sentiments* simply cannot be understood as the Declaration of Independence extended to women; it contains a broader, more radical understanding of oppression and of revolution.

I take a thematic approach to the work of Goldman (Chapter 6) and Astell (Chapter 7) as well, tracing one theme in each (childhood and power, respectively). In the chapter on Goldman I consider connections between childhood and politics. Goldman is, I argue, useful as one model of how to include children's lives more fully in political theorizing and why it is important to do so. In the chapter on power I ask what social relationships political theory studies through the lens of power dynamics and contrast the answers of Astell and Thomas Hobbes. Finally, Chapter 8, "Equality: Quilted Voices," is a sort of experiment in which I collect feminist ideas on equality and put them next to one another for the first time to see what kinds of patterns and emphases we get.

Overall, I show feminist thinkers throughout history wrestling with what the canon has recognized as core topics but has treated narrowly (power, equality, revolution), as well as those it has dismissed (childhood) or minimized (community) without sufficient cause and with undesirable consequences. I demonstrate what it means to search the works of a foremother for insight into a single concept (Goldman on childhood) and to join their analyses of core ideas to one another and to contemporary discussions (Cooper and Wollstonecraft on community). Throughout, I argue for more attention to documents, essays, books, and theorists that could enrich the field of political thought, and maybe make us all a bit smarter.

The women I chose as the main figures in this volume cover different time periods and political perspectives. They were selected after many rewarding years of teaching their work. Included are some (not all) of the figures that had a great impact on me and my students; those I found myself enthusiastically coming back to, to teach and study again and again; those who intrigued me; those from whom I learned important things; those I wanted to talk about with colleagues: women whom political theorists should know. While I focus on but a handful, I make repeated references to a wide range of others in order to offer readers a fuller sense of the number and variety that exist, opinions to the contrary notwithstanding.

CONTRIBUTIONS TO POLITICAL THEORY

The Study of Individual Women Thinkers

Indisputable evidence of the growing attention being given to women political thinkers can be found in the exciting new editions of their original writings being published, including the papers of Harriet Taylor Mill (Jacobs 1998), Margaret Cavendish (James 2003), Anna Julia Cooper (Lemert and Bhan 1987), Maria W. Stewart (Richardson 1987), Lydia Maria Child (Karcher 1997), and Jane Addams (Elshtain 2002b). Thanks to the Internet, we also have easy access to resources such as the Emma Goldman Papers Project, where the entirety of Goldman's writings is available. Ever more inclusive anthologies of selected and excerpted women's writings are available as well, a contemporary trend that perhaps started with *Feminism: The Essential Historical Writings* (Schneir 1972) and *The Feminist Papers: From Adams to de Beauvoir* (Rossi 1973) and progressed to *Words of Fire: An Anthology of African-American Feminist Thought* (Guy-Sheftall 1995), *The Neglected*

Canon: Nine Women Philosophers First to the Twentieth Century (Dykeman 1999) and *Women's Political and Social Thought* (Smith and Carroll 2000). We now even have texts limited to certain time periods, such as the modern era (Atherton 1994). This trend needs to be continued, accelerated, and expanded to cover more works by more writers from different countries in varied languages with a broader range of foci across the centuries. Ready access to the entirety of their works is utterly essential if debate about their political thought is really to take off in earnest.

As another part of this trend of attention to women thinkers, anthologies of critical essays about their work are coming out, both collections on single authors such as Wollstonecraft (Falco 1996), Beauvoir (Marso and Moynagh 2006) and Pizan (Brabant 1992), and on groups of thinkers (Spender 1983; Tougas and Ebenreck 2000), though the fact that we still encounter titles such as *Introducing Women Philosophers* and blurbs such as "The first book devoted exclusively to Beauvoir's politics" shows the early stage we are in at present. Perhaps most important as a sign of and contribution to serious treatment of women in the history of political thought, a few single-authored texts devoted in their entirety to the study of the ideas (not the lives) of a single woman thinker are finally beginning to appear, among them works on Wollstonecraft (Sapiro 1992; Gunther-Canada 2001), Beauvoir (Simons 1999; Bauer 2001), Pizan (Forhan 2002), Astell (Springborg 2006), Arendt (Canovan 1994), and Addams (Elshtain 2002a). Progress is undeniable.

Smallest of all the subgroups of books on women thinkers are those that, like mine, have a single author examining a number of historical women thinkers. Many books exist in which an author examines a number of canonical *male* thinkers from a feminist perspective, but there is only recent and rare precedent for a broader view of women's contributions to the history of political thought. Catherine Gardner's *Rediscovering Women Philosophers: Philosophical Genre and the Boundaries of Philosophy* (2000) covers Catherine Macaulay, Pizan, Wollstonecraft, George Eliot, and Mechthild of Magdeburg, a list that overlaps with mine only twice. More important, unlike mine, Gardner's book examines a single issue—genre—through the works of these authors; readers here will see that I make modest use of its utterly fascinating and persuasive ideas in my own chapter on "the politics of form," but otherwise I treat more figures on more topics from a more political perspective. In her recent work, *Eight Women Philosophers: Theory, Politics, and Feminism,* Jane Duran discusses Hildegard of Bingen, Anne Conway, Astell, Wollstonecraft, Harriet Taylor Mill, Edith Stein, Simone

Weil, and Beauvoir, a fascinating collection. Again our lists do not overlap much, and Duran is less interested in political theory than in philosophical subfields such as "metaphysics and ontology, theory of value . . . [and] feminist theory of knowledge" (2006, x). Lori Marso's recent *Feminist Thinkers and the Demands of Femininity: The Lives and Work of Intellectual Women* (2006) focuses on Wollstonecraft, Germaine de Staël, Goldman, and Beauvoir. Hers, too, overlaps with my list of thinkers only twice and also differs in its approach—a focus on the intersection between the theorists' ideas and their lives. I tend to shun biography, a stubbornness born of frustration with the way women's lives trump their ideas, though Marso shows that in studying both each can shed light upon the other. I am thrilled and humbled by the opportunity to add to this growing scholarship.

A Conceptual Approach to Political Theory

There is a group of texts in feminist theory that addresses specific concepts in the field of political theory. Sometimes they take an issue already understood as core in political thought and reassess it from new angles—from feminist perspectives. For example, feminist thinkers have tackled such basic political ideas as authority (K. B. Jones 1993), obligation (Hirschmann 1992; Pateman 1979), privacy (Ackelsberg and Shanley 1996), rationality (Lloyd 1984), community (Weiss and Friedman 1995), and power (Hartsock 1983; Janeway 1980). They reassess the meaning of our most central political ideas or their place in the political world. Additional theoretical perspectives and experiences are joined to previous discussion of these concepts, effects on more parties are included, and their compatibility with various forms of equality is newly prioritized.

Work in this broad category sometimes pays increased attention to issues that feminist political thinkers claim have wrongly been neglected or underestimated. Really challenging the boundaries of the political itself, texts here cover ideas and practices such as reproduction (O'Brien 1983), parenting (Rich 1976), misogyny (Dworkin 1974), embodiment (Bordo 1993), care (Tronto 1993), and voice (Griffin 1981). In a way, everything is at stake in determining the boundary lines, both intellectually and in the ways we live. We have repeatedly to reconsider whether to treat an idea or practice as private or public, individual or social, idiosyncratic or systemic, and with what consequences. We analyze them differently depending on their categorization, and we weigh them differently in political life.

A conceptual approach to political thought is central to my work, as shown in the very organization of Part 2 by theme. Unlike most contemporary feminist work on political concepts, mine is grounded in the history of feminist thought; unlike most historical work on political concepts, mine is based on the work of women theorists. In addition, my work includes well-recognized as well as contending ideas. Further, I do not limit my inquiry to what others have narrowly defined as the subject matter of feminism (motherhood, family, love, etc.) or of political theory (the state, justice, etc.), but have let the authors themselves determine the range of topics.

The History of Political Theory

There are feminist reinterpretations of every classic thinker, ancient (*Women and the Ideal Society: Plato's "Republic" and Modern Myths of Gender* [Bluestone 1987]) and modern (*Gendered Community: Rousseau, Sex, and Politics* [Weiss 1993]), more obviously feminist (*Mill and Sexual Equality* [Tulloch 1989]) and much less so (*Fortune Is a Woman: Gender and Politics in the Thought of Niccolò Machiavelli* [Pitkin 1984]). It makes sense that feminist academics turned their attention earliest and frequently to the canon in which we were educated. Numerous volumes have made evident certain patterns by covering multiple figures. Among the earliest of these, appearing in rapid succession, were *The Sexism of Social and Political Theory: Women and Reproduction from Plato to Nietzsche* (L. Clark and Lange 1979), *Women in Western Political Thought* (Okin 1979), and *Public Man, Private Woman: Women in Social and Political Thought* (Elshtain 1981). Among the most recent additions are volumes in the Pennsylvania State University Press series Re-Reading the Canon, which are in fact still being issued.[4]

As I will discuss in Chapter 2, although few of these recent books make adequate reference to it, contemporary scholarship on works now considered

---

4. At present, the series has feminist interpretations of the following canonical male thinkers (their editors and dates of publications are given parenthetically): Plato (Tuana, 1994), Hegel (Mills, 1996), Kant (Schott, 1997), Kierkegaard (Leon and Walsh, 1997), Aristotle (Freeland, 1998), Nietzsche (Oliver and Pearsall, 1998), Descartes (Bordo, 1999), Sartre (Murphy, 1999), Hume (Jacobson, 2000), Levinas (Chanter, 2001), Heidegger (Holland and Huntington, 2001), Dewey (Seigfried, 2001), Wittgenstein (Scheman and O'Connor, 2002), and Rousseau (Lange, 2002). The series has also published volumes on more contemporary male theorists (Foucault [Hekman, 1996], Derrida [Holland, 1997], Gadamer [Code, 2002], Quine [Nelson and Nelson, 2003]), as well as several historical and contemporary women (Beauvoir [Simons, 1995], Arendt [Honig, 1995], Wollstonecraft [Falco, 1996], Rand [Gladstein and Sciabarra, 1999], Daly [Hoagland and Frye, 2000] and Goldman [Weiss and Kensinger, 2007]).

canonical is part of a long feminist tradition. Historically and today, feminist work on the canon has multiple purposes, including discussing often-neglected subjects such as how and with what consequences women and the feminine are characterized, exploring how supposedly gender-neutral ideas such as rationality or political participation are in fact gendered, and seeking in sometimes surprising locations useful "antecedents to feminist philosophy" (Witt 2003, 3).

Because many of the women theorists I cover were often in dialogue with the canon, that is among the aspects of them I explore. In addition, I continue to find comparisons of feminist theorists with canonical male counterparts useful. There is no one right way to introduce feminist theorists to scholars whose training excluded study of them, but certainly it is helpful to build on knowledge we already have as we discuss the unfamiliar. In the chapter on revolution, I compare the Declaration of Sentiments with the (somewhat) more famous Declaration of Independence. The latter document has long been understood to contain important ideas on everything from revolution to political legitimacy. I approach the Declaration of Sentiments searching for its different takes on those same topics, and for places where it introduces ones not addressed by the Declaration of Independence. The essay on power, too, is built on a comparison of feminist and nonfeminist texts, contrasting the relationships of relevance to a political community in the writings of Mary Astell and Thomas Hobbes. The chapter on childhood asks about the place of children in political thought and political life and compares the approach of Emma Goldman to some commonly found in the canon.

These conversations between canonical and noncanonical thinkers restore and reflect the kinds of interaction between them that existed but have been lost to us, losses that distort even our understanding of the endlessly studied main characters. My approach is generally utilitarian: I pick comparisons that can help us read the women who are my central focus. I am aware of and try to skirt two dangers: first, lest my use of the canonical figures distract us from the women, I try not to put forth particularly controversial interpretations of the men. They function here as familiar means to the end of introducing and incorporating women thinkers with whom they contrast fruitfully, and means are self-defeating if they distract us from the goal. Second, I am aware of the danger of using frameworks to read the "newer" figures that are alien to their thought. The men are not the standards here—positive or negative—by which to measure the women, but ways to make the latter visible and comprehensible in their similarities and their differences.

Feminist Theories

Another body of work in feminist political thought explores one or more distinct theories within feminism, such as radical feminist theory, black feminist theory, or ecofeminism. Here, too, there is variety and evolution. Alison Jaggar's relatively early categorization (*Feminist Politics and Human Nature* [1983]) covered liberal, Marxist, radical, and socialist feminisms, for example, while Josephine Donovan's typology (*Feminist Theory: The Intellectual Traditions of American Feminism* [1985]) excluded socialist and added cultural, Freudian, and existential feminisms, and Rosemarie Tong (*Feminist Thought* [1989]) added consideration of psychoanalytic, existentialist, and postmodern feminisms. Texts devoted to a single school of thought may have as their primary purpose to document its debut (*Reweaving the Web: The Emergence of Ecofeminism* [Diamond and Orenstein 1990] and *Opening the Gates: A Century of Arab Feminist Writing* [Badran and Cooke 1990]), to criticize it (*Nothing Mat(t)ers: A Feminist Critique of Postmodernism* [Brodribb 1992]), to push it politically (*The Radical Future of Liberal Feminism* [Eisenstein 1981]), or to make available new developments within it (*Making Face, Making Soul: Creative and Critical Perspectives by Women of Color* [Anzaldúa 1990]). Work today in this broad category continues to define and evaluate distinct approaches to understanding oppression and liberation, to clarify differences between feminist thinkers, to establish the coherence of feminist analytical frameworks, and to link theory and activism.

Reading these contemporary works, one would have to conclude that in the history of feminist theory there is little attention paid to differing feminist frameworks. Perhaps because we have not yet engaged in much comparison of one historical feminist theorist with others, and have frequently treated so many as isolated, anomalous "first feminists," we have simply not delved into how *they* understood their similarities to and differences from one another. I suspect that as we move away from comparing them predominantly to the canonical male theorists, we may find that our typologies of feminist theories have historical precedents. After all, many of our foremothers were familiar not only with the canon but also with challenges to its antifeminism, as the chapter on Pizan, among others, demonstrates.

Further, recent categorizations of feminist thought often misuse or fail really to study the history of feminist thought; most commonly, our foremothers are hastily twisted into categories that are not of their own making, and ideas that do not fit tend to vanish. Readers here will find scattered sections that challenge some categorizations of historical theorists, especially in the chapters on Wollstonecraft and Cooper, Astell, and the Declaration of Sentiments. Even if indirectly, I hope that my attention to these historical figures and texts will contribute to a reassessment that may ultimately lead to relocations of some, and novel use of others. In addition, the essays that compare feminists more with one another than with the usual cast of male political thinkers allows inquiry into feminist traditions, continuities, and conversations that can challenge some of the categories and shift emphasis to common ground rather than difference. Overall, then, my work questions the centrality as well as the comprehensiveness and accuracy of certain categorizations of feminist theory.

CONCLUDING THOUGHTS

I am not arguing for the inclusion of this particular set of women thinkers over another in some eternal canon; like Virginia Woolf, explored later, I am deeply ambivalent about such a project. I am decidedly less interested at this point in "weeding out" than in "reading in," in being open-minded to what can be learned from the reappearance of the disappeared. I do, however, make clear here the politics and costs of the preposterous exclusion of women in general.

As a professor I get to select books every semester for classes in political theory. Who should we read, and why, and in what combinations? I change my book list constantly. I switch to different texts by the same authors and add others by authors I've never taught before. True to the arguments of this book (because my classroom is where I learned these things) I choose not only standard political treatises but also autobiographies and speeches and novels and, when I am feeling particularly brave, poetry and (gasp) even an occasional film. I challenge myself and my students to read from a list dramatically more diverse in a number of ways than that by which I was educated. Sometimes my students are shocked to discover that feminist theorists actually existed as far back as we have records of political writings.

PART 1

RETHINKING POLITICAL THEORY

1

THE POLITICS OF THE CANON:
GATEKEEPERS AND GATE-CRASHERS

How can we understand the invisibility of women in the history of political theory?[1] We might say of this or that particular philosopher that there was some unfortunate or unusual situation that led to her being unpublished or untranslated, unread or misread, or even some perfectly reasonable question about her merit, but how can we understand virtually every single one being overlooked or underappreciated? The rationalizations that have been offered are not simply unconvincing; they testify to the presence of a damaging and dangerous system of preferences and prejudices, injustices and abominations, in which this (usually) semiconscious but determined exclusion plays an important part. The fate of a Mary Wollstonecraft or a Mary Church Terrell is in some ways the fate of an Ida Wells-Barnett or a Rokeya Hossain, and it is a gendered fate. In this chapter I consider several explanations for the male monopoly in the canon of political theory, focusing on those explicitly put forth by editors and authors of all-male anthologies in the history of philosophy and political theory, who are among the gatekeepers of the traditional canon. I respond to these justificatory stories with a variety of historical counterexamples. I also discuss the criteria for inclusion put forth by editors of all-female anthologies in political theory and philosophy to see if they offer anything better, or even interestingly different.

In her 1915 *Are Women People? A Book of Rhymes for Suffrage Times,* Alice Duer Miller responded to opposition to women's suffrage with "Our Own Twelve Anti-suffragist Reasons," composed of "six pairs of antisuffragist 'reasons'... [that] are strictly accurate statements of commonly expressed opinions" (Kraditor 1968, 216). They read:

---

1. This chapter contains several paragraphs from "The Gendered Fate of Political Theorists" (Weiss 1996). The two chapters ask similar questions, but the answers are framed quite differently, and the present chapter is much broader in approach.

Because no woman will leave her domestic duties to vote.

Because no woman who may vote will attend to her domestic duties.

Because it will make dissension between husband and wife.

Because every woman will vote as her husband tells her to.

Because bad women will corrupt politics.

Because bad politics will corrupt women.

Because women have no power of organization.

Because women will form a solid party and outvote men.

Because men and women are so different that they must stick to different duties.

Because men and women are so much alike that men, with one vote each, can represent their own views and ours too.

Because women cannot use force.

Because the militants did use force. (Miller 1968, 218–19)

This skillful arrangement of "commonly expressed opinions" neatly demonstrates that, in pairs, they cancel each other out. Politically, the contradictory pairings reveal the backseat taken by logic and consistency and integrity and rational argument in the face of serious threats to a system of different and unequal rights and duties, a familiar occurrence in both political theory and practice.[2]

Marilyn Frye looks at systemic contradictions from a related angle: the double bind.

> One of the most characteristic and ubiquitous features of the world as experienced by oppressed people is the double bind—situations in which options are reduced to a very few and all of them expose one to penalty, censure or deprivation. For example, it is often a requirement upon oppressed people that we smile and be cheerful. If we comply, we signal our docility and our acquiescence in our situation. We need not, then, be taken note of. We acquiesce in being made invisible, in our occupying no space. We participate in our own erasure. On the other hand, anything but the sunniest countenance exposes us to being perceived as mean, bitter, angry or dangerous. This means, at the least, that we may be found "difficult" or unpleasant to work with, which is enough to cost one one's livelihood; at worst, being seen as

2. For example, Pateman writes: "Political theories that were, ostensibly, universalist gave women powerful intellectual weapons, but men disregarded the claims of reason where their rule was at stake" (1998, 372).

mean, bitter, angry or dangerous has been known to result in rape, arrest, beating and murder. (1983, 2–3)

When options are limited, and each alternative is restricting or self-defeating, you cannot win. When, over and over again, the power and integrity of one's arguments fail to convince and the charges of injustice go unheard, whether the issue is suffrage or dress or sexual behavior or ethics or work or family or inclusion in the canon, only a political explanation will suffice, a macroscopic view. Feminist political theory is especially suited to provide analysis of how both official policies and unofficial practices relate to systems, structures, and power relationships. As seen in the Declaration of Sentiments, which I explore later in this book, it understands patriarchy as a form of rule and as an organism that adapts as circumstances require. It also understands the "governmental" to cover only a small fraction of the territory of the "political," as the later chapter on Astell discusses, and sees the critical, the profound, and the theoretical often residing and embodied in what others have deemed trivial. It confronts phenomena that are widespread, are systemic, have a severely differential impact on different populations, and contribute to various forms of inequality.

In Miller's clever pairing of antisuffragist arguments, she shows that women sometimes cannot win. It does not matter if one proves that women are different from men or establishes that they are the same as men; either way, they do not deserve to vote. Whether women agree or disagree with their husbands about politics, they should not vote. Regardless of whether women are portrayed as pure or corrupt, peaceful or violent, the bottom line is that the rights and duties of men and women should differ. "Reasons" will be used to defend this inequality as they are useful, not because they are valid. When such politics allow a "win," the accepted rationale for it often blesses and reinforces gender inequality and delegitimizes further demands.

Returning now to women political theorists, I offer my own pairs of "explanations" for their absence from the canon of political thought, all of which one can too easily actually encounter in academic discourse and dialogue.

Because women philosophers have not existed for most of human history.
Because there are so many women who might be called political thinkers
    that including them would make the canon unwieldy or lead to the
    exclusion of deserving men.

Because women did not write about politics.

Because women's writings are too political.

Because women have not written theory.

Because women have "only" synthesized, amended, adjusted, adapted, and expanded others' ideas and theories.

Because works by women fit into no established traditions or schools.

Because they are all derivative from the works of men.

Because women's writings are narrow, focused too heavily on gender concerns.

Because they address too many issues.

Because women thinkers were not influential.

Because they influenced only other women.

As in Miller's list, here, too, proffered "explanations" cancel each other out. After they negate each other, what remains seems to be merely a determination to exclude women rather than legitimate or even genuinely thoughtful reasons for doing so. In the end, the issue is not that women theorists are too political or not political enough, write like men or do not write like men; as with suffrage, the bottom line is that the canon should contain the already recognized men and their supposedly universally acknowledged classics, and whatever reasons effectively exclude women will be used, the dubious validity of the reasons notwithstanding. Let us turn to the words of the canon's supporters and gatekeepers as found in all-male versions of the history of political theory and philosophy.

CONFUSION AND VAGUENESS

The selection has been confined to a few authors, for reasons not only of space, or of limitations of my own knowledge (though either of these reasons would have been sufficient), but because it is part of the plan of the book to concentrate attention upon the most important works.

—Michael B. Foster, *Masters of Political Thought*, vol. 1

In saying that the limits of his present personal knowledge would be an unproblematic basis for choosing authors for his history, Foster marks the matter of selection as one of relatively little significance and shows how we often merely inherit our lists of "important works." In fact, many authors are silent about why they chose certain works and individuals over others, as if either it were an obvious no-brainer without need of explanation, or it never even occurred to them that there were debatable preferences to consider and controversial decisions to make, ultimately with far-reaching consequences. "The restriction of names and of subject matter is easy enough," Clark assures us (G. Clark 1957, vi).[3] Trust me.

Looking over Thiele's text, one wonders if his inattention to women, like his relative neglect of non-Western figures, is also "owing to the author's own restricted exposure to other traditions of political thought" (L. P. Thiele 2003, xii). These editors are not owning up to some merely inevitable limits of how much material any individual can master, but are acknowledging a pattern of ignorance, a bias resulting in the exclusion of distinct groups of thinkers that they nevertheless do not feel called upon to remedy. They mention the deficiency as if it was unproblematic, even inconsequential. Presses apparently agree. But such complacency signals a kind of intellectual laziness and a dereliction of philosophical duty. If it truly makes no difference who is chosen (a view with which I admit some sympathy, finding adequate opportunities to philosophize in all sorts of places), are we to think it just an inconsequential coincidence that the same folks keep getting reserved seats while others are consistently turned away at the door (perhaps for appearing without a coat and tie)? At the very least we need to explore the effects on theory of these biases, and more to the point, we need to correct them.

Up one step from those who perpetuate the canon without much defense are texts with criteria so vague as to create meaningless standards. Included in this category would be Dagobert D. Runes, who includes almost four hundred individuals in his 1959 *Treasury of World Philosophy* out of "about ten thousand men and a score of women who have some claim to be classed as philosophers." Not one of that underestimated "score of women" made the cut. If one looks to see what test they failed, here is what Runes tells us about the "difficult . . . process of selecting": "All these men whom I have brought together under the roof of this volume have, at certain times in their lives, sat down to meditate upon the wondrous themata that came to their minds in uncharted realms" (xxiii). I am not certain what that accomplishment even means, but it seems dramatically unhelpful; I imagine one could conjure reasons for or against inclusion of any particular thinker based on it. He does convey some consciousness about his choices, noting

---

3. In a similar way, editors, authors, and teachers often speak uncritically about the division of political philosophy into historical eras and fundamental concepts. Yet in these processes, too, like canon construction, women can indirectly be erased with hardly a mention of their existence. This contrasts forcefully with the idea that decisions about the canon are the product of open, rigorous, and sustained reflection.

that he has "listed American philosophers" (xxiv) and "taken care to include in this anthology a considerable number of Hebrew, Chinese, and other Oriental minds who have generally been ignored by our Western-focussed historians" (xxiii–xiv). Why he felt that that was justified and necessary as opposed or in addition, say, to including women ignored by male-focused historians of philosophy, remains a mystery. He acknowledges "the unavoidable coloring of choice by personal taste" (xxiv), but also fails to reveal what his personal taste is for, or how those whom he selected conform to it. Runes is not alone.

A third and much larger group of histories including only men of distinction offer assertions of greatness as reason for inclusion. Too often, decisions about whom to include in a survey text or course syllabus are simply based upon who is included in other survey texts and course syllabi. Some supposed "consensus" about who is worthy almost simultaneously emerges and is appealed to in a dizzyingly self-reinforcing circle. As one editor explains his choices, "The usual problem with a book of readings is that it is difficult to have a consensus on the selections, but by listing only the indisputable classics and by having lengthy selections this problem is solved" (Porter 1997, xiv). No need to loiter. Porter's process of following the road more traveled appears uncontroversial, as indisputable as the chosen classics themselves. Over the decades, appeals to something like Porter's universally agreed upon "indisputable classics" appear repeatedly, as vague as it sounds, and as empty of independent judgment or explicit standards. In 1949, Lodge claimed to include the few thinkers "whose essential greatness is universally conceded" (ix). The editor of *A History of Modern European Philosophy* says he includes "the leading postmedieval philosophies" (J. D. Collins 1954, iii) and "the great modern thinkers" (iv). Jones refers to "concentration on the major theorists, on the *real* masters (W. T. Jones 1959, 6; emphasis added), Bowle includes "the outstanding ideas of the great masters of political thought" (1961, x) and Harmon focuses on "the fundamental ideas of the major political philosophers" (1964, v). In explaining his choices, W. T. Jones says, "There will probably be no difference of opinion about the great figures of the remote past. Everyone will surely agree that Plato and Aristotle are the masters of their ages. And perhaps there will be general agreement that Augustine and Thomas occupy similar positions in the Middle Ages" (1959, viii). It is fascinating how seamlessly the probable unanimity of opinion that Jones first mentions slips into possible "general agreement"; consensus regarding greatness cannot be used to justify choices while lack of it is allowed to have no impact on the selection process.

How much agreement *is* necessary? How do we know that the asserted concord appealed to even exists? Who is the "everyone" in supposed harmony? Is there a shred of evidence that in coming to their supposedly unanimous conclusions "about the great figures of the remote past" "they" even considered figures such as Hypatia, "perhaps the greatest woman philosopher of all time" (Kersey 1989, 5), or Pan Chao, whose "lasting fame rests partly on the work *Lessons for Women,* a feminine ethic consisting of a system of theoretical moral principles together with rules for their practical application [that] . . . exhibits a pronounced philosophical eclecticism and incorporates elements of Han Confucianism, Taoism, and thoughts of the Lao-Chuang school of nature" (Kersey 1989, 6)? Apparently not, because according to the texts used in classes on every college campus, the reason there are no women in the histories and canon of political theory and philosophy is that everyone (or nearly everyone) agrees (probably) that none are worthy of inclusion, none having received unanimous or overwhelming support confirming greatness from a self-appointed group of unnamed voters in a secret election based on an incomplete slate that no one else ever sees.

INFLUENCE

Selection has been necessary, and not every one, we may be sure, will agree with all of Dr Lancaster's choices. Is Kropotkin really a master? he will be asked. Why include the Fabians? Dr Lancaster would answer—and rightly—that a theory is to be judged not merely by its internal consistency (or lack of it), but by its influence—by its impact on other writers, and on events.

—W. T. Jones, *Masters of Political Thought,* vol. 3

Influence is quite frequently cited as a clear and specific justification for inclusion in textbooks, syllabi, and the canon itself. Lodge chose "the greatest works in the world of thought" as judged by "vitality and creative influence" (1949, ix). It is the only criterion explicitly mentioned in Alexander's 1922 *A Short History of Philosophy:* "I have included in the History an account of some German writers who, though not strictly regarded as philosophers, have exercised a powerful influence upon speculative thought as well as upon general culture" (vi). Influence outweighs being "strictly regarded" as a philosopher for Alexander and "internal consistency" for Lancaster; Bertrand Russell considers "influence" so decisive that it outweighs "merit":

> The importance which [I] give to a philosopher is often not that which he deserves on account of his philosophic merit. For my part, for example, I consider Spinoza a greater philosopher than Locke [for unstated

reasons], but he was far less influential; I have therefore treated him much more briefly than Locke. Some men—for example, Rousseau and Byron—though not philosophers at all in the academic sense, have so profoundly affected the prevailing philosophic temper that the development of philosophy cannot be understood if they are ignored. Even pure men of action are sometimes of great importance in this respect; very few philosophers have influenced philosophy as much as Alexander the Great, Charlemagne, or Napoleon. (1946, ix–x)

Two things are especially striking in these examples. First, being regarded as a meritorious philosopher, or even a philosopher at all, is neither a necessary nor a sufficient condition for inclusion in the history or canon of philosophy. This idea seems in at least some tension with the previously mentioned philosophical "greatness" that supposedly determined inclusion. Second, the "influence" that overrides these factors is not simple to define; is influence crucial "upon speculative thought [and] . . . general culture" (Alexander 1922, vi), or upon "the prevailing philosophic temper" (Russell 1946, ix–x), or "on politics" (Ebenstein 1966, vi), or on "other writers" or "events" (W. T. Jones 1959, 7)? This is an astonishingly fundamental issue about which to find such a lack of clarity and consensus among the defenders of the standard themselves.

In *Eight Women Philosophers: Theory, Politics, and Feminism,* Jane Duran says that the figures she chose to include "have been selected . . . in part because . . . these thinkers *were* recognized as having contributed to philosophical thought during their own era, and it was only at a later point that their names ceased to be listed among those who wrote during a given period" (2006, 1–2; emphasis added). Perhaps surprisingly, Duran's celebrated female figures *did* have to be considered philosophers, at least during their lifetimes, while Alexander's, Jones's, and so on, did not. Her purpose seems to be to remove an objection made by skeptics—that there were no women philosophers—by giving as evidence not only explication of their texts, but also previous evaluations of them, perhaps by (recognized male?) authorities with more credibility than that of the thinkers themselves.

That feminists might not have the option of picking more freely those we would deem "theorists" is itself evidence of inequality, and Duran's response to it contains a cautious challenge. Other editors, however, including Smith and Carroll (2000) and Collins (P. H. Collins 1990) think it crucial to reexamine who and what counts as theorists and theory, as part of the political struggle. Gardner's project is precisely to challenge "the reasons for the assignment of non-philosophical status to certain forms" of writing (2000, 2). In fact, this second approach is more common than Duran's (and Spender's [1982]), though hers has the benefit of confronting us with a different history of the reception of women's theoretical works, the revelation of which is, hopefully, a prod to read them.

Interestingly, reasons for going outside those previously deemed political theorists or philosophers are different in anthologies of women's writings from those in men's. In the anthologies of women, inclusion of "nonphilosophers" is a response to the unjust fate of their works and the unreasonable boundaries drawn in various disciplines; by comparison, in the anthologies of men it is because nonphilosophers influence philosophy, too, without staking legitimate claim to the lofty title of philosopher. The first expands boundaries, while the second at least also protects certain existing ones.

So, among those attempting to use "influence" as the guide for choosing whom to include, we encounter not only vagueness and question-begging, but also genuine difference of opinion about whom or what the contestants should have influenced, whose recognition of them as exactly what really matters. "Being written about by academics" is essential "influence" in some histories. That the secondary literature colored the figures included in Cahn's large text might be inferred from his notes on the literature for each theorist. "The secondary literature on Smith is vast" (1997, 521). "The secondary literature on Machiavelli is immense" (4). "There is an immense and growing literature on Mill's moral and political theory" (930). In fact, no figure is included who does not have library shelves dedicated to discussion of his work.

Consider Cahn's helpful introductory notes in some detail. Among the references cited for Hegel, it is noted that one book "sets Hegel's political philosophy in the context of the religious and political culture of old Wurttemberg," others "provide good introductions to Hegel's philosophy," another "is an extremely helpful guide to Hegel's technical vocabulary," one offers "a very good analysis of Hegel's social and political philosophy," another "approaches Hegel's social and political philosophy from the standpoint of reconciliation," and a final one "provid[es] an excellent treatment of Hegel's contribution to ethics" (736). A short sample of the literature on Hobbes mentions one "overview of Hobbes's work . . . three detailed examinations of the validity of Hobbes's social contract argument . . . [a work on] the nonpolitical aspects of Hobbes's thinking . . . a discussion of Hobbes's religious arguments . . . [and] a collection of classic interpretive essays on Hobbes's work" (80). Only on Spinoza are the "studies of [his] political thought available in English . . . sparse" (200), but even here Cahn lists a book that "puts Spinoza's political theory within the context of his critique of theology . . . [a book that] examines Spinoza's excommunication against the background of the Marrano community and its influence on his manner of writing . . . [one that offers] a useful guide to Spinoza's relation to radical currents within Dutch politics of his time . . . [and an essay that] attempts to understand Spinoza's neglected role within the history of democratic theory" (200). Students of Locke can find works that "include an extensive discussion of his ethical and natural law theories . . . reliable *historical* accounts of his political thought . . . a most accessible, brief, general overview . . . [a book on] Locke's theory of property . . . [one in which the] attack on Filmer is put into a larger theoretical and historical context . . . and [t]wo works [that] examine Locke's political thought and some of its implications from a nonhistorical, contemporary, philosophic perspective" (217). On Hume one can find "excellent general studies of Hume's thought . . . [a work that offers a] lucid introduction to Hume's ethical thought, helpfully placing it in the context of the British moral tradition . . . [one in which] Hume's ideas about value, virtue, and justice are carefully examined in light of their psychological underpinnings . . . [another l]ooking at Hume from the perspective of contemporary political philosophy . . . [one that] interprets Hume as a political conservative . . . [while another provides the] opposite case for regarding Hume as a would-be reformer . . . [and a final one] shows how Hume treats history and experience as sources of political value" (489–90). The pattern is clear. Those we will read in today's anthologies are those we have written about repeatedly, in tremendous detail, from a number and wide range of perspectives. Academic interest is a form of influence and proof of worthiness of continued attention.

The simple, incontrovertible fact of the matter is, however, that we do not possess such numerous, varied, specialized, philosophical analyses of a single female political thinker. Not one. There are only a handful of women (and from before the twentieth century only one—Wollstonecraft—and only recently) on whom we have more than a few theoretical books; for most we have multiple biographies and assorted scholarly articles that do not always even engage one another (literature on Emma Goldman is an excellent example [Weiss and Kensinger 2007]). If secondary literature is to be the standard for inclusion in political theory textbooks, and if (as we know from the outset) there is no woman for whom there exists anything like the range and number and depth of commentaries that is present for men, then "logically," "reasonably," without a trace of malevolence or misogyny, no women will be included. The cycle will continue. But not only is the outcome predictable, the method is suspect. It "safely," lazily renders no or minimal independent judgments on the writings of political theorists; it appeals to criteria of influence that, as we have seen, are vague and contradictory; and it applies these standards both inconsistently and uncreatively.

Are feminists (like me) attempting to resurrect women who had no impact on the worlds in which they lived or that came after them? Hardly. There is little connection between the acclaim many of them received during and after their lifetimes and their ultimate fate in the secondary literature or the canon, as Duran suggests. They experienced popular success: "In a London that boasted only two theatres, [Aphra Behn] had seventeen plays produced in seventeen years [and] . . . wrote thirteen novels (thirty years before Daniel Defoe wrote *Robinson Crusoe,* generally termed the first novel) and published several collections of poems and translations" (Spender 1982, 34). Behn's *The Rover,* in particular, was performed seventy times "between 1700 and 1725" (Link 1967, xiii). Their work received worldwide recognition: "in 1898 [Charlotte Perkins Gilman's] *Women and Economics* was published, to immediate acclaim. It went through seven English-language editions and was translated into seven other languages" (W. L. O'Neill 1972, ix); more generally, "in the first decades of [the twentieth] century, Charlotte Perkins Gilman was recognized internationally as a major theorist and social commentator (Lane 1990, 3). They influenced political life: "at her death [Jane] Addams was America's best-known and most widely hailed female public figure. . . . The mourning at her death was international. Tributes poured in from prime ministers and from ordinary men and women whose lives she had touched in some way by her life and work" (Elshtain 2002a, xxi). They interacted with other major political figures: "Mercy Otis Warren, her brother, and her father were players on a revolutionary stage inhabited by Samuel Adams, John and Abigail Adams, King George III, John Hancock, James and Dolley Madison, and Thomas Jefferson. Many of the revolutionary leaders . . . corresponded with her (Waters 2000, 172). They were often heroic:

> Simone Weil is one of the most selfless and courageous figures of our time. Her life, though very brief, was an action-crowded life and a many-sided one, involving matters intellectual, creative, social, philosophical, scientific, moral, religious and, by no means least of all, physical—physical, in the sense of moving actionally, often directly and decisively, for example, into the affairs of the working-classes. It

was a life that moved suspensefully from the search for simple justice and humaneness in the world to periodic disappointments that
came close to disillusionment and despair. . . . Out of compassion for
her captive and undernourished fellow-countrymen, she insisted upon
limiting herself to the meagerest kind of diet that proved harmful to
her already frail system. (Ellert 1958, vii, viii)

The influence of women is not nonexistent but ignored, downplayed, or
interpreted as unrelated to their ideas.

"Influence" only appears to be an objective criterion for inclusion among
the greats. What we mean by it in practice is narrow: "constitutive relations
of descent and *influence between men* define what philosophy is—Aristotle
inherits from Plato the problem of universal essences, Ockham corrects
Abelard's treatment of logical truth, Locke revises Descartes's rationalist
grounding of scientific knowledge, and so on through the history of philosophy" (Nye 1988, xiv; emphasis added). It matters if those influenced
were male. Consider Catherine Macaulay. "It was not just Mary Wollstonecraft who acknowledged her debt to Macaulay . . . but also Elizabeth Cady
Stanton, Susan B. Anthony and Matilda Joslyn Gage, who made much of
her contribution" (Spender 1982, 128). Wollstonecraft had an essay written
about her by Emma Goldman and another by George Eliot. She was read
by Judith Sargent Murray (Harris 1995, xxv); was cited as a precedent by the
authors of *The History of Woman Suffrage;* and had an introduction to her
Vindication of the Rights of Woman penned by Olive Schreiner (First and
Scott 1980, 369), the same book that was positively reviewed by Mary Hays
(Poston 1988, 223) and said by Virginia Woolf to be "so true" that along with
the *Vindication of the Rights of Men,* "their originality has become our com-
monplace" (Poston 1988, 269). If we are going to use influence as a standard,
we need to look for influence in different places, and to be both more precise and more open-minded in answering, "Influence on whom, or what?"
Otherwise, innocently or not, we create a distorted history.

One reason influence counts is that it is supposed to be an indicator of,
or proxy for, worthiness. But other considerations besides unworthiness can
also explain someone's lack of due influence, a lack that academics should
remedy rather than *reinforce:* "The most important element in fostering the
development of abstract thought has been the existence of an intellectual
history of men, which has enabled male thinkers to begin where other men
left off, and to argue with the male thinkers before them. This condition
has never been available to women and we are barely beginning, through the

development of women's history, to make it available today" (Lerner 2000, 12). If women's work disappears, goes out of print and out of conversation, then it is not *allowed* to have the long-term influence that would mark it as meritorious and significant. We cannot, after making some forms of influence on certain people nearly impossible, judge them deficient and ignorable for not having had sufficient influence on them. At least, we cannot do so and also claim that influence matters because it is an indicator of merit.

When we do our homework, however, we can in fact make all kinds of connections. For example, "Dorothy Day described her philosophy as 'gentle personalist' or 'constructive socialism. . . . Personalism assumes the supreme dignity of the individual and therefore a moral stance is making oneself available to the other—a notion that prefigures Nel Noddings's concept of caring. . . . Day's political philosophy was a unique blend of anarchism, communism, and Christianity. In many ways, Day's brand of political philosophy anticipates Latin American Liberation Theology that was not to develop until the 1960s" (Hamington 2007, 170). Here a woman is linked to a later philosopher and a later school of thought; such connections are rare, but unfortunately, in this case neither Noddings nor liberation theology have the status to lift that of Day. There is a reason such cycles are described as "vicious."

The criteria for inclusion in collections of women political thinkers are almost the exact reverse of those in collections of canonical thinkers. The editors of these collections tend to choose precisely those writings *not* easily available and *not* repeatedly discussed in the literature. Nye writes, "I propose the work of three women [Luxemburg, Weil, and Arendt] who have received only marginal attention from feminists and philosophers" (1994, xvi). Anthologists of feminist collections *all* remark on the difficulties in obtaining access to work by women: "The majority of works by women have not been republished since they were originally written and they can be found only in a few research libraries or on microfilm" (Atherton 1994, 1). Berenice Carroll explains: "We have sometimes *omitted the best-known writings of a given theorist, so as to bring to attention and make available other of her works.* Thus, for example, we excluded Mary Wollstonecraft's *Vindication of the Rights of Woman* (1792) in favor of her earlier and more neglected *Vindication of the Rights of Men* (1790), in which she had already signaled some of the central arguments of the later work" (Smith and Carroll 2000, ix, x; emphasis added). Beverly Guy-Sheftall used similar criteria for determining inclusion and exclusion in *Words of Fire: An Anthology of African-American Feminist Thought:* "I have omitted from this collection fiction, poetry, and literary criticism.... The literature of contemporary black women is *more accessible*... widely read, frequently taught, and increasingly the object of critical inquiry [citing Cheryl Wall]. *Words of Fire* is a highly selective collection of feminist essays by African American women some of which have appeared in a variety of places and are often *difficult to retrieve*" (1995, xiv, xvii; emphases added). The writings of women are not being collected today in order to reproduce those already replicated in every other anthology; instead, one *purpose* is "to make available to interested readers a selection from the writings of women philosophers of the period" (Atherton 1994, 1). The process of collection and selection becomes, among other things, an opportunity to make less available work more visible. Rather than looking for the works that most political thinkers are already teaching and reading and writing about, Nye, Smith and Carroll, Atherton, and Guy-Sheftall self-consciously look to include ones that readers are less likely to know or to obtain easily, but that *deserve* recognition. In that way the works themselves contribute to an ongoing, additive process of recovery, providing resources for current readers and future scholars and continuing to allow "influence" the opportunity to emerge. Other practices continually rewrite women out of history.

There is one final twist. Even were we to reach consensus about how much of what kind of impact on whom matters, and to apply such standards fairly, "influence" is utterly rejected by some as a relevant factor at all. Speaking about the process used to select works for the 1990 edition of the *Great Books of the Western World,* Adler simply asserts that "we did not consider the influence exerted by an author or a book on later developments in literature of society" (1997, 3). Compare this with the earlier position taken by Russell, that influence outweighs greatness in the selection process, and the circularity and politics of the often hidden standards of the canon are impossible to deny.

ORIGINALITY

The World will hardly allow a Woman to say any thing well, unless as she borrows it from Men, or is assisted by them.

—Mary Astell, *Reflections upon Marriage*

Astell sees that a political environment that attributes women's ideas to men, regardless of their actual source, makes it impossible for women to be acknowledged as original. Beyond the problem of inaccuracy in attribution, "originality" is as problematic a criterion as "influence," for as many and similar reasons. Whether something is deemed original depends upon that with which it is compared. As I mention later in the chapter on Astell, phrases from Rousseau for which he is celebrated appear earlier in Astell without comment. Yet because most scholars have read him repeatedly and never heard of her, he alone is admired as original, even when he is undeserving.

In addition, originality is only looked for in certain places and on certain subjects. Some of the original ideas of women were ignored as trivial ("Why," for example, "is she talking about sex?" Kropotkin seems to have asked about Goldman, as Lenin did of Zetkin [Nye 1988, 46]), or were the very cause of their being dismissed as theorists, rather than recognized as pathbreaking (Haaland 1993). In such instances, the problem is not that women were unoriginal, but that they were sometimes "too" original—inconveniently, insistently, daringly, and provocatively so.

More generally, it should go without saying, but, of course, does not, that works by women were every bit as original (and every bit as collaborative and derivative) as works by men. Aphra Behn was "a sexual pioneer who contended that men and women should love freely and as equals" and "was an early abolitionist whose novel *Oroonoko* contained the first popular portrayal of the horrors of slavery" (Spender 1982, 34). According to Doris Stenton, Macaulay "was the first to attempt the writing of history on a large scale, based on materials, in manuscript as well as in print" (cited in Spender 1982, 129). Ida B. Wells was "the earliest and most effective critic of lynching in the South and the widespread loss of political rights for African Americans in the late nineteenth and early twentieth centuries (Smith and Carroll 2000, 261). Gilman was "the first social thinker who tried to understand social conditions and social consciousness from the perspective of human evolution, economic change, and women's conditions" (W. L. O'Neill 1972, ix). Phillis Wheatley "launched two traditions at once—the black American literary tradition *and* the black woman's literary tradition" (Gates 1988, x). Mercy Otis Warren's "chief accomplishment . . . *History of the Rise, Progress and Termination of the American Revolution* . . . constitutes the only major contemporary anti-federalist account of the American Revolution, and it does so from the standpoint of someone concerned with philosophical issues" (Waters 2000, 172).

As with "influence," we have to ask of "originality" such questions as, What does it mean to be original? How much of one's work has to be original? Is newness itself greatness, and if not, what else is implied in granting the title? What connections to previous thought preclude one being deemed original? "Novelty" can come from new information, new combinations, new applications and extensions; from taking a different turn or going farther down an old road or traveling with a different companion who generates different discussion. One can say new things, and also can say old things to new audiences, translating, interpreting, applying, incorporating, and connecting. Old ideas put to new uses are new again, door openers and pathbreakers.

The "originality" of theorists we have deemed to be great cannot even be accurately determined when no women with whom to compare them have been on the reading list. Too, the "originality" of women's contributions to political thought cannot be evaluated if the subjects judged worth being original about, and the methods deemed appropriate for discussing them, are decided upon using narrow, predetermined, racist, or patriarchal definitions, frameworks, or visions. Ultimately, however, we should celebrate originality with some caution—our desire for "firsts" can lead us to erase more history, which we are hardly in a position to afford; can make collaborative accomplishments seem second rate, as if they or their producers were somehow less magnificent; and can conflict with the recovery of alternative traditions, since it celebrates an imagined solitary thinker rather than glorying in connections and incremental progress.

BREADTH

The breadth of certain thinkers is part of what makes them great, for they are able to cross the boundaries of disciplines and bring methods and insights from one to bear on inquiry into another. Breadth is testimony to an intellectual ability to grapple with diverse issues and ways of knowing. Among political theory's "greats," Plato wrote not only the *Republic,* which is on justice, but also dialogues covering issues from beauty, law, and knowledge to friendship, virtue, and love. Aristotle wrote not only the *Politics* but also works on logic, rhetoric, poetry, and ethics. In addition to the *Social Contract,* Rousseau wrote a popular novel; an opera; an autobiography; and works on political economy, education, and the arts. Perhaps the problem, the basis for their exclusion from the canon, is that women only wrote about women?

Like originality, "breadth" in women is sometimes actually held against them—it becomes a criticism of them, a justification for inattention rather than evidence of intellectual range and integration. Gilman "wrote so much on so many different topics that occasionally the corpus of her work seems diffuse and eclectic" (Ceplair 1991, x). Not unrelated, Margaret Fuller is criticized for "her tendency to digression" (Chevigny 1976, 10); perhaps one man's digression is one woman's way of making new connections. It has been said of Olive Schreiner that "the range and seeming incompatibility of her imaginative work and her political writing have placed her at continuing risk of being fragmented by admirers and detractors alike" (First and Scott 1980, 17). One commentator considers the possibility that the reason Susanna Langer's "pioneering and evocative" work "has been undervalued [and] . . . even virtually ignored for periods of time" relates to its breadth (Hart 2004, 239, 244). "In order to appreciate its significance, the whole of her interconnected system must be studied patiently, with an extremely open mind and with a reasonable degree of interdisciplinary sophistication." This, Hart thinks, is both difficult for many specialized thinkers and even what some consider "beyond the boundaries of philosophy" (241). "Within philosophy she made major contributions to a diverse array of sub-fields, ranging from symbolic logic . . . to symbolism and semiotics, to aesthetics, [and] philosophy of mind (239). . . . Langer readily infused her writings with material from the social sciences, art, cultural studies, religion, and myth, and moved about within such realms with an ease and mastery most readers are scarcely up to" (244).

Wollstonecraft was interested in the social, political, and marital equality of the sexes; in education; in the French Revolution; and in issues of morality, freedom, and rationality in human nature and social life. Jane Addams wrote books on democracy (*Democracy and Social Ethics*, 1902), peace (*Newer Ideals of Peace*, 1907; *The Long Road of Woman's Memory*, 1916; *Peace and Bread in Time of War*, 1922), urban youth and government (*The Spirit of Youth and the City Streets*, 1909; *A New Conscience and an Ancient Evil*, 1912), settlement houses (*Twenty Years at Hull-House*, 1910; *The Second Twenty Years at Hull House*, 1930), and political change (*Women at the Hague*, 1915), as well as biographies (*The Excellent Becomes the Permanent*, 1932; *My Friend, Julia Lathrop*, 1935). "In addition to books, Addams's published work includes more than five hundred essays, speeches, editorials, and columns" (Elshtain 2002a, xvii). Mentioning *only* her early works, McFarland and Van Ness describe a selection of texts by Simone Weil:

> "Science and Perception in Descartes" (1929–30), a formidable dissertation Weil wrote as a twenty-one-year-old philosophy student; . . . "The Situation in Germany" (1932–33), a ten-article extravaganza of dissident Left journalism on the subject of Hitler's rise to power and Comintern

politics; "Factory Journal" (1934–35), Weil's unedited, almost daily record of the "year" she spent as an unskilled factory worker; "War and
Peace" (1933–40), a selection of essays and fragments reflecting aspects
of her pacifist thought; . . . and "Philosophy" (1941), a light [?] essay
that accurately reflects some of the breadth of her mature thought on
Eastern and Western art, mysticism, science, and philosophy. (McFarland and Van Ness 1987, xi)

In many cases, the breadth of the work of women theorists has simply been
ignored. We tend to know only their most obviously feminist work, and we
grant their fiction more attention than their non-fiction. To the extent that
women have been allowed to speak they have been allowed to speak on wom-
en's issues narrowly understood—generally as those issues have been defined
by certain men. Simone de Beauvoir is better known for her landmark 1949
feminist text, *The Second Sex* (Beauvoir 1986), than for any of her numerous other works, which include travel books, memoirs, novels such as *She
Came To Stay* (1943) and *The Mandarins* (1954), and nonfiction political and
philosophical texts such as *Force of Circumstance* (1963), *The Ethics of Ambi-
guity* (1947), and *The Coming of Age* (1970). Gilman is more famous for her
utopian novel *Herland* and her short story "The Yellow Wallpaper" than she
is for her remarkable treatises on economics (*Women and Economics: A Study
of the Economic Relation Between Men and Women as a Factor in Social Evolution* [1898]), labor (*Human Work* [1904]), culture (*The Man-Made World;
or, Our Andocentric Culture* [1911]), ethics (*Social Ethics* [1914; serialized in
Forerunner]), or religion (*His Religion and Hers: A Study of the Faith of Our
Fathers and the Work of Our Mothers* [1923]). Interestingly, her philosophy
commits her to breadth: "Hers was an organic view of society. . . . Society is
one living thing; we cannot ignore poison in one part of it and think we can
escape because it is a long way off. She wrote about ethics . . . about mothering . . . about the home . . . about work" (Lane 1990, 6). Yet "she is still seen
as a commentator concerned only with issues of women's emancipation and
women's social role. Her scope and creative imagination are as yet unappre-
ciated even by today's admirers and supporters. A careful reading of the full
body of her work demonstrates the immense breadth of her vision and the
enormously ambitious character of the project she set for herself" (8).

In contrast, what men have said about women is often utterly ignored.
Some translations of Rousseau's *Emile*, for example, simply drop book 5,
the one that discusses women's education, despite all the interesting problems it raises for most interpretations of the book as a whole (Weiss 1993).

And, until very recently, rare indeed was the commentator who found much of anything worth pondering in interpreting Rousseau's views on the sexes. His derogatory remarks about women were treated as unfortunate but understandable and as ultimately irrelevant asides to his "real" political theory. When men have said negative things about women, the most common responses have been to ignore them or, in passing, to call them "unfortunate anomalies" and, in general, to blame it on the times. All such responses beg the reader to see that in no case do the male writer's views on women have any relevance to his politics or philosophy. Interestingly, if men said something positive about women, there, too, the response has generally been to ignore such remarks, though when acknowledged they are often "blamed" on the female company such men kept. There are books about John Stuart Mill and lists of his writings that make no mention of his *Subjection of Women*, or that explain his feminism away as something Harriet Taylor somehow forced him to endorse. In general, whatever men say about women is irrelevant, and whatever women say about anything other than women is irrelevant. Both (what some men define as) women's issues and women writers are ghettoized, forced into narrow quarters and largely ignored except when it is convenient to acknowledge them, often to ridicule or pigeonhole them, or to mask bias through token inclusion.

The consequences of this pattern are severe. When women are allowed to speak only about child care or abortion or women's rights, it allows those in power to say, falsely but usefully, "See how we are bringing women in?" The terms on which women are included are not their own. And "permitting" women to address women's issues shows where control lies, and it can be a way of justifying the exclusion of women everywhere else. When foreign policy, for example, is defined as outside the rightful range of women's issues, that definition or location perpetuates the expectation and acceptance of attitudes and actions in that arena that disproportionately reflect the training received by men in patriarchal cultures: training in one-upmanship, physical violence, competitiveness, saving face, flexing muscle, and drawing lines. And, on the other hand, when child care, for example, is defined as the paradigmatic women's issue, we come to expect and justify men's more marginal participation in rearing children or thinking knowledgably about childhood. Others are deciding when women may speak and on what subjects (also, of course, in what tone). That is silencing, not inclusion; it is a strategy for perpetuating, rather than challenging, women's subordination.

Further, what does it mean to be broad or narrow, to have great or little breadth? If Wollstonecraft "only" wrote about the roles and relations of the sexes, would that somehow justify excluding her from the canon? Was Marx narrow and dismissible for "only" writing on economics? Was Aquinas one-dimensional and irrelevant for bringing a Christian perspective to bear on everything he wrote? Stature is not merely a question of the number of subjects treated. Even if Wollstonecraft had "only" considered gender, it seems misguided to label her as narrow. In all her writings she contributes something relatively rare: thoughts about the implications of various practices, social structures, and political changes on the status of and relationships between the sexes. In at least that regard, she is not narrower than others who have written on these subjects, but more comprehensive. In fact, her works show how narrowly many ideas and practices had been treated before; they thus contribute to a broadening of the scope of the discipline. That, it seems, is hardly an insignificant contribution, though some may find it a burdensome one.

Ignoring most of Wollstonecraft's or Astell's or Pizan's or Beauvoir's or Gilman's work perpetuates a distorted version of feminist philosophy in general and of these individuals as political theorists. Assigning women to theorize on women in the ways in which the dominant tradition of Western political theory has done diminishes our understanding of feminism by putting boundaries on the topics feminists may inquire into. It detracts from our understanding of individual theorists who are, like Addams, Langer, and Weil, denied their depth and breadth, misrepresented and underestimated, through selective inattention. We cannot even find Wollstonecraft the feminist in the narrowest sense without looking beyond the relatively famed *Rights of Woman,* since, for example, part of her critique of the institution of marriage is found in *Maria* and of economic inequality in *Rights of Men.* Some of the writers offering interpretations of Wollstonecraft who treat her so critically might even arrive at different conclusions were they to gain an appreciation for the way her thought developed in her short life, the ways in which a range of issues come together in each work, the ways each work sheds light on the others. These are not unusual tenets of interpretation to insist upon.

PERENNIAL ISSUES

Patrick Gardiner's *Nineteenth-Century Philosophy* contains an all-male selection of philosophers. When he notes that "the omission of authors" is explicable by his choice "to give prominence to certain salient themes and tendencies" (1969, n.p.), the reader might reasonably conclude that no women wrote on such important themes, but they would be incorrect to do so. Gardiner simply did not do them justice.

The circularity that repeatedly surfaces in defenses of the canon reaches a peak on the subject of perennial issues, as seen in Mortimer Adler's discussion of "Great Ideas." He lists 102 "ideas basic and indispensable to understanding ourselves, our society, and the world in which we live" (1997, 1), and like others whom we have encountered, insists that consensus exists: "Different groups of persons will, if called upon to do so, construct different lists of books that deserve the status of 'great.' This is not the case when we consider ideas rather than books. Take the list of the 102 ideas exhibited here. There may be some disagreement about them, but it will be very slight, indeed; there are few of these ideas that anyone would recommend dropping and few that anyone would recommend adding" (4). Adler arrived at the list of "Great Ideas" by looking at what the authors of the "great books" were talking about: "These ideas were derived from an extremely close analysis of 44 works by 73 authors from Homer to the twentieth century. This analysis was performed by a staff of specialized indexers under my direction, and the works analyzed were later published as Great Books of the Western World" (5). Who decides what are perennial, critically important, discipline-defining subjects? According to Adler, there actually are some specific authors who get to "vote" on this, whose votes are carefully counted by specialists. Why do these authors decide what the great ideas are? Although he has just admitted that there is disagreement about what books are great, the answer appears to be that the authors determine the great ideas because they wrote great books. Later, however, he says that "it is the set of great ideas that determines the choice of the great books" (2). Remember Alice Duer Miller's antisuffragist arguments?

If we had had experts scan the works of women political thinkers for recurring themes (a good dissertation project!), would lists identical to Adler's have emerged? Adler simply asserts that there would be no difference. There would, of course, be a great deal of overlap, though discussing the same issue does not necessarily entail treating it from the same angles, based on the same stories, or speaking to the same set of social concerns. But we have studied enough to say that the answer is that the lists would vary some, and importantly, because Adler's "consensus" is based on a systematically biased sample. Women theorists have been fighting for the inclusion and relevance of their lives and their insights, their questions and their assigned duties, while men have been fighting to keep the turf almost exclusively composed of issues relevant to their lives, their duties, their needs, and their desires. The method of which Adler seems so proud is in fact another way of erasing women from the history of political philosophy. Childhood, child rearing, marriage, sex, sexuality, intersectionality, dress, care, the body, health, respect, and sympathy are intrinsically no less relevant to the well-being of individuals and political associations than are the structures of executive power or the competition for economic power. Dismissing women thinkers on the grounds that they are not speaking enough to political theory's core concepts is often less a commentary on the political nature of their work than an expression of the politics of the discipline.

The canon itself—its categories and mode of reasoning, its truth claims and conditions—determines what we accept as political theory as well as what we expect of political writing and political writers. "I read Wollstonecraft's texts as an immanent critique of the canon, a war of words that serves to caution us, as we work to place worthy women among the great men on the syllabus and add their writing to the curriculum, that we should carefully consider the politics of membership and exclusion within the canon" (Gunther-Canada 2001).

The question of "perennial issues" is linked to the previous one of "breadth." Labeling someone a feminist is automatically supposed to indicate a narrow range of interests. But that is not based on the author's writings and flies in the face of the recurring theme that "women's interests" are inextricably linked with the whole range of political concerns.

> Amelia Jenks Bloomer belonged to a generation of women concerned with the moral issues of their day as well as with the issue of reform. These women believed that they had a job to do in freeing the slaves, moderating the use of alcohol, and ultimately in providing women with the tools necessary to accomplish these tasks—legal and social emancipation. The individual reforms that Amelia Bloomer and her contemporaries espoused must be seen as part of a larger social movement to fully appreciate their significance. (Kleinberg 1975, v)

INVISIBILITY

Artemis March (1982) constructed a typology of forms that women's "invisibility takes in andocentric sociology" (B. Thiele 1986, 30). Beverly Thiele "extend[ed] this analysis to political theory" (30–31). In both cases, the authors look at the fate of women *in* social theories. However, the categories they offer can also be useful in summarizing the fate of women as social theorists, as discussed in this chapter. The fact that the two fates are analogous perhaps reveals the role each plays in the sustaining of sexual inequality.

The three forms of invisibility in sociological theory that March discusses are exclusion, pseudoinclusion and alienation. Applied to women political thinkers, "exclusion" captures instances when the very existence of historical women theorists is denied, as well as when their existence is mentioned but breezily dismissed because of the supposed inappropriateness or triviality of their subject matter. The subjects about which men theorists have written are equated with what is important, or what is political. Thus understood, "the exclusion of women is an active process. . . . [They] are structurally excluded from the realm of discourse" (32). Any women thinkers who are not rendered nonexistent, whose names or work somehow cannot be made to disappear completely, are effectively dismissed, reduced to irrelevance. We see this in every text that presents us with an all-male roster of great thinkers, as well as in many sketchy comments about how no women were political enough, or broad enough, or deep enough, to make the cut.

"Pseudoinclusion" in social theory occurs when women are discussed but treated differently from men, "defined as a 'special case,' as anomalies, exceptions to the rule" (33). Applied to women political thinkers, pseudoinclusion most frequently takes the form of acknowledging them only if the subject is gender or is something else that is deemed to be a feminine concern, such as children or family. In this way, women theorists become as peripheral as the subjects about which they write, and they are silenced on the subjects that are considered core to the discipline. Pseudoinclusion might also capture the times when a woman thinker is treated as having no predecessors, no history, as well as when her accomplishments are attributed to her "masculine" mind or said to be actually the product of a male colleague.

The final form of invisibility is alienation. In social theory, alienation captures work in which women's "experience is interpreted through male categories because the methodology and values of the theorists remain androcentric" (33). "Alienation" of historical women political thinkers occurs when they are forced into the frameworks of their philosophical brothers, regardless of the ill fit. It is unsurprising that the first women political thinkers to get any significant recognition are read within schools of thought created by men. Addams is always compared with Dewey, Wollstonecraft is read as extending the liberalism of Locke and others to women, Beauvoir is never discussed without prior examination of Sartre. By contrast, a book on Sartre would be unusual if it began with chapters on Beauvoir's philosophy, Locke is not treated only as "applying" or "extending" Hobbes but as himself helping define liberalism, and Dewey can be written about without mentioning the political theory of Addams. These phenomena get considerable attention in the rest of this book.

CONCLUDING THOUGHTS

There are both philosophical and political purposes informing who is included in feminist anthologies. Carole McCann and Seung-Kyung Kim reveal their standards:

> maintain a balance of old and new material that represent[s] pivotal moments of theoretical insight;
> balanc[e] the writings of women of color . . . with those of Western women and white women . . . to reframe discussion of feminist theory;
> shift away from a narrow focus on gender to emphasize some of the ways in which race, ethnicity, class, nationality, and sexuality intersect with gender;
> incorporate[] global perspectives throughout the anthology in order to continually challenge Western hegemonic concepts and categories; [and]
> not merely incorporate the challenges made by women of color and women of the South to themes and agendas defined by white and Northern feminists. . . . [but] include[] conversations among women of color about issues of gender, race, colonialism, and sexuality. (2002, 4)

Feminist anthologies are themselves *doing* political theory, not simply presenting it as a frozen, unchanging collection of the indisputably classic.

Charles Taylor claims that the basis for demands "to alter, enlarge, or scrap the 'canon'" is the assertion "that women and students from the excluded groups are given, either directly or by omission, a demeaning picture of themselves, as though all creativity and worth inhered in males of European provenance" (1994, 65). He concludes that "enlarging and changing the curriculum is therefore essential not so much in the name of a broader culture for everyone as in order to give due recognition to the hitherto excluded" (65–66). I argue throughout this book exactly the contrary: the problem is precisely that "all students may be missing something important through the exclusion" of women from political theory. We can do more than "presume" that women "have something important to say" (66). We already know enough to argue for their worth with more evidence than is needed, if that is what is sought. For example, discussing only selected writings from merely seven women from but one era, Atherton writes that what "the ideas of these various seventeenth-century women fill in for us is the richness of the existing debates" (1994, 5), asserting that they offer "examples of the wide variety of positions found within the epistemological debates of the period" (6) that are simply not represented by the current canon.

It is not unreasonable to wonder at this point about the fate that is desirable for the canon as we know it. Three options exist. They mirror the possibilities Woolf laid out for higher education after her analysis of the unfortunate and unavoidable role that higher education played in war: "Rebuild the [canon] on the old lines . . . rebuild it, but differently . . . or burn [it] to the ground" (1938, 33). Following my analysis of women thinkers as canon fodder, to reconstruct it on the old lines would mean opening the door to those who previously were wrongly excluded, making the canon truer to itself by more consistent application of rules for inclusion. Women, that is to say, would be admitted on the same terms as men. "The canon is looking for a few good women," the advertising campaign would run. "It is now an equal opportunity employer, guaranteeing equal treatment of canon law, in search only of sex-blind, race-neutral greatness." Those debating whether particular individuals should be incorporated into the canon are pursuing this path, asking whether each is sufficiently significant, influential, broad, original, and timeless.

To rebuild the canon differently means reopening the debate not only about who gets in, but also about what criteria one has to meet. Previously excluded women can reapply for membership, but also necessary is reconsideration of previously included men. Justification for a different constitution of the canon is based on the argument that the very standards for admission were biased, tainted, narrow, or incomplete, and the assumption is that they are capable of some significant degree of purification. The problem is perceived as corrupt rules rather than inconsistent application of objective, neutral, fair, well-founded standards. Here, women as canon fodder is understood as an unjust, unreasonable, predictable outcome that can and should be remedied. As Woolf would criticize it, works are not getting in that "teach the arts of human intercourse; the art of understanding other people's lives and minds, and the little arts of talk, of dress, of cookery that are allied with them . . . the ways in which mind and body can be made to cooperate." Instead, it is "the arts of dominating other people . . . the arts of ruling, of killing, of acquiring land and capital" (34).

The third possibility is to do away with the canon. This alternative might be defended on grounds that the existence of a canon itself brings about undesirable effects. Consider Woolf's words: "We can say that for educated men to emphasize their superiority over other people, either in birth or intellect, by dressing differently, or by adding titles before, or letters after their names, are acts that rouse competition and jealousy—emotions which . . . have their share in encouraging a disposition toward war. . . . Such distinctions make those who possess them ridiculous and learning contemptible. . . . We can refuse all such distinctions and all such uniform for ourselves" (21). If new female canonical figures basically offer what men have taught, how much does it matter that women be included? It matters some, of course, recalling Taylor (1994); it matters some that women be seen as capable of the same political and philosophical accomplishments. That is part of why Woolf sent a guinea to the college despite the fact that the authorities "must follow the old road to the old end" (Woolf 1938, 36), a "lame and depressing" conclusion. The real hope for change, however, stayed with outsiders who could still "refuse to bolster up the vain and vicious system" (37).

Why have a canon at all? How else could we organize, represent, and pass on authors, ideas, cultures, masterpieces? How else could we choose readings, applaud the great? Do we want a world that does not glorify? In which we do not compete to be first, best, most, outstanding? Woolf thinks that bestowing prizes itself degrades both author and learning. Wollstonecraft adds a "firm persuasion that every profession, in which great subordination of rank constitutes its power, is highly injurious to morality" (1988, 17). And yet prizes multiply. Those in the academy must cite and study those in the canon. Thus is not culture but legitimacy passed down; thus is one's academic standing established.

Of what value is the outsider, and to whom? Outsiders have "a different training and a different tradition" that "put more easily within our reach than within yours" (Woolf 1938, 21) certain opinions, refusals. It requires "training" and constitutes a "tradition." We must "do our utmost to use our influence in the universities where it properly belongs" (26). Use our influence. Do something, together, for change.

Patricia Hill Collins speaks of the African American woman intellectual as "the outsider within." They are "prevented from becoming full insiders" (1990, 12). As one of the consequences, they are "individuals whose marginality provides a distinctive angle of vision on the theories put forth by such intellectual communities" (12). "And yet marginality is not the only influence on [their] work" (13).

2

THE POLITICS OF IGNORANCE:
CHRISTINE DE PIZAN

In an attempt to understand deeply ingrained racist behaviors and ideas, Charles Mills introduced the intriguing concept of "an epistemology of ignorance": "a particular pattern of localized and global cognitive dysfunctions" that results in whites generally being "unable to understand the world they themselves have made" (1997, 18). The epistemology of ignorance is made up of such phenomena as "structured blindnesses and opacities . . . misunderstanding, misrepresentation, evasion, and self-deception on matters related to race" that function to justify and perpetuate white superiority. Among other things, it allows whites to "act in racist ways *while* thinking of themselves as acting morally" (93). These are not occasional happenings or minor misperceptions, but frame our very way of seeing and judging the world. "Evasion and self-deception thus become the epistemic norm," resulting in "a tortured ignorance so structured that one cannot raise certain issues" (97).

Two aspects of Mills's epistemology of ignorance especially capture my imagination. First, it easily has a gendered equivalent. As he explains his project, in fact, he appeals to work in feminist theory: "What is needed is a global theoretical framework for situating discussions of race and white racism, and thereby challenging the assumptions of white political philosophy, which would correspond to feminist theorists' articulation of the centrality of gender, patriarchy, and sexism to traditional moral and political theory" (2–3). While it is true that feminist theory has examined the impact of gender, patriarchy, and sexism on political theory from numerous vantage points, it has not done so using Mills's framework or the relative of it that I explore here.

Second, dominated races are not entirely free from the epistemology of ignorance: "*One has to overcome* the internalization of subpersonhood prescribed by the Racial Contract and recognize one's own humanity, resisting the official category of despised aboriginal, natural slave, colonial ward. *One has to learn* the basic self-respect that can casually be assumed by Kantian persons" (118; emphases added). Building on this understanding of racist norms internalized by the dominated, I look in this chapter at the invisibility of women thinkers not in the canon but, perhaps surprisingly, in contemporary feminist theory: "The 'history' of political thought to which I was introduced thirty years ago is thus (very slowly) being recognized as truncated and partial. Curiously, although feminist political theory has been flourishing for two decades, albeit to a large degree alongside the standard approaches, few feminist scholars have been concerned with their early predecessors" (Pateman 1998, 367).

I want to add to Mills a more explicit *politics* of ignorance that focuses on practices that sustain the cognitive distortions even among those working to overcome them. I turn for help to Christine de Pizan, for she began to build a political framework for understanding issues such as what counts as knowledge and ignorance and who has epistemological credibility and authority.

THE PROBLEM

In the concluding chapter of *Feminist Challenges: Social and Political Theory,* Elizabeth Gross writes, "In the [nineteen] sixties feminists began to question various images, representations, ideas and presumptions traditional theories developed about women and the feminine" (1987, 190). Among those who might find this an utterly astonishing claim is Christine de Pizan, who six hundred years ago documented and questioned precisely the ideas written about and images drawn of women in philosophy and politics, among numerous other fields.[1] The stronger argument can even be made that her theorizing *"starts from* these uncomfortable realities" (Mills 1997, 130), for Pizan's 1405 *The Book of the City of Ladies* opens with the following response by Christine to browsing a volume of poetry:

1. Hereafter, "Pizan" refers to the author of *The Book of the City of Ladies,* and "Christine" refers to the character in it. In addition to using "Pizan" to keep this distinction clear, I also use it to counter the pervasive tendency in secondary literature to refer to women thinkers by their first name (Emma, Mary) and men by their second (Locke as John?). I understand that in her case the parallel is with Aquinas, who is indeed often referenced as Thomas.

Just the sight of this book, even though it was of no authority, made me wonder how it happened that so many different men—and learned men among them—have been and are so inclined to express both in speaking and in their treatises and writings so many wicked insults about women and their behavior. . . . Philosophers and poets and . . . orators . . . speak from one and the same mouth. They all concur in one conclusion: that the behavior of women is inclined to and full of every vice. . . . I could hardly find a book on morals where, even before I had read it in its entirety, I did not find several chapters or certain sections attacking women, no matter who the author was. (Pizan 1982, 3–4)

Did women profoundly "question . . . traditional theories" (Gross 1987, 190) before the 1960s?[2] If women engaged in such epistemological and political ventures but no one acts as if they did, then have we lost a trail that could help us out of patriarchal jungles? Are women only allowed in the philosophical forest if they don't make any noise? Did Gross's 1960s feminist critics spring up overnight like mushrooms on the forest floor or, like so many TV children then and now, have only fathers?

Weighing her positive personal knowledge about women against the negative verdicts of the "authorities," Pizan's character Christine "finally decided," despite the unhappiness it caused her (1982, 5, 15), that "God formed a vile creature when He made woman" (5). After this, three virtuous figures appear to Christine—Ladies Reason, Rectitude, and Justice. Their mission, they inform Christine, is "to bring you out of the ignorance which so blinds your own intellect that you shun what you know for a certainty and believe what you do not know or see or recognize except by virtue of many strange opinions. . . . Fair daughter," they ask, "have you lost all sense" (6)?[3] Their goal is larger than the education of Christine: "to vanquish from the world the same error into which [she] had fallen" because of "various assailants" (10).

These passages begin to define the ignorance of a reader, and they clearly contain both epistemological and political elements. Multidimensional, such ignorance includes the blinding of one's intellect, the silencing of what one knows to be the truth, the loss of sense that could guide one through error

2. The earliest version of this chapter was actually titled "Did Women Know Anything Before the 1960s?" I am indebted to the participants of the 2003 NEH Seminar on Feminist Epistemologies, with whom that rant was shared, for their encouraging response.

3. Charles Mills notes that it is by agreeing with "what counts as a correct, objective interpretation of the world" that one is "granted full cognitive standing in the polity, the official epistemic community" (1997, 18). Lady Reason, fully aware of such epistemological politics, here subtly and powerfully redefines having sense as disagreeing with that "objective" interpretation.

and conflicting perspectives, and acquiescence to the alien opinions of others. Critically, the ignorance of a reader does not pertain primarily to mere unthinking acceptance; instead, it refers to conscious acceptance that follows "thinking deeply [and] . . . judg[ing] impartially and in good conscience," but that ultimately turns on the weight of "the testimony of so many notable men" (4). Christine's ignorance, like ours about Pizan, can be attributed to the granting of epistemic authority—of credibility itself (5, 7)—to the socially legitimate, well-coordinated voices of misogynist and nonfeminist authors and their interpreters across the ages. Lady Reason insists, however, that "women [readers] *can* clearly know with proof that certain things which [an author] treats are not at all true, but pure fabrications . . . [and] outright lies" (22; emphasis added). Women can respond to any such falsity both by "contradict[ing] it, and mak[ing] fun of it" (23).[4]

There is a necessary counterpart to the ignorance of a reader: the ignorance of opinion givers. Authors who attack women even for a presumably "laudable intention," Lady Reason declares, display a "sweeping ignorance [that] never provides an excuse" (17). Their ignorance causes "damage or harm" (17), involving as it does "exploit[ation of] the rights of others" (18). The "rather loose[] . . . arguments" (17) of such authors could have been avoided "if these writers had only looked" a little harder (18). But they are sidetracked by "their own vices . . . pure jealousy, [and] . . . the pleasure they derive in their own personalities from slander" (18). Pizan describes what has been written about women as "heresy" (7), "absurdit[y]" (8), "sin" (10), "deception" (31), and "slander" (23).[5] The authors of such "foolishness" she describes as suffering "overweening madness [and] . . . irrational blindness" (23).[6] In comparison with what she has described as the ignorance of a reader, the ignorance of an author can have a variety of intentions, but its effects—and its effects are what first draw Christine to the subject—are uniformly damaging. Ignorance on the part of authors is blameworthy, while the same is never said of readers. Readers silence what they know in favor of the reputed wisdom of authors, while authors blindly, madly pen often self-serving words that silence others—not only specific readers, but

4. "Contradicting" seems to appeal to more formal reasoned argument than does "making fun of," though the latter can involve logic and insight just as the former can use humor or ridicule. Perhaps Pizan leaves open to us a range of responses to patriarchy that can rightly and effectively vary according to factors from context to mood.

5. These characterizations imply that patriarchal descriptions of women's nature and "proper" role contradict moral and religious doctrine ("heresy," "sin"). "Slander" and "deception" not only point to the falseness of charges against women, but also speak to an intention to mislead.

6. Like the references to "absurdity" and "foolishness," above, those to "madness" and "blindness" emphasize irrationality and incomplete knowledge, with a possible inference of subterfuge.

also potentially whole classes of people. At best, their works are "of no use in developing virtue or manners" (3). At worst, they contribute to and rationalize the superiority of men over women. As for a reader, the ignorance of a writer is avoidable.

In this chapter I apply Pizan's understanding of what I am calling the "politics of ignorance" to contemporary feminist ignorance of historical women political thinkers like Pizan herself. Overwhelmingly, feminists doing philosophy and political theory today either do not know or do not use historical women philosophers. Books and articles reveal a most remarkable, nearly universal, and terribly unfortunate lack of conversation between contemporary and historical women philosophers. If judged by references in feminist theory and epistemology, before around 1960 virtually every philosopher was male. At least every one worth engaging in dialogue, looking to for inspiration, citing as authoritative, wrestling with in disagreement, or using as precedent. Yet there is nothing in the character or quality of the work of historical women philosophers that makes sense of our disregard of them. How could there be, when most of us have never even read most of them? Understandably, predictably, as readers we have been taught "many strange opinions" (Pizan 1982, 6), but when we become writers we have an obligation to reconsider them, a responsibility to do more than merely repeat, recycle, and reinforce them. Our ignorance, too, is inexcusable, harmful, deceptive, and repairable.

The blameworthy opinion givers Pizan cites—Matheolus, Ovid, and Cicero among them—are all men. In fact, in *Cupid's Letter* of 1399, Pizan writes, "But if women had written the books, I know for sure that things would be quite different; for they know well that they have been falsely blamed" (cited in Blumenfeld-Kosinski 1997a, 299). In this speculative assertion, she is mostly correct. Many, many philosophical texts written by women in the centuries between her time and ours are profoundly different—and more philosophical—on the subject of women from those written by men. But in our ignorance of those philosophical texts the writings of women today are *no* different from those of men criticized by Pizan.

The three ladies suggest a number of ways for Christine to remedy her ignorance, to be "wakened from sleep" (Pizan 1982, 6). Among the recommendations are self-knowledge (9), enhanced interpretive skills, and a healthy skepticism that does not accept "all the words of the philosophers [as] articles of faith" (7). The remedy that I focus on here fascinates me because of its connection to the history of political philosophy itself: telling stories of the "many women . . . who have been very great philosophers" and the "great women rulers who have lived in past times" (2). This remedy puts theory into conversation with practice, allowing practice the possibility of correcting theory. Christine's first reaction to the misogynous texts she read was to compare their pronouncements to her own "character and conduct" and that of other women (4), but no amount of evidence could outweigh for her the authority of the texts. Lady Reason, however, allows experience-based knowledge to be decisive "regardless of what you might have read," in part because experience includes not only what you see "with your own eyes" (7), but stories of women past as well. These stories, Pizan is claiming, have power—tremendous power—which is why her own work "established an authoritative 'alternative' genealogy for herself, an anterior line of authoritative female ancestors, exemplars of superlative achievement in politics, science, scholarship, literature, and religion" (Brownlee 1997, 373). When we ignore our philosophical foremothers, we fail to recognize and use this power.

In the realm of politics, for example, many believe that "women do not have a natural sense for politics and government" (Pizan 1982, 32). Pizan, however, responds to this claim by telling us of such now-forgotten but "great women rulers" (32) as Empress Nicaula, the countess of La Marche, the duchess of Anjou, and Queens Fredegund, Blanche, Jeanne, Thamiris, and Semiramis. Similarly, in the realm of philosophy, while "men maintain that the mind of women can learn only a little," Lady Reason insists that Christine "know[s] quite well that the opposite of their opinion is true" and offers "to show . . . this even more clearly . . . [by] giv[ing] proof through examples" (63). She tells us about "the wise Sappho," whose "learned books can only be known and understood by men of great perception and learning" (67). She mentions Cornificia, who "was not only extremely brilliant and expert in the learnedness and craft of poetry but also seemed to have been nourished with the very milk and teaching of perfect philosophy" (64), and the Greek Leontium, who was "such a great philosopher that she dared, for impartial and serious reasons, to correct and attack the philosopher Theophrastus, who was quite famous" (68).[7] These stories contradict and,

7. In the introduction to Ninon de l'Enclos's *To the Modern Leontium*, the ancient Leontium is described as follows: "Leontium was an Athenian woman who became celebrated for her taste for philosophy, particularly for that of Epicurus, and for her close intimacy with the great men of Athens. She lived during the third century before the Christian era. . . . She added to great personal beauty, intellectual brilliancy of the highest degree, and dared to write a learned treatise against the eloquent Theophrastus, thereby incurring the dislike of Cicero, the distinguished orator, and Pliny, the philosopher, the latter intimating that it might be well for her 'to select a tree upon which to hang herself.' Pliny and other philosophers heaped abuse upon her for daring, as a woman, to do such an unheard of thing as to write a treatise on philosophy, and particularly for having the assurance to contradict Theophrastus" (l'Enclos 1903, 1).

in combination, overrule the misogynist theories. Politically, they are essential to know, and epistemologically, they are essential in order to have knowledge. *The Book of the City of Ladies* not only begins but also ends with Christine urging all women to "be well-informed" (256).

Pizan's alternative genealogy of authoritative female ancestors has not, in fact, taken root, for there remain today both puzzling absences and problematical presences of women actors and knowers in the literature of every field. The list of authors caught in the politics of ignorance has only grown, reinforcing itself. Critically here, among the names on the list are feminists who might have been expected—because uniquely equipped professionally and unusually invested politically—to continue Pizan's tradition of uncovering and studying and using women thinkers.[8] Nonetheless, feminist theorists and epistemologists today almost across the board write as if they find historical women thinkers "full of every vice" (Pizan 1982, 4) when worth mentioning at all. Perhaps, according to Pizan, we continue too readily to accept the verdicts and interpretations of canonical philosophers toward whom we ought to be more skeptical and against whom we ought to have more evidence. At some level, it appears, we still pay homage to the seemingly disreputable androcentrism of traditional "man the philosopher," where intellectually strong men alone have the vital and dangerous task of hunting big ideas to provide us with the central source of food for thought, the meat of philosophy, and in which women merely gather the ideas of others. Are ideas "game"? Is that why philosophers like to shoot down the ideas of others? Is that why women are not supposed to play?

Interestingly, the same feminist authors who avail themselves not at all of their foremothers tend to quote *contemporary women and men* theorists quite regularly. There is genuine, admirable conversation going on especially among academic feminist thinkers today; it contains praise as well as criticism, allows writers to build and improve upon each other, and treats female and male authors as equally credible. There is also regular citation of *historical male* philosophers and political theorists. This, too, is admirable, locating recent work in larger frameworks, patterns, and traditions and based on careful scholarship, even if the same names appear time after time. But if neither using historical figures nor using women thinkers is uncommon, where are the *historical women* thinkers?

Lady Reason stressed that such absence, such ignorance, "stems from a failure to learn . . . about women who have possessed great learning and

---

8. I should be clear that I include myself here. Most egregiously, I wrote a book on Rousseau with scant mention of the powerful critiques of him written by historical women political thinkers.

profound understanding" (Pizan 1982, 64). *We* have failed to overcome the ignorance of past writers, perhaps in no small part because we have not remedied our ignorance as readers, which would seem to be a necessary prior step.[9] We display in our published work a rather sweeping ignorance of our philosophical foremothers when, looking a little harder, and actively educating ourselves, we could do far better. Most critically, according to Pizan, our actions cause harm, both to our readers in particular and to women in general. As Mills notes more recently with regard to racial practices, "the *lack* of appropriate concepts can hinder learning, interfere with memory, block inferences, obstruct explanation, and perpetuate problems" (1997, 7). In light of Pizan's analysis of the causes and consequences of the politics and epistemology of ignorance, we should reexamine our own work and consider the remedies she recommends.

THE EVIDENCE

It is actually somewhat unpleasant to provide the evidence to support my rather broad charge that sadly, if in some ways unsurprisingly, even feminist theorists ignore our female predecessors. Whatever examples I choose sound like indictments of those particular authors, though each is only a useful illustration of a much more general pattern and though I include my earlier work as part of that troubling pattern. That said, I resolve the problem as follows: I try to "pick on" some of the "big girls" rather than those more institutionally vulnerable, to use individual authors only to make visible larger trends, and to acknowledge that they have a tremendous amount to offer despite the few specific passages cited. Most usefully, I use Pizan's own style from *The Book of the City of Ladies* to present the case, a style that is wisely, strategically, both conversational and confrontational. In addition to using Pizan's theory, that is to say, I also adopt something of her style.

Among the aspects of her literary approach I admire and imitate is its conversational character. Christine recounts a conversation between herself and the three ladies. Her role (like that of "Penny" in what follows) is to raise questions and file complaints. Her frank questions are sometimes

---

9. Blumenfeld-Kosinski writes that "the function of the three allegorical ladies in the *City* is to console Christine. On a first level, Christine's complex relationship with her authors is bound up with the question of consolation; consolation is an achievement that requires Christine's active participation: the correct evaluation of her own experience, the shedding of her blindness, *and finally, writing*" (1997a, 308; emphasis added).

about the claims of specific authors, but also refer to general ideas embodied in proverbs, legal practices, and customs. She is not easily persuaded. She often follows up a lady's answer with another more pointed question. The queries tend to be about various aspects of women's nature and social roles. When she is convinced, Christine draws out what conclusions she considers to have been reached.

The answers Christine receives are an amazing and varied collection of stories. All aim at correcting popular and learned opinions about women. A response might ridicule an author's personality and motives for insulting women or reinterpret an insult against women so that it becomes a compliment. Most valuably, the answers are themselves an education about women's history. Pizan "does not merely reason away prejudice, she also aims to promote a positive conception of women's nature and abilities," to draw the reader into the possible through a retelling of the past (Gardner 2000, 51). I (the "Professor" in what follows) join her in that retelling.

PENNY POINTS FIRST TO PERHAPS THE MOST INDISPUTABLY PROB-
LEMATICAL TENDENCY IN RECENT FEMINIST PHILOSOPHY REGARDING
HISTORICAL WOMEN THINKERS—ERASURE—AND USES GENEVIEVE
LLOYD AS AN EXAMPLE.

Genevieve Lloyd's landmark and much cited *The Man of Reason: "Male" and "Female" in Western Philosophy* reveals the gendered nature—the maleness—of ideals of reason claimed by their authors to be gender neutral, objective, and universal. But this marvelous critique of what the book's cover calls "the nature of our Western beliefs about 'reason'" is actually a critique of Plato, Aristotle, Philo, Augustine, Aquinas, Bacon, Descartes, Hume, Rousseau, Kant, Hegel, Sartre, and (ta-da!) Beauvoir, of whom there is even a "partial defence" (1984, 99). The "Western philosophy" of the title is of theories, traditions, and schools established by men. Did no women contribute to "Western philosophy"?

THE PROFESSOR RESPONDS, SHOWING SOME OF WHAT THIS ACCOUNT
OMITS.

Despite their absences from these texts, many women throughout the centuries thought that they were part of the history of Western philosophy, and many of the males on the list you cited acknowledged the role of these women. Further—and here the substantive argument is truly amazing—many of the criticisms leveled by Lloyd against Western philosophy are *untrue* of Western women philosophers; in fact, centuries earlier, numerous

women made points about reason similar to Lloyd's, though unacknowledged by her. "Let me tell you about women who have possessed great
learning and profound understanding" (Pizan 1982, 64) on the subject of
reason. Christine de Pizan's *The Book of the City of Ladies* defends both
women's rational nature and women's "educated reason . . . [as] a guide to
truth" (Green 1995, 27). In the 1700s Mary Wollstonecraft's rich analysis of
reason analyzes its critical connections with virtue, passion, and community,
and she "reflected positively on other ways of understanding the world,"
such as through sensibility (Sapiro 1992, 63). Later that same century, Germaine de Staël, somewhat suspicious of abstract reason and objective truth,
"*redefines* reason in order to include passion, engagement, and interdependence (with certain identifiable others) as integral to moral political action"
(Marso 1999, 99, 106). The overgeneralization that equates certain male,
misogynist, canonical thinkers with "Western philosophy" systematically
excludes specific women too numerous too count and too dear to discount
in terms of their substantive ideas about reason.

PENNY BRINGS UP ANOTHER EXAMPLE OF ERASURE OF WOMEN FROM
THE HISTORY OF IDEAS.

I see now that, ironically, "Western philosophy" as used by Lloyd is as subtly
and problematically male as the "reason" her book critiques.

Professor, I see the same thing done with regard to "modern philosophy"
and "the history of ideas." However the broad category is described, it is inhabited only by men. Consider Arlene Saxonhouse's 1985 accomplishment,
Women in the History of Political Thought. Saxonhouse establishes the important fact "that women do appear consistently throughout the history of
political thought," and that "it is the inadequacies of modern scholarship"
rather than of the original texts that made them vanish (vii). But the authors
whose views on "the role of the female" in political life (1) she explores are
all male: Plato, Aristotle, Cicero, Seneca, Saint Paul, Saint Augustine, Saint
Thomas, and Machiavelli. Like Lloyd's "Western philosophy," Saxonhouse's
"history of political thought" was written exclusively by men. She admits
that "obviously lacking" in her analysis "is any work by a woman," but says
that "to flagellate history for what was not, accomplishes little" (viii).

THE PROFESSOR RESPONDS.

"Now you see an example of someone . . . very wise coming out with something very foolish" (Pizan 1999, 23). To use Saxonhouse's own idea, we must
look to the "inadequacies of modern scholarship" rather than "history" to

explain the absence in her book of "any work by a woman." "Flagellate history" indeed.

PENNY CONTINUES, ADDING ANOTHER EXAMPLE.

It is not just a handful of writers who do this. The same is true of Nancy Tuana's 1992 *Woman and the History of Philosophy*, which covers what a different list of men—Plato, Aristotle, Descartes, Rousseau, Kant, Hume, Locke, and Hegel—say about women. Again, the aim is philosophically noble and politically spot on: "to demonstrate that feminist critiques of traditional philosophy will require . . . extensive transformations of the discipline itself" (xiv). Women appear in all these books as subjects, not as speakers, not as authorities even on themselves, and the impression they leave, especially in combination, is that no women did write authoritatively, or notably differently, or perhaps at all. If we do not even look for women to be credible authorities when the subject is their own political role and perspectives, it seems less likely that we will search them out for their views on more legitimated subjects of political discourse such as justice or freedom.

THE PROFESSOR DISCUSSES TUANA'S "EXTENSIVE TRANSFORMATIONS."

I agree with Tuana that "feminist critiques" mandate "extensive transformations" of varied disciplines; I am joined by feminist thinkers across the centuries. Feminist scholarship on works now considered canonical is part of a long, if, according to what you bring up, unacknowledged, feminist tradition. It is a mark of the political theorist to be engaged in debates of the day and over perennial political questions; thus, the writings of feminist theorists, like those of nonfeminist theorists, usually include responses to and criticisms of the influential ideas of others.

The history of theory contains, for example, Margaret Cavendish's 1664 reflections on Thomas Hobbes (*Philosophical Letters*), Mary Astell's 1694 examination of John Locke (*A Serious Proposal to the Ladies*), and Mary Wollstonecraft's 1790 critique of Edmund Burke (*A Vindication of the Rights of Men*) and more famous 1792 one of Jean-Jacques Rousseau (*A Vindication of the Rights of Woman*).[10]

---

10. Jean Grimshaw writes: "Since the time of Wollstonecraft, feminist questions and concerns have always had a dialectical relationship to dominant or influential philosophical or political traditions; they have both used but also been critical of them" (1986, 11). Although she wrongly begins with Wollstonecraft, and although she does not mention that influential thinkers also used and criticized feminist theorists as well, she is on the right track.

Not only have historical feminists tackled each canonical figure, they have also done so on a wide range of political and philosophical issues. To cite some specific issues, Emma Goldman "rejected the long-standing bifurcation of private and public held by her anarchist predecessors . . . [Peter] Kropotkin, Michael Bakunin and Pierre Joseph Proudhon" (Haaland 1993, 22). Margaret Fuller "emphasized art over philosophy, the reverse of what Emerson did" (Rosenthal 1971, v). Rosa Luxemburg "disagreed with Marx. . . . [She] maintained that nationhood divides rather than unites workers . . . stressed an ethical dimension and the idealism of workers while Marx stressed the inexorable laws of history . . . refuted Lenin's basic doctrines . . . [and] created a concept of socialism that was her own" (Ettinger 1986, 47, 166, 167).

PENNY NOTES THE ERASURE OF FEMINIST FOREMOTHERS EVEN WHEN THE TEXT IS DISCUSSING FEMINISM.

I see now that those who ignore women in the history of ideas or philosophy or political theory or Western thought misrepresent that history and leave out all varieties of important ideas.

Professor, I notice that even on the subject of feminism historical women are not cited. For example, Carole Pateman's historical essay, so promisingly titled "Feminism and Democracy" (1989), is not a study of what our foremothers wrote on democracy but an exploration of the historical John Stuart Mill. Jane Addams's landmark *Democracy and Social Ethics* (1902) is never mentioned, nor is Harriet Taylor's work on intolerance, though it has been said that in Taylor "many will, no doubt, recognize . . . elements foreshadowing the discussion of eccentricity in [Mill's] *On Liberty*, written more than twenty years later" (Jacobs 1998, 135). The literature on democratic theory generally conveys the impression that the "seventy-year struggle for woman suffrage . . . contributed nothing to the course of American democratic thought" (Kraditor 1968, 4).

THE PROFESSOR ADDS EXAMPLES OF WOMEN POLITICAL THEORISTS WHOSE VIEWS ON DEMOCRACY HAVE BEEN IGNORED.

To explore women thinkers on the subject of democracy is a mammoth task. Perhaps unexpectedly, the eloquent Voltairine de Cleyre "saw the seeds of anarchism in Jeffersonian democracy" (Glassgold 2001, 29). Even Frances Wright's "political misrecognition" of U.S. political culture as "a veritable utopia of democracy" (Bederman 2005, 441) is informative. Eleanor Roosevelt's spiritual take on democracy is also noteworthy (Cahill 1997, 171–74).

And then there is Lydia Maria Child, who "protested against Indian dispossession and genocide" (Karcher 1997, 25); "shift[ed] the scene of . . . transcendentalist explorations from rural nature to urban streets and slums" (299); "essentially created American children's literature, which she used as a vehicle for combating racial prejudice" (3); "anticipate[d] today's multicultural approach to Women's Studies by exploring commonalities and differences in the status of women across the globe" (336); "publicized the plights of the urban poor[,] spoke out against capital punishment and the imprisonment of women for prostitution[,] called for prison reform [and] eliminating poverty" (3); campaigned for women's suffrage; and had "a vision of community that extended the bonds of family beyond blood kin" (5).

PENNY INTERRUPTS, SMILING.

But was she a theorist?

THE PROFESSOR LAUGHS, THEN CONCLUDES.

"I could cite you so many cases that my testimony would be endless!" (Pizan 1999, 128). Such unwarranted exclusions of women are not, of course, unique to democratic theory, but exist with regard to every subject and in every school of thought.

PENNY INSERTS SOME HOPEFULNESS.

I see now that "so much good has come into the world by virtue of the understanding of women" (Pizan 1982, 77). Pateman's book as a whole, subtitled *Democracy, Feminism, and Political Theory,* is better than most. A look at the index shows one reference apiece to Beauvoir, Vera Brittain, and Woolf; two references to Arendt; three to Mary Astell; and seven to Wollstonecraft.

NOW THE PROFESSOR REFUSES TO BE SOOTHED.

That is progress. On the other hand, according to that same index, meriting one mention among historical male theorists are Dewey, Du Bois, and Engels, while Mill the father gets two, Marx five, Filmer and Freud eight, Hegel nine, Hobbes ten, Mill the son thirteen, and Rousseau twenty. More inclusive of women than most, yes, but still quite a contrast.

PENNY MENTIONS A FINAL EXAMPLE OF ERASURE IN WORK ABOUT FEMINISM.

Consider, as well, the anthology *Revisioning the Political: Feminist Reconstruction of Traditional Concepts in Western Political Theory.* From the history of political theory one will encounter, among the men: Aristotle, Augustine, Machiavelli, Mill, Rousseau, Weber, Marx, Montesquieu, Bentham, Burke, Hobbes, Hume, Locke, Montaigne, and Engels. Among its thirteen chapters, the history of women in political theory does appear: there is one reference apiece to Gilman, Beauvoir, Ida B. Wells, Mary Follett, and Simone Weil and three to Arendt, whose earliest cited work, from 1958, just squeaked in under the pre-1960 criterion. I was especially disappointed because I had excitedly anticipated before reading the text that as feminists reconsidered core concepts in political thought, they would look to our philosophical foremothers for inspiration.

THE PROFESSOR POINTS TO SOME RECURRING PROBLEMATICAL ASSUMPTIONS.

Again, the assumptions behind so many reclamation projects seem to be that "traditional concepts" come exclusively from traditions that exclude women, and "reconstructions" come only from contemporary sources. The literature assumes that no female theorist before 1960 thought about political philosophy either very deeply, or very differently from men.

HERE PENNY NOTES THAT SOMETIMES FEMINISTS DO MENTION THEIR HISTORICAL FOREMOTHERS BUT DISMISS THEM WITHOUT SUFFICIENT EXPLANATION AND OFFERS DONNA HARAWAY AS AN EXAMPLE.

In her famous essay on cyborgs, Donna Haraway makes a passing reference to Virginia Woolf: "Students facing Joanna Russ for the first time, students who have learned to take modernist writers like James Joyce or Virginia Woolf without flinching, do not know what to make of *The Adventures of Alyx* or *The Female Man*" (1990, 220). In this sentence, the incredible Virginia Woolf becomes merely a representative of "modernism," something bad, mundane (222). I *never* read her without flinching, and most students never read her at all, so I do not know this foremother as Haraway presents her. Haraway's Woolf is irrelevant. Mine is brilliant.

THE PROFESSOR REPLIES TO THE CHARGE AND DEFENDS WOOLF.

"My dear daughter, such a deduction is totally invalid and unsupported" (Pizan 1982, 36). Not a single book has yet been written on Woolf's political or philosophical opus—though biographies and literary studies abound— so it certainly seems premature at best to dismiss her as simplistic. Do not conclude that since she has read Woolf—though any specific works she is thinking of remain unnamed—we need not bother. Why, even I flinch a bit at Woolf's "photographs of dead bodies" (1938, 10); her discussion of how "culture is prostituted and intellectual liberty sold into slavery" (92); her analysis of how, "when a brain seller has sold her brain, its anaemic, vicious and diseased progeny are [still] let loose upon the world to infect and corrupt and sow the seeds of disease in others" (93); and her arguments about how society "distorts the truth[,] deforms the mind[, and] fetters the will" (105), to mention just a few nonmundane ideas from a single one of Woolf's numerous flinch-inducing books. Perhaps what we wrongly read without flinching are such dismissals of women thinkers.

PENNY CONSIDERS WHY, EVEN WHEN DISMISSIVE COMMENTS ARE MORE SPECIFIC, THEY SEEM SOMETIMES TO SERVE NO REAL PURPOSE AND STILL TO LACK JUSTIFICATION. SHE OFFERS ANN SNITOW AS AN EXAMPLE.

In a most unusual and wonderful move, Ann Snitow in her 1990 "A Gender Diary" makes relatively extended use of Mary Wollstonecraft—nearly two pages out of thirty discuss her—as she insightfully explores historical varieties of what she terms the "central feminist divide . . . about just how gendered we choose to be" (9). But in an equally surprising move, at least to me, Snitow spends a fair amount of this time dismissing aspects of Wollstonecraft that are not really even related to Snitow's project. She writes that "we . . . have rejected Wollstonecraft's call for chastity, for the end of the passionate emotions 'which disturb the order of society'; we have rejected her confidence in objective reason and her desire to live as a disembodied self . . . [and *Vindication*'s] appeals to God and virtue are a dead letter to feminists now" (29). Further, she describes Wollstonecraft's *Vindication* as chaotic, suffering "structural disorganization" (29).

THE PROFESSOR TRACES SUCH IDEAS BACK THROUGH TIME.

You know, my dear, while the widespread praise and fame of historical women thinkers repeatedly seems magically to disappear (Spender 1982), criticisms and dismissals of them travel through time with ease, each version reinforcing the previous ones. Remarks about the supposed disorganization of *Vindication,* for instance, go back to William Godwin's 1798 *Memoirs of the Author of "The Rights of Woman."* Without a single example, Wollstonecraft's husband declared the book "eminently deficient in method and arrangement" (Godwin 1987, 232). Biographers two centuries later continue the pattern. Claire Tomalin, for example, claims that the *Rights of Woman* "is a book without any logical structure" (1974, 103). Yet one reads the rest of Tomalin's chapter in vain if one is looking for her reasons for finding its structure so deeply flawed.

PENNY CONNECTS THIS POINT WITH AN EARLIER ONE.

Such recycled but not reconsidered criticisms remind me of another example. To return to Haraway, the authors whom she contrasts with Woolf are applauded because *they,* supposedly unlike Woolf, satisfyingly engage in "serious politics" (1990, 220). Decades earlier, I recall, Leonard Woolf similarly wrote that "Virginia was the least political animal that has lived since Aristotle invented the definition" (cited in Black 1983, 297). The charges do get repeated, gaining in potency, even if they are never really defended.

THE PROFESSOR REFUTES THE CHARGES AGAINST WOOLF AND WOLLSTONECRAFT.

Regarding Woolf, "her interests and occupations did not fit the classical Aristotelian definition of politics as activities relating to public governance . . . [and] the issues that attracted her attention and the solutions that she preferred were not the ordinary ones" (Black 1983, 298). Leonard apparently was tripped up by the narrowness of his authorities.

As far as Wollstonecraft's work is concerned, I judge the book to have an easily observable structure. As a "vindication," it is a defense of what has been denied or challenged: women's rights. The first chapter provides us with a theoretical perspective from which to think about the subject—an unfamiliar perspective on freedom. In the next three Wollstonecraft lays out the familiar attacks on equality in order to respond to them. She describes "prevailing opinion" in two chapters, and "animadversions" in a third, thus describing what women are "supposed" to be like and how certain writers have defended that. She then adds her own distinctive critique of women's and men's lives, as subsequent chapters trace the undesirable social and moral effects of women's degradation. The final chapters speak to solutions, from domestic arrangements to national education.[11]

PENNY RESPONDS.

That so many should comment on how "badly organized" (Sunstein 1975, 207) the text is remains something of a mystery. "But please tell me exactly what it is that makes so many different authors slander women" (Pizan 1999, 17).

11. This is a one-paragraph summary of a talk I gave, "Wollstonecraft's *Vindication of the Rights of Woman:* The Structure and the Argument" (2005).

THE PROFESSOR DARES TO INTRODUCE AN UNCOMFORTABLE POLITI-
CAL VANTAGE POINT FROM WHICH TO VIEW THE SITUATION.

I fear there may be some politics of the academy involved here. I have
said elsewhere, regarding authors' motives, that some "men have criticized
women . . . because they like to flaunt their erudition: they have come across
these views in books and so like to quote the authors whom they have read"
(Pizan 1999, 18). If it is plausible that these authors cite certain writers to
prove themselves well educated, then is it not plausible that other authors
make use of male and neglect female ancestors in order to establish their
own credentials and "objectivity"? In a case like Snitow's, there may even be
"good intentions" (17)—an attempt to justify or make palatable the positive
use of one aspect of a woman philosopher's thought by showing ability and
willingness to dismiss the rest.

PENNY INTERRUPTS WITH A QUESTION.

Are such authors "right to do so, since they were acting with good intentions" (17)?

TO ANSWER, THE PROFESSOR CONSIDERS THE CONSEQUENCES.

First of all, "attacking one party" or section "in the belief that you are ben-
efiting" another simply "is unfair," potentially even an "abuse[of . . .] power"
(17). Even more troubling, it "stops anyone else from using the material" (18),
a result "completely unjust" (17) and exactly opposite that which we hope for.
Too, I find it most fascinating how this strategy stands in rather stark opposition to the widely spread notion that feminists do not subject other feminists to critical analysis—supposed political correctness, you know—and in
deeply troubling contrast to feminist use of historical male theorists.

PENNY PROVIDES EVIDENCE IN SUPPORT OF THE PROFESSOR'S SUG-
GESTION ABOUT DIFFERENTIAL TREATMENT, CITING AN ESSAY BY
LINDA ALCOFF.

In contrast with the negative references to Wollstonecraft and Woolf just
discussed, among endless other examples, think about the extraordinary degree of generosity, and the nearly monumental effort, put forth to "rescue"
male philosophers. Consider Linda Alcoff's imaginative essay exploring the
usefulness to feminist theory of Gadamer's epistemology. Alcoff says that
Gadamer is a "conservative" (2003, 231), that he is not by intention a feminist (232), and that he may not even have an epistemology (231, 232). Despite all these deficiencies, she says, in an essay *on* feminist epistemology,

it is worth it to advance a different interpretation of Gadamer, to "follow Gadamer's definitions of tradition and meaning carefully" (234), and to "maximize the coherence" of his thought (235). When will we bring this spirit of interpretive generosity and open-minded exploration to the texts of historical women philosophers? When will we take the "God" out of "Gadamer," so to speak?

THE PROFESSOR SUGGESTS ANOTHER UNPLEASANT BUT PLAUSIBLE EXPLANATION OF THE DIFFERENCE IN HOW WE READ TEXTS.

I harbor a persistent, nagging suspicion that there is "women's work" even in philosophy. As I read contemporary feminist theorists repeatedly, hopefully, appealing to schools of thought not made for us or by us, I wonder if what we are doing is exercising traditional female virtues: accommodating, redecorating, appreciating, excusing, adapting, fitting in, focusing on the positive, not really disagreeing with so much as making men into their best selves, almost letting them take credit for our ideas, even seeking protection in them for our own work.

PENNY LAUGHS. THE PROFESSOR CONTINUES.

I know, I'm getting carried away. But I wonder, does it *ever* seem that way to others?

PENNY CONSIDERS ANOTHER POSSIBILITY.

Maybe we should consider these acts philosophical virtues rather than shortcomings?

TO WHICH THE PROFESSOR RESPONDS.

Maybe I would, *if* we exercised them in readings of women as well as men. *And* if we sometimes had sufficient legitimacy to say to the male philosopher-kings: "Forget this, it's not worth it; what you have to offer is not enough to offset the distortions, omissions, misinterpretations, slander, and disingenuousness."

PENNY POINTS OUT HOW SOMETIMES EVEN WHEN OUR FOREMOTHERS ARE MENTIONED, IT IS IN PASSING AND USES SUSAN MOLLER OKIN AS AN EXAMPLE.

"I understand and clearly see that women are overwhelmingly innocent of what they are so frequently accused" (Pizan 1982, 110). I did have a moment of excitement. Scanning the index to Susan Moller Okin's 1989 *Justice, Gender, and the Family,* I found the names of Abigail Adams, Susan B. Anthony, Astell, Beauvoir, Olympe de Gouges, Gilman, Elizabeth Cady Stanton, and Woolf. But looking through the text to see what use Okin had made of these figures erased the smile from my hope-springs-eternal visage. These historical women appeared almost exclusively in lists of "bold feminists . . . [who] have occasionally challenged the tradition" (14), "great feminist thinkers" (61) and "those throughout history who dared suggest that accepted principles about rights and equality be extended to women . . . [and who] were all ridiculed for such suggestions" (67). While I applaud practically any references to them, I have to wonder, if these women were so bold, such great thinkers, so daring, why does Okin do no more than mention them, while there is plenty of time to delve more deeply, once again, into Aquinas, Aristotle, Rousseau, and Mill?

THE PROFESSOR REPLIES.

"I can readily believe you, for whoever wants to look for intellectually sophisticated women can find many in the world" (Pizan 1982, 85–86).

PENNY EXPLORES HOW RECENT FEMINIST THEORY OFTEN REPEATS WHAT OUR FOREMOTHERS HAVE SAID, BUT MAKES NO MENTION OR USE OF THEM, CITING FRYE.

Marilyn Frye examines the situation of women reading philosophy that "makes women's experience appear[] anomalous, discrepant, idiosyncratic, chaotic, 'crazy,' . . . unintelligible or intelligible only as pathological or degenerate" (1992, 59). Frye is especially troubled by the fact that individual women readers "tend[] to trust the received wisdom and distrust her own senses and judgment" (59). She comments how, in "the present era" women's "most fundamental act of . . . emancipation was granting ourselves authority as perceivers" (61). While I appreciate so much in Frye's essay, I cannot but notice and mourn the fact that she is, apparently without ever suspecting, repeating the words of Christine de Pizan from six hundred years earlier: "They say . . . [woman] is the vessel as well as the refuge and abode of every evil and vice. . . . I detested myself and the entire feminine sex, as though we were monstrosities in nature" (1982, 5). But are we, in "the present era," the first really to grant ourselves "authority as perceivers"?

THE PROFESSOR OFFERS NUMEROUS EXAMPLES FROM HISTORICAL WOMEN POLITICAL THINKERS TO COUNTER THIS CLAIM REGARDING WOMEN'S AUTHORITY.

How could we be, when in 1405 Pizan checked the accuracy of misogynist texts by "thinking deeply about these matters . . . examin[ing] my character and conduct . . . and . . . consider[ing] other women whose company I frequently kept, princesses, great ladies, women of the middle and lower classes, who had graciously told me of their most private and intimate thoughts" (1982, 4)?[12] How could it be true when, in 1706, Mary Astell "insist[ed] on this natural Right of Judging for her self" (1986b, 72)? What about Margaret Fuller, who, in 1845, said to her women readers, "I ask them, if interested by these suggestions, to search their own experience and intuitions for better" (1971, 14)? How can it be true when, in 1893, Matilda Joslyn Gage told people to take her book and "read it; examine for yourselves; accept or reject from the proof offered, but do not allow the Church or the State to govern your thought or dictate your judgment" (1980, 5)?

THE POLITICS OF IGNORANCE

As the previous conversation has shown, ignorance can manifest as absence: silence, erasure, and invisibility. Ignorance is passed on by marginalization: shunning, minimizing, making token references, underestimating, using without citation, criticizing without argument, and criticizing gratuitously. Another form of ignorance is misrepresentation (which may include many of the former), which we practice through lies, distortion, and relatively careless analysis.

Adrienne Rich writes:

> Suppose we were to ask ourselves, simply: What does a woman need to know? Does she not, as a self-conscious, self-defining human being, *need a knowledge of her own history,* her much-politicized biology, an awareness of the creative work of women of the past, the skills and crafts and techniques and powers exercised by women in different times and cultures, a knowledge of women's rebellions and organized movements against our oppression and how they have been routed or diminished? Without such knowledge women live and have lived without context, vulnerable to the projections of male fantasy, male

---

12. Beatrice Gottlieb adds, "Christine's defense against both literary attacks and shabby treatment was, first, to deny the truth of what was said. She could see with her own eyes that women were not what they were said to be" (1997, 281). Even more strongly, Patricia Phillippy says that Pizan's project directly "involves a turning away from traditional authorities" (1997, 330).

prescriptions for us, estranged from our own experience because our education has not reflected or echoed it. I would suggest that not biology, but *ignorance of our selves, has been the key to our powerlessness.* (1979, 240; emphases added)

The thread connecting Pizan and Rich is an understanding of what is at stake in the knowledge of our history, a lesson this chapter says we have not yet put into practice. The politics of ignorance contains epistemological elements—questions about what constitutes knowledge and what counts as ignorance, as not knowing; issues of what is knowable and of what is worth knowing; questions about not only how we can know but also what maintains our ignorance—and political ones: social forces that legitimate and perpetuate misrepresentation, neglect, absence, and marginalization, from the conventions of universities and various disciplines to the standards of publishing houses. The political aspect has to do not only with causes but also with consequences, the effects on individuals, groups, and social relations that feminist thinkers from Pizan to Rich have made central.

Pizan uses examples of historical women theorists to preserve, reinterpret, or recover their ideas, as well as to counter arguments commonly used to justify sexual inequality. Pizan, of course, is not alone in employing this strategy, but herself follows some and precedes others engaged in similar ventures. In 1691 Sor Juana Inés de la Cruz wrote about books from which she received "no little inspiration" (1987, 64), stories of "many and illustrious women" (64). Among those she cites are "a most wise Queen of Saba, so learned that she dares to challenge with hard questions the wisdom of the greatest of all wise men" (64). She refers to the Sibyls, Minerva, Polla Argentaria, Zenobia, Nicostrate, Aspasia, Hypatia, Leontium, and Proba Falconia, noting their wisdom, their accomplishments as teachers, their quests for knowledge. She points out that these women were "held, and celebrated— and venerated as well" (66), but she necessarily stops short of "mentioning an infinity of other women whose names fill books" (66). In the eighteenth century Judith Sargent Murray also spoke of the power of "accumulating examples" and thought that "knowledge of women's abilities and accomplishments is the greatest tool for empowering young women in the new republic" (2006, 1). She published four essays as a follow-up to her famous "The Equality of the Sexes," each a compilation of stories and examples she thought would overturn prejudices about women's virtues and merits. She speaks of Corinna; Sappho, "addressed as the tenth Muse" (9); Hypatia, whose "wisdom was held in universal esteem" (9); Cassandra, "proficient in the philosophy of her own and preceding ages" (9); Anna Maria Schurman, "mistress of all the useful and ornamental learning of the age which she adorned" (10); Margaret Cavendish, Duchess of Newcastle; Lady Masham; Mary Astell; and Catharine Macaulay, "witnesses" (11) with a host of others, to women's past and future.

Keeping this lineage alive through such references was and is but one strategy in countering the politics of ignorance. There is no single project, of recovery or otherwise, in which all feminists must engage, so diverse are the contributions to be made to sexual equality. Nonetheless, there are political causes and consequences of widespread ignorance and neglect of our foremothers; a product of androcentrism, the ignorance also perpetuates patriarchy, and it does have to be addressed.

To study the ideas of historical women thinkers is not to assume that they got everything "right"—they did not, just as we will not. To build on their contributions is not to assert that we should establish an identical agenda or use the same methodologies. As Pizan says, and as my use of Pizan is meant to demonstrate, what these predecessors indisputably *can* offer us is intellectual insight and political power. Charlotte Perkins Gilman talks about honoring our predecessors by surpassing them: "They knew less than we do. If we are not beyond them, we are unworthy of them—and unworthy of the children who must go beyond us" (1979, 111). We can better go "beyond" them if we know and use and build upon them.

In the end, is contemporary feminist disregard of foremothers such as Pizan any different from contemporary antifeminist ignorance of them in cause, character, or consequence? There is definitely overlap in causal factors. The number one claim from both is that, because of a variety of factors, women did not write political theory. The lack of familiarity with women thinkers is traceable to the fact that few people of any political stripe encounter them in school at any level; or find them in bookstores or libraries; or hear of them as important to whatever historical eras, social movements, or schools of thought organize their academic disciplines, guide their personal lives, shape their political systems, or inspire their heroes. Most people conclude that the reason they do not see something is because nothing is there.

The all-male version of the history of political thought is like the emperor who wore no clothes. Both are convinced that they are dressed in the most elegant garb, which only the wise and elite can see, making it rather tough for either to admit that something is missing even when, at some level, they know. The politically astute townspeople, like most political theorists, know or enjoy their place too well to push the embarrassing truth, though there are whispers. Relative outsiders, a child in one case, feminists in the other, persist in breaking the news, in neither case gratefully received.

Without doubt, we can convince ourselves and be persuaded by others that something exists when it does not, or that something does not exist when it does. On a social level, the deceit is often linked to political advantage to be had by the deceivers. While general knowledge of such events— from undercover operations, cover-ups, and smear campaigns to hidden treasures, intrigues, and cabals—is readily admitted, most tend to see themselves as beyond manipulation. Who will suspect untruths and sense the invisible in what situations and why? Who will speak up, at what costs? What are the potential sources of knowledge that can counter widespread, deeply ingrained ignorance?

Feminists are usually more suspicious of gendered claims (such as "there have been no women political thinkers") than are nonfeminists. We have become accustomed to various political frameworks that talk about the unconscious, false consciousness, and consciousness-raising and usually ask questions about who really gains and loses from certain social arrangements purportedly established for the common good. But there has been precious little evidence of women thinkers to the contrary (few stories about or books by women, even fewer with commentaries written about or myths built around them). Much feminist energy *has* gone into related tasks: explaining what—other than women's inferior nature—accounts for women's absence from political theory, detailing the maleness of much philosophical work thought to have nothing to do with gender at all (Lloyd 1984), exploring the consequences of patriarchal perspectives (Pateman 1988), and struggling to establish conversations about what male theorists have said about women, as if women mattered to political life (Saxenhouse 1985). Therefore, it is fair to conclude that while there are some causes of ignorance in common between feminist and nonfeminist neglect of women philosophers, revealing differences exist as well.

The supposed absence is often seen by antifeminists as evidence of women's inability to engage in philosophical work or of their natural disinterest in it compared with their interest in more appropriately feminine concerns. Further, it tends to be reported by nonfeminists as simple fact, rather than a starting point for related inquiries, and often a rather uninteresting fact, philosophically speaking: "Philosophy has been a male preserve. This is a fact which one would have to take account of if one were interested in the historical background of philosophy. It forms part of the social setting, and a history of thought and culture would have to take note of it. But, although feminists may not like my saying so, it is a point of no importance for the *history of philosophy*" (Hamlyn 1987, 11; emphasis in original). The unspecified feminists Hamlyn assumes might disagree with him are indeed more likely to find the exclusion of women philosophically relevant.

Feminists tend to note women's absence, to discuss alterable social causes of their supposed nonparticipation, to treat what canonical thinkers say about women as politically and philosophically important, and to bring a feminist perspective to bear on other philosophical issues. Perhaps this tempers the consequences of neglect of women thinkers. It certainly does not eliminate the negative effects.

FINAL THOUGHTS

If I said that a new work of Descartes or Dewey had just been unearthed, and that *you* were to be among the first to work with the manuscript, that would easily be seen as an amazing opportunity. Why are we—apparently still—not as excited by the prospect of being among the first today to work out Sappho's theory of love, to compare Pizan's advice to princes with Machiavelli's, to describe what pragmatism looks like when Jane Addams and Charlotte Gilman are considered its founders, to explore the roots of situated knowledge in Anna Julia Cooper's *A Voice from the South,* or to examine the challenges to Platonic epistemology in Sor Juana's seventeenth century *First Dream*? Why are we more comfortable writing the ten millionth essay on Rousseau (as I have done) than a trailblazing interpretation of Emma Goldman or Emma Mashinini?

I hesitate. I see a specter of feminist guilt being inflicted by me: "Bad feminists. Too enamored of big boys." I consider taking advantage of women's socially overwrought sense of responsibility by adding my concerns to others' work. I know I am a little off the charts when I flinch at yet another reference to Foucault, a bit extreme for scouring texts for references to the history of women philosophers. I know the research agendas of others are trustworthy and often more enlightened than my own. But who is *ever* going to pay attention to the women if not people such as those discussed in this essay and reading this book?

I urge all scholars who use the history of philosophy in their work to put a five-year moratorium on references to historical male thinkers. If we are to grant women epistemic authority—deemed essential by writers from Pizan to Frye—we must refuse to recreate patriarchy by repeatedly if unwittingly reinscribing men as single-parent fathers of every tradition, giving men pride of place in every philosophical narrative. Ultimately, it is by focusing on them that we can ask not only how women fit into malestream categories and schools of thought, but also how they reorganize, rewrite, repel, and reimagine them: "One has to learn to trust one's own cognitive powers, to develop one's own concepts, insights, modes of explanation, overarching theories, and to oppose the epistemic hegemony of conceptual frameworks designed in part to thwart and suppress the exploration of such matters; one has to think *against the grain.* . . . So we need to see differently, ridding ourselves of class and gender bias, coming to recognize as political what we had previously thought of as apolitical or personal, doing conceptual innovation, reconceiving the familiar, looking with new eyes at the old world around us" (Mills 1997, 119, 123).

What we have instead is a politics that can go so far as to make one's appeal to historical women theorists evidence of the triviality of one's project, justification for the marginalization of the contemporary author along with the historical one. Epistemic authority is a political accomplishment. There is not only an epistemology of ignorance, but also a politics of ignorance, and the two are connected.

We can all do something, even short of my five-year moratorium, without having to become historians of philosophy. We can order for ourselves or our libraries some of the wonderful new editions of the works of women thinkers so that presses will continue to keep them available. We can avoid generalizing about "the history of philosophy" or "modern epistemologists" when we exclude women, so that we do not make women invisible and irrelevant. (Better yet, we can think about how some particular women do and do not challenge those generalizations.) We can exhibit the same degree of generosity and exert as much effort in reading women philosophers as we do men. For every five references to historical male philosophers in our work, we can make one to a woman. Or even every ten. There is a citation politics. And someone might see our reference to Sojourner Truth or Mercy Otis Warren, Mary Church Terrell or Alexandra Kollontai, and then read her. We can break the cycle.

More informally, we can say something like this over drinks at a conference: "I see what you mean in your paper. But have you considered the perspective of Ida B. Wells (or Josephine Butler or Maria Stewart) on the subject?" We do not have to feel responsible for detailing their work, any more than we do for teaching our companion about overlapping systems of oppression or how rape is violence, not just sex. A sketchy comment ("I'm not certain, but I seem to recall that she had something a bit different to say on the subject of X"), wonderfully, may send both parties to the library. We can start new conversations.

Those of us who teach can begin, slowly, to include some or additional women in our syllabi. Those of us at Ph.D.-granting institutions should quite reasonably require students to be conversant with historical women theorists before the former go out and start teaching; otherwise, the next round in the politics of ignorance begins. Their education should be considered incomplete without it. As Pizan urged, we can be enlightened and empowered by learning and using this history.

Pizan knows that our task is difficult, as it always is for those who "started instruction in my school late" (1997, 306). But "difficult" is not the same as "impossible," and starting late is much more desirable than never starting at all. Six centuries ago Pizan made "a choice to write works defending women" (Quilligan 1991, 2) in the face of various traditions that "obscured and misrepresented" (Phillippy 1997, 330) women's lives. In this alone, she is an example of a foremother worth following.

The world has been divided up in many different ways. Philosophically we divide it temporally, into ancient, medieval, and modern. Sometimes we divide it by theorists, so that the world becomes inhabited by Marxists and Aristotelians, Thomists and Heideggerians. Or we cut it into schools of thought, so that we look out into a world of pragmatists and realists, empiricists and idealists, liberals and conservatives. But *none* of the ways of divvying it up is based on women. We don't look around and think, Are they Astellian or Cooperites, Pizanians or Cruzers? It is men who mark philosophical territory, and that should piss us off more.

3

THE POLITICS OF FORM:
SEI SHŌNAGON

To write well, a man must, then, possess his subject fully; he must reflect upon it sufficiently to see clearly the order of his thoughts, and to make of them a sequence, a continuous chain, of which each point represents an idea; and when he has taken up his pen, he must guide it with due sequence along this chain, without letting it wander, or bear too heavily anywhere, or make any movement save that which will be determined by the ground it has to cover. It is in this that severity of style consists, and it is this also that will make unity of style, and regulate its flow; and this alone also will suffice to make the style precise and simple, even and clear, lively and consecutive.

— Comte de Buffon, 1753

I. ACCORDING TO BUFFON

According to Buffon (1707–1788), renowned author of a landmark thirty-six-volume work on natural history, good writing requires knowledge of and reflection upon the author's subject. The writing, exactly like the thinking that produces it, is

    sequential;
    unified;
    precise;
    linear;
    parsimonious; and
    orderly.

Above all, it seems, the pen must not wander. One could hardly hope for (or dread finding, as the case may be) a starker contrast to use to introduce Sei Shōnagon (circa C.E. 965–?), Empress Sadako's lady-in-waiting from about

993 to 1000. *The Pillow Book,* Sei Shōnagon's masterpiece, is described as a "lengthy collection of notes, stories, comments, and descriptions of everyday life" (I. Morris 1991, 317). Her pen roams, her style varies, the order is not apparent. "The datable sections are not in chronological order, and the lists have been placed with little attempt at logical sequence" (12). Yet without Buffon's "severity of style," and despite the academy's general assessment of "engaged, socially situated, and sometimes literary styles as inimical to serious knowledge" (Stone-Mediatore 2007, 56), Sei Shōnagon, I will show, produces a work worthy of notice by political thinkers.

2. THE LIST TITLED "THINGS THAT HAVE LOST THEIR POWER"

Sei Shōnagon's list titled "Things That Have Lost Their Power" includes a stranded boat, a toppled tree, a defeated wrestler, a woman waiting in vain, and a balding man. What an unusual entry into the notion of power. It encompasses defeat and retreat, lost rank and lost love, every example simple to feel, easy to visualize. The useless boat stranded in a dry creek has not permanently lost its ability to move and carry, but is at the mercy of elements over which it has no control. Even after the water rises and the boat sails again, it will remain eternally vulnerable, a message perhaps about the fleeting nature of abilities and sometimes even of incapacities. The tree felled by winds, lying "on its side with its roots in the air" (Shōnagon 1991, 145), on the other hand, is a permanent loss, and a slow death. The roots have nothing to grab on to; their defeat is obvious, like the bug that is on its back and helpless to right itself. Even the great go down, and that which causes the fall may be sudden, natural, overwhelming. Does Sei Shōnagon imagine the life to which the dead tree contributes, from soil for other growth to homes and food for many species? Or is giving, even giving life, at the expense of one's own life, something akin to but distinct from power? More public yet is the losing sumo wrestler, walking off, undoubtedly aware of eyes on his back. Even almost unimaginable physical power, like personal and political power, is insecure. We set up contests that guarantee losers. We do not immediately disappear without victory. Our losses can touch others.

The boat and the tree were "defeated" by nature, one permanently and one temporarily. Both are obviously helpless, unable to cover up their losses. In contrast, the woman combing her "short hair that remains" after removing a wig (Shōnagon 1991, 145) had "hidden" her loss in public, but in her isolation and privacy still has to confront an unpleasant reality. Power has public and private dimensions in more than the sense of different realms; losses successfully covered up must eventually be faced. Although it seems similar, in the example of the "old man who removes his hat, uncovering his scanty topknot" (145), the emphasis is on how others view him, while in the woman's case it is on her confrontation with herself. Power encompasses both. Similarly, in the case of the woman who realizes she waits in vain for her husband to "rush about looking for her" (145), her confrontation with the fact that she has lost her sway over him, or is less dear to him, is the moment of loss, the feature Sei Shōnagon captures, perhaps more than the actual decrease of influence or how the woman appears in her husband's eyes.

The examples capture sadness and resignation more than fighting back. Because of the category, every example contains its opposite, a stage before the loss. The category itself emphasizes change. Overall, power includes flourishing, health, holding on against and moving with opposing forces, being useful, sustaining oneself, public recognition, being heard and heeded, victory, being loved. On the last point, however, the examples under "People Who Seem to Suffer" include a "woman passionately loved by a man" who is "absurdly jealous" (171). The answer for the woman whose husband is now indifferent to her is not simple, for love can also oppress the beloved. There is just so much to think about here.

Sei Shōnagon's entry into power is interesting to compare with more common images of power in political theory. Both Aristotle's *Politics* and Locke's *Second Treatise* open with discussion of numerous household hierarchies, delineating who has what form of power over whom and why, from parent and child to sovereign and subjects. Plato's *Republic* is framed by the situation of a perfectly just man severely punished for supposed injustice, who is used as a vehicle to discuss the worthiness of justice regardless of its costs. Mill's *On Liberty* begins with a history of clashes between liberty and authority, from ancient Greece to modern Europe. Publius's solution to government abuse of power envisions mutually suspicious branches of divided government resisting each other's perpetually anticipated encroachment. From brutish states of nature to the nature of brutes, these examples are more extreme than quotidian, more abstract than real, more institutional than interpersonal. Lost power is rarely so poignant as in Sei Shōnagon, for the focus is usually on such matters as the causes of the decline of various regimes or varieties of corrupt states. Emotion is muted, even in more intimate examples, as when Plato's aging Cephalus leaves the conversation, or when Rousseau's autobiographical young self learns of his parents' fallibility. Although perhaps it comes closest, Socrates' condemnation to death is more moving in his companions' responses than in his own, which turn to reflections on political obligation.

3. SEI SHŌNAGON IS DESCRIBED

Sei Shōnagon's work is described as "the precursor of a typically Japanese genre known as zuihitsu" (I. Morris 1991, 11) (also, to clarify the muddiness, its "earliest example" [Miyake 2002, 1] and elsewhere yet its "inventor" [Daugherty 1999, 1]). *Zuihitsu*, a still-existing form of writing, is variously defined as "a term of Chinese origin that literally means 'following the brush'" (Fukumori 2003, 1), or "'the brush moving with the mind'" (Greer 2000, 5). The author's mind either follows or moves with the brush. In either case, mind does not lead or fly alone. It is a collaborator, and emphasis is strongly on the process of writing/thinking rather than on writing as the product of thinking.

4. *ZUIHITSU* PUTS BUFFON TO THE TEST

Zuihitsu puts Buffon to the test, for we might be stretching to call it a "form" of writing at all. In what might be ascending Buffonian order, its product—Sei Shōnnagon's *The Pillow Book*—has been said to be

"hardly coherent as a continuous narrative" (Greenaway 2005, 2);
"unsystematic and disordered" (I. Morris 1991, 13); and
"structured in but the loosest fashion" (Dalby 2001, 1).

But some portrayals continue up the continuum, describing it as

"intuitively, as opposed to systematically, structured" (Sullivan 2003, 2) and
structured in the ren "order of themes linked . . . semantically" (Tanaka 1993, 4).[1]

David Greer connects it to Joseph Campbell's myths, writing that is unsymmetrical and purposely unfinished, leaving room for the reader's imagination (Greer 2000, 1). Also hinting at its depth and coherence, Carroll

---

1. Tanaka defines *ren* as "not only a mechanism in which words were linked creatively . . . but also in which people were linked themselves provoking and changing each other" (1993, 6).

writes that Sei Shōnagon's "varied forms are not easily recognized today as 'political theory.' [But o]ne must ask whether this doubt arises because *The Pillow Book* does not meet essential criteria for what constitutes political theory, or rather because our assumptions and notions (stated or unstated) of political theory's forms are too limited" (Smith and Carroll 2000, 20). That is, indeed, what we must ask.

In this chapter I pursue some possibilities inherent in these later more positive comments. As Tanaka indicates, the absence of one easily recognizable kind of order is not simply the equivalent of incoherence but may hold the possibility of another kind, maybe even conceptually deeper, and especially useful for rethinking the customary. Arguably, pursuing Greer's point, theoretical works that "leav[e] room for the reader's imagination" surpass those that convey the author's conclusions; more interactive, they encourage the reader to talk back in a philosophical conversation. And finally, along the lines Carroll suggests, narrow ideas of forms appropriate to political theorizing deprive us of the insights of quite profound political thinkers who found alternative genres more useful, more suitable, or necessary for raising certain issues, perspectives, possibilities and connections.

5. THREE TYPES OF WRITINGS

It is generally agreed that *The Pillow Book* contains three types of writings: catalogs, essays, and diary entries. In the first, catalogs, Sei Shōnagon inventories items of interest to her under a general topic heading, with varying degrees of comments upon them. The lists range from "Herbs and Shrubs" to "Things That are Unpleasant to See." The second category, essays, often contains Sei Shōnagon's observations, speculations, and explanations of people, events, and things around her, with titles ranging from "When a Woman Lives Alone" to "Men Have Really Strange Emotions." Finally, the diary element comprises memoirs, primarily about her years at the imperial court, with descriptive titles, for example, "Gentlemen of the Fifth Rank" and "On the Tenth Day of Each Month." While these three types of passage are distinguishable, "more than one style of writing can be interwoven into a given passage" (Fukumori 1997, 2), as when, for instance, an item on a list itself becomes an essay.

Other commentators have found similar but still divergent ways of classifying the content:

"Reminiscences; opinions and imaginative sketches; and lists, some with comments, others merely lists of words" (Disse 2005, 1)

"A collection of lists, gossip, poetry, observations, complaints and anything else she found of interest" (Wikipedia 2005, 1)

"Stray thoughts and impressions . . . informal collections of notes. . . . Insights, gossip, character sketches, poetic fancies . . . anecdotes and stories" (Dalby 2001, 1)

"Names of things . . . thoughts on place, life, human affairs and nature; diary accounts and narrative sections concerning Sei Shōnagon's experiences at the palace" (globaled 2000, 1)

Clearly, some descriptions of Sei Shōnagon's form are negative ("no set of writing could be more miscellaneous," says Washburn [2001, 1]), others more positive ("the outstanding quality . . . apart from her incomparable prose, is precisely the freedom with which she offers her opinions on absolutely everything," declares Delacour [2002, 3]).

6. STRAY AND INFORMAL NOTES

"Stray" and "informal" "notes" and "lists" (no less "gossip") is not what Buffon suggested constitutes good writing. On the other hand, "cataloging," "commenting," "recollecting," "speculating," "explaining," "observing," "opining," and "criticizing" seem rightful—some even essential—parts of theoretical work. Fascinatingly, Fukumori writes that Sei Shōnagon's book "offers the scholar a wealth of approaches in its myriad subjects, observations, and writing styles. Indeed, what seems to be the primary difficulty in scholarship of *Makura no soshi* is the formulation of a method for encompassing this very diversity" (1997, 1).

What Fukumori describes is an intellectual difficulty for scholars, not a problem with Sei Shōnagon's writing, Buffon notwithstanding. Ivan Morris, in contrast, locates the problem squarely in Sei Shōnagon's brush. He considers the "structural confusion" of the book "its main stylistic weakness," though he also finds "part of its charm . . . precisely in its rather bizarre, haphazard arrangement" (1991, 13). Fukumori sees in *The Pillow Book* especially challenging material for the scholar, while Morris, marking the text as "charming" (not to mention "weak," "bizarre" and "confused"), almost undermines its scholarly worth—and both verdicts are largely in reference to its form.

7. SEVERAL QUESTIONS PRESENT THEMSELVES

Several questions present themselves. If Buffon is correct, why would Sei Shōnagon choose to write in any way other than that which he prescribes? If Buffon is correct, can Sei Shōnagon be of value? Can she, in particular, be considered a political thinker? If Buffon is incorrect, why did he mistake a particular form for the whole of theory? If he is incorrect, can Sei Shōnagon serve as a corrective? Either way, what connection has any form to the substance of political theorizing? Are there any restrictions on form in what we will call theory? How do issues of gender intersect with questions of form?

8. THERE ARE THREE MAIN ISSUES

I see three main issues, or risks, for political theorists in what I am calling the politics of form: first, being irrational, namely, arbitrarily associating only certain forms of writing with philosophical investigation; second, being unjust, that is, exercising political bias, consciously or not, in silencing voices that write in certain forms, given "that texts that present alternatives to dominant worldviews also tend to defy scholarly norms (Stone-Mediatore 2007, 56); and third, being unwise, because of the "loss to our philosophical endeavors that would accompany such an exclusion" (Gardner 2000, 17). The problem with the politics of form to date, I will argue, is not the idea that *how* one writes is linked to *what* one writes; instead, what is troubling is that the associations it makes between style and substance are incomplete at best, erroneous at worst. Further, the gaps and errors have a pattern to them: what the politics of form is most likely to comprehend and appreciate is theorizing within Buffon's comfort zone, while the majority of political writings by women and many by non-Western men are likely to reside outside it. Sei Shōnagon, for instance, who has virtually never been studied as a political thinker, uses language and forms that simultaneously mark her work as feminine and nonphilosophical.

9. SEI SHŌNAGON'S STYLISTIC CHOICES

Was there a politics to Sei Shōnagon's stylistic choices? "Japanese men considered the writing of prose in their native language to be beneath them, and so they concentrated their literary efforts on poetry and Chinese prose" (globaled 2000, 1). But while men wrote "in Chinese, in kanji . . . men discouraged women from learning Chinese characters" (Greer 2000, 3), though Morris states that Sei Shōnagon simply "*prefers* to avoid Chinese characters, the so-called 'men's writing'" (I. Morris 1991, 306n190; emphasis added). As "Logic 101" informs us, if all philosophy is written in form Y, and no women write in form Y, then women do not write philosophy. The exclusion of women from Chinese letters involved assumptions about what the sexes *should* do, questions of appropriateness and propriety, as well as about what they *could* do, issues of ability and nature. "Chinese literature, even the poetry of such a popular writer as Po-Chu-I, was supposed to be beyond women's ken" (I. Morris 1991, 306n190). Sei Shōnagon wrote *The Pillow Book* "in the same characters lovers wrote their tanka in, *hiragana*. . . . Heian noblemen sniffed at hiragana, though. They called it *onnade*, the women's hand. Good for poetry and love letters, maybe; but for the Heian man to write 'something serious' in hiragana was . . . unseemly" (Greer 2000, 3) The fact that Sei Shōnagon wrote in a style both reserved for women and associated with the nonphilosophical makes her an extraordinarily useful test case of the politics of form.

In Sei Shōnagon's own time, style was inseparable from substance. It was not uncommon even to have "regarded handwriting as the mirror of a person's soul" (I. Morris 1991, 184), based on "the belief that a person's handling of his brush was a better guide to his breeding, sensitivity, and character than what he actually said or wrote" (183–84). In the rest of this chapter I focus exclusively on Sei Shōnagon's lists, or catalogs, a form indisputably even less studied and more suspect than the essay and diary. I not only write about Sei Shōnagon but also employ her method in my argument, as is hopefully already evident. Using some of her style allows me to advocate for it both by argument and by example.

In the end, I believe that the politics of form has been used as an exclusionary strategy—it has certainly functioned that way in practice. In most of what follows I discuss how it has excluded women from being treated as serious political thinkers. Much of the argument also applies to the exclusion of many non-Western men, for overlapping though not identical reasons. I leave it to others, however, to more systematically develop that angle, since this will take me in some different directions.

10. NORMS OF FORMS

Tuana writes that "to the extent that we have elevated the rational, objective, universal style of much of contemporary philosophy, the personal, situated, individual style of [nontreatise] writings renders their philosophical status questionable" (Tuana 2004, 67). A correlation exists between our elevation of certain forms, such as that of Buffon, and the diminution of other forms, such as that of Sei Shōnagon. Because we equate philosophy with certain forms, anything that departs from them risks being labeled unphilosophical (too, we may mistake "good" form for good content). The operating assumption is that philosophical investigation requires certain styles and is incompatible with others.

There is a second, more hidden but more revealing correlation between certain forms and philosophizing. Buffon's recommendations lend themselves to a certain set of virtues, or at least characteristics; they work well with writing inclined to universalize, for example, and to follow a particular form of rational argument. But such writing also leaves out, or is less compatible with, a different set of virtues or characteristics that other forms capture better; included here is writing inclined, for instance, to personalize. It would be difficult to find a text that is more "personal, situated [and] individual" (Tuana 2004, 67) than *The Pillow Book,* which lists what Sei Shōnagon deems embarrassing, surprising, and elegant, and details happenings under titles such as "One Day When the Emperor Visited Her Majesty's Rooms" and "Travelling in My Carriage One Day." Is political theorizing compatible with the forms employed by Sei Shōnagon, forms that lend themselves to the more "personal, situated [and] individual"?

II. VIRTUALLY ANYONE CAN WRITE A LIST

Virtually anyone can write a list. We compose them without a moment's hesitation and on a daily basis. We make lists of "pros" and "cons" to help us reach tough decisions and produce "to do" lists to organize our projects. We create shopping lists to help us navigate the grocery story and birthday lists to remind us to send someone a greeting. Writer's block for someone trying to create a list of household chores is almost unimaginable (unlike cleaner's block for one actually trying to accomplish the tasks on that terrible list). A more accessible, less threatening form of writing is difficult to conjure up. What is its possible relevance to political theorizing?

Things ordinary people commonly use lists for:

To organize (days, inventory)
To remember (tasks, events)

To rank in importance (qualities, goals)
To weigh (sides of a question, options)
To facilitate decision making (give reasons, consider alternatives)
To be more efficient (with time, resources)
To clarify one's thinking (break the complex into manageable parts,
    brainstorm)

Lists are connected with rational processes such as weighing, evaluating,
mapping out, sorting, and clarifying. They are also linked with philosophical goals such as exploring and "uncover[ing] . . . possibilities" in oneself and
in different ways of living with others (Segalove and Velick 2000, 2). They
invite us to be more observant and imaginative, sometimes unexpectedly
and excitingly so, as lists proceed beyond the obvious or superficial. There is
no necessary limit on subject matter.

The Pillow Book contains about 164 lists. Some are simply catalogs of
names, such as those of mountains, offered without comment; many of these
were omitted in Ivan Morris's popular translation.

Sei Shōnagon's lists that present items with minimal elaboration:

Things That Cannot Be Compared (laughter and anger; the little indigo
    plant and the great philodendron)
Annoying Things (thinking of something to add to a letter after having
    sent it; forgetting to knot a thread)
Depressing Things (persistent rain; a wet nurse out of milk)

Even with minimal commentary, Sei Shōnagon shows herself to be an astute
observer of the everyday and the unusual, the natural and the social, the
ritualistic and the idiosyncratic. Without question, she appears in her lists
as capable of the most precise description in few words and as a wise and
fascinating selector of items. Even more critically, the choice of items is a
strategy for challenging the reader to see diverse relationships and to suggest
common ground between them that can lead to a reconsideration of both
the individual items and the subject of the category itself. The headings of
many lists are unique to Sei Shōnagon.

Among Sei Shōnagon's most unusual and intriguing categories:

Things That Are Distant Though Near (relations between members of a
    family who do not love each other; the last day of the twelfth month
    and the first of the first)

Things That Are Near Though Distant (paradise)
Things That Were Good in the Past But Are Useless Now

In these instances the unfamiliar grounds for classification help us to create new analytic categories for seeing and understanding the world, an alternative mental filing system. This seems quite a philosophical accomplishment.

In some lists, it takes a sentence or two to describe an entry (Hateful Things: "An admirer has come on a clandestine visit, but a dog catches sight of him and starts barking. One feels like killing the beast"). Often such elaborated-upon items refer to especially specific incidents, and frequently they combine description and evaluation.

While lists seem the most mundane product of writing and a far cry from the political theory treatise, Sei Shōnagon's lists are unlimited in content (public and private; natural and human-made; concrete and abstract), and bring together in unexpected and provocative ways ideas and events that seemed disparate. There are reasons an author might prefer to use them over other alternatives.

Why someone chooses lists over other forms:

A list is adequate for the task: it gets the job done
It is perfect for the task: it captures exactly what one is after
There are time constraints on the writer (from inconvenient interruptions to fear of being caught writing)
There are time constraints on the readers one desires
A list is a useful stage of writing that may develop further
It reflects a way of thinking one has mastered
It is an easy form in which to include the unexpected, bury the controversial, and so on
It is accessible and inviting to the audience one wants to reach
It is thought-provoking—invites the reader to participate, add on
It matches the author's strengths
It is compatible with certain kinds of thinking
It is an efficient means
It can be used to make a point about style
It can help to personalize the writing

The idea of a fit between author and form is provocative, leading us to consider authors as in possession of knowledge not only of their subjects but also of themselves. "One respect in which Hannah Arendt differs conspicuously from most contemporary schools of political study is her fondness for the essay form as a means of expression. *The freedom of the essay suits admirably her manner of discursive reflection,* exploring the implications of a subject into unlooked-for ramifications" (Canovan 1974, 110; emphasis added). So it may be said with regard to Sei Shōnagon: the catalog is a form that fits well with her "keen powers of observation, a rapier wit, and wicked sarcasm" (Paris 2004, 2), among other qualities.

The idea of a fit between reader and form is also interesting. As the editors of *Lists to Live By* suggest, "You can read them one at a time, pondering and reflecting on each point. Or you can read them in bunches. Start at the beginning and work your way through to the treasures at the end, or jump around to your favorites. Read them when you're on the run, or curl up with a steaming cup of hot chocolate" (Gray, Stevens, and Van Diest 1999, 9). They suggest not only that a certain type of reader might be drawn to lists, but also that the various moods and situations of each reader are compatible with different uses of the book. Further, the flexibility of lists not only accommodates readers, but also invites them to put the material to a variety of uses. "Some will cause you to reflect. Some will bring excitement. Some will make you smile. Some will move you to action. Some might even change your life" (9).

12. POLITICAL THEORIZING

Political theorizing certainly shares such goals, for it is work intended to move people to think and to act, to care and to converse, about and in light of "dynamic ideas covering a gamut of topics from contentment to friendship, from family to virtue" (Gray, Stevens, and Van Diest 1999, 9). Consider one exemplary example of a passage describing a trip on a boat that becomes material for political theorizing: Sei Shōnagon's list called "Times When One Should Be on One's Guard."

The first item on the list warns us about people with bad reputations who give "a more sincere impression than those of good repute" (Shōnagon 1991, 246), individuals who also fascinate canonical theorists such as Plato and Rousseau. The second item tells us to be wary "when one travels by boat" (246). This item becomes an elaborate story about a "delightful" excursion Sei Shōnagon had taken with a light heart on a calm day. Again, appearances and assumptions are deceiving and dangerous, for "a violent wind blew up" and the sea transformed. These events lead Sei Shōnagon to reflect on some of her own assumptions about people and situations, touching on our tendency to under- and overestimate certain people and tasks and also to be oblivious to the very different lives even of those right around us. "When one thinks of it," one sees the bravery and skills of "common people," such as those working on the boat in rough seas (246). It is through telling the story of her journey that Sei Shōnagon encourages her readers to confront, literally and metaphorically, the fearful waves that overtake smooth waters, to reflect on our own unacknowledged dependence on others, and to really see how different people live.

This last theme leads to a story about a second journey, this time on a boat with a cabin, used by "people of quality" (246). Here again she is led, through her new vantage point, to reevaluate what is safe and what is dangerous. Again, she is "very moved to observe people" (247) and this time considers the different lives people lead in relation to the water, from the pleasure-seeking travelers to the risk-taking, resourceful sailors to the courageous "poor women divers who have to plunge into its depths for their livelihood" (247). Concluding the tale, she writes that the experience she had watching the divers was "enough to make even an outsider feel the brine dripping. I can hardly imagine this is a job that anyone would covet" (248).

In the end, the list has provocatively, seamlessly, moved from the familiar "people who have a bad reputation" but who nonetheless misleadingly "give a more sincere impression" (246) to the newly appreciated strengths and hardships of people too easily overlooked. She has offered a thoughtful reconsideration with political overtones and ramifications. She has engaged, and through her vivid recounting invited her readers to engage, in political theorizing.

13. WHAT AN AMAZING CONTRAST

What an amazing contrast between this unstudied list and Plato's much-analyzed parable of the ship in the *Republic,* book 6. In Socrates' parable, the common people are ignorant even of what knowledge is required for sailing, yet they nonetheless struggle for position and power and ridicule the one true sailor. In Sei Shōnagon's story, "people of quality," including herself, are ignorant of what the "common people" know until they realize in a dangerous situation how skilled the sailors are and how dependent upon them the travelers are. What radically different politics the stories embody. But why is one of these competing visions part of the canon of political thought while the other either goes unnoticed or is declared irrelevant to the discipline? Allan Bloom writes that "the image Socrates presents to Adeimantus has a double function: it tells him a lovely tale which charms him into a more favorable disposition toward philosophy; and it causes him to think about the meaning of the image. . . . Thus he is beginning to think about philosophy, and in a way he is philosophizing" (Bloom 1968, 398). But Sei Shōnagon's, too, has a double function: it grabs us with a dangerous adventure and leads us into a more favorable disposition toward the knowledge and abilities of "commoners." We reconsider the character and location of wisdom, thereby also engaging in political philosophizing.[2] We become more aware of those whose lives, like those of Sei Shōnagon's sailors and pearl divers, intertwine with ours without recognition, likely at their cost. And this list is but one example of the potential contribution to political theory that *The Pillow Book* might make

14. ALTHOUGH IT IS NOT MUCH NOTICED

Although it is not much noticed, Sei Shōnagon is not the only politically relevant writer to employ catalogs.

Other political thinkers who used lists and catalogues, and why:

Aristotle. Ernest Barker describes three "type[s] of Aristotelian writings," one of which "may be called the compilation or catalogue" (1975, xxxvi), such as in the *Constitution of Athens.* Von Fritz and Kapp consider that text "a sketch written mainly for private use" (1950, 6). Despite a consistently negative tone to their evaluation, they see that the form is particularly useful for a survey and for work that is "historical and descriptive" (6). Further, they notice that it not only lends itself to a "detailed account of the constitutional set-up and of the governmental machinery" (7), but also allows "two different sketches of the same constitution, one from a more evolutionary, the other from a more stationary, point of view" (10–11), almost but not quite grasping its profound potential to alter viewpoints and offer a look through multiple lenses.

Hobbes's *Leviathan,* especially the definitions. "Hobbes assumes that definitions are the only principles we need to treat as requiring no argument" (Curley 1994, ix). His use of lists thus reflects a philosophical position he is arguing for. Also, the definitions are supposed to build compellingly, step

2. I do not mean to imply that she is a great democrat, though passages like this one do raise questions about the frequent characterizations of her as unremittingly elitist.

by step, what will ultimately be political consensus. The lists contribute to the appearance of irrefutable logical demonstration. Finally, they teach readers "habits of thought and action which were required if his scheme for the organization of political society was to work" (Johnston 1997, 366).

Susan Griffin, in *Woman and Nature.* In her own explanation for her choice of form, she writes: "In the process of writing I found that I could best discover my insights about the logic of civilized man by going underneath logic, that is by writing associatively, and thus enlisting my intuition, or uncivilized self. Thus my prose in this book is like poetry, and like poetry always begins with feeling. One of the loudest complaints which this book makes about patriarchal thought (or the thought of civilized man) is that it claims to be objective, and separated from emotion, and so it is appropriate that the style of this book does not make that separation" (1978, xv).

Griffin's style, like Hobbes's (and perhaps Sei Shōnagon's), is itself an argument, a criticism of other styles that Griffin is consciously trying to go "underneath," even though they are associated, variously, with "logic," objectivity, and civilization itself, recalling Buffon. Consider her characterization of the alternative she rejects: "Patriarchal thought . . . represent[s] itself as emotionless (objective, detached and bodiless). . . . This voice rarely uses a personal pronoun, never speaks as 'I' or 'we,' and almost always implies that it has found absolute truth, or at least has the authority to do so" (xv–xvi). "The other voice . . . is an embodied voice, and an impassioned one" (xvi). In each case, the choice of a list or listlike form is associated with substantive goals. The two men use it differently from how the two women do: to get the reader to see from a particular perspective, using an analytical style where wholes are broken into definite parts, and descriptions and definitions are made to appear as simple fact. The women, by contrast, use it to complicate rather than simplify, to tax themselves as writers and their readers, to incorporate feeling rather than make it seem to disappear. But all four authors provide evidence that diverse forms are associated with specific philosophical insights and inquiries, with distinct effects on readers, and with certain topics and goals of inquiry.

15. THERE IS, THEN, A PROBLEM

There is, then, a problem in limiting political theory to certain forms. The problem goes beyond missing theorizing that exists outside those forms, though it certainly does include that. According to political writers and commentators from Aristotle and Sei Shōnagon to Hobbes and Griffin, openness to form is *required* if we want a fuller range of political philosophy, for form *is* associated with content, and disregarding certain methods entails eliminating certain philosophical insights and impacts.

We have perhaps always practiced a modest degree of openness to form in political theory. Especially when engaged in by canonical thinkers, but even for those a ring or two outside center stage, we have indulged or at least overlooked their excursions into nontreatise writings. But very few of those formally adventurous works are rated as highly as ones the same authors wrote in more standard genres and formats, though a few were best sellers in their own day.

Examples of mainstream male theorists using nontraditional forms:

Epistolary novel: Montesquieu, *The Persian Letters* (1721); Jean-Jacques Rousseau, *Julie* (1761)

Dialogues: Plato; Rousseau, *Rousseau, Judge of Jean-Jacques—Dialogues* (1780 and 1782)

Autobiography: Saint Augustine, *The Confessions* (401); Jean-Jacques Rousseau, *Confessions* (1781); Peter Kropotkin, *Memoirs of a Revolutionist* (1899)

Fable: Machiavelli, *Belfagor: The Devil Who Took a Wife* (composed 1515–20); Bernard de Mandeville, *The Fable of the Bees* (1705)

Novel: William Godwin, *Things as They Are; or, the Adventures of Caleb Williams* (1794); Jean-Paul Sartre, *Nausea* (1938) and *No Exit* (1944)

Essays: William Godwin, *The Enquirer* (1797); Bertrand Russell, *Sceptical Essays* (1928) and *Unpopular Essays* (1950)

Poetry: Friedrich Nietzsche, *The Gay Science* (1882) and *Zarathustra* (1891), sections

Short stories: Sartre, *Intimacy and Other Stories* (1938)

Plays: Machiavelli, *Mandragola* (*The Mandrake Root*) (1515)

Virtually across the board, formally diverse works do not get the attention that is given to works that conform to norms of forms in political theory, regardless of the gender or reputation of the author. Yet we may be working with incomplete understandings when we ignore these men's less traditional (in form) writings. The problem takes on more dramatic dimensions when everything, or nearly everything, in an author's corpus is outside the boundaries; for many women, we miss their thought entirely. They have two strikes against them. Add to their being female and beyond the borders of accepted form an author being non-Western, like Sei Shōnagon, and she is likely out.

Disinterest in or disdain for nontraditional forms of political theorizing alone does not explain why we have disregarded women theorists, for many have written in forms that are more traditional.

Among the innumerable historical examples of women using traditional forms of political and philosophical writing:

> Treatise: Catherine Macaulay, *Treatise on the Immutability of Moral Truth* (1783); Mary Wollstonecraft, *A Vindication of the Rights of Men* (1790) and *A Vindication of the Rights of Woman* (1792); Harriet Taylor Mill, *Enfranchisement of Women* (1851); Aisha Ismat al-Taimuriya, *The Mirror of Contemplation on Things* (1892?); Matilda Gage, *Woman, Church, and State* (1893); and Charlotte Perkins Gilman, *Women and Economics* (1898)
>
> Political pamphlet: Catherine Macaulay, *Loose Remarks on Certain Positions to Be Found in Mr. Hobbes's "Philosophical Rudiments of Government and Society"* (1767) and *Short Sketch of a Democratic Form of Government in a Letter to Signor Paoli* (1769)
>
> Utopias/dystopias/satires: Margaret Cavendish, *The Blazing World* (1655); Rokeya Sakhawat Hossain, *Sultana's Dream* (1905); Charlotte Perkins Gilman, *Herland* (1925)

But according to the arguments here, we need to do more than look past form—we need to understand what diverse forms are capable of grasping, asking, teaching, and expressing (Gardner 2000).

16. THE HEGEMONY OF PATRIARCHAL THOUGHT

"The hegemony of patriarchal thought in Western civilization is not due to its superiority over all other thought; it rests upon the systematic silencing of other voices. Women of all classes, men of different races, ethnicities, or religions, and the vast majority of laboring people were kept out of the intellectual discourse" (Lerner 2000, 7). One of the ways of maintaining that hegemony is through the politics of form. "I think we need to be sensitive to the possibility that women's thought, just like women's art, would find different modes of expression than would men's" (11). The justice claim I am most interested in here is that limiting theory to certain forms systematically silences *particular* voices. Tuana declares that "if we are to accurately understand women's contributions to philosophy, then we must foreground the venues in which women pursued philosophical inquiry" (2004, 66). Her claim is that women used different "venues," that what took place in those venues constitutes "philosophical inquiry," and that we have not looked in the right places, leading us to erroneous calculations of "women's contributions to philosophy" and, therefore, to a partial history of philosophy.

Reasons women might have for choosing/using different forms from those employed by men:

Women have different educations

They have different publishing opportunities

They are less focused on the abstract, impersonal, "the impartial, the coolly reasoned . . . the universally applicable" (Gardner 2000, 1)

The chosen forms are "more intimate, more personal, more particular" (Gardner 2000, 1), concrete

They attract different, desired readers. Lists and diaries would seem to be especially accessible, inviting forms

Philosophical writing in traditional forms are deemed especially inappropriate for women

The chosen forms evoke different, desired responses in hoped-for readers

Traditional forms set unwanted boundaries for philosophical investigation

Diaries invite personal opinions that can guide readers to specific conclusions

Patricia Hill Collins writes that "reclaiming the Black feminist intellectual tradition also involves searching for its expression in alternative institutional locations and among women who are not commonly perceived as intellectuals" (1990, 14). Gerda Lerner supports this approach: "Yes, there have been great women philosophers. . . . To find them we have to stop looking for women in the male model. We have to be willing to look at small-scale work, at messages delivered 'slant,' as Emily Dickinson said. We have to look at partial attempts, at aborted insights, at *women searching for new forms of expression*" (Lerner 2000, 11; emphasis added).

This last idea—of women consciously seeking alternative forms in which to express their ideas—is especially intriguing. Consider, for example, the "formally experimental" writings of Margaret Cavendish (Lilley 1992, xi). Frequently Cavendish "assembles a collection of short prose pieces and poetry . . . signal[ing] her concerted expansion into other prose genres" (x).

Nature's Pictures, Lilley notes, "is Cavendish's most ambitious and copious generic experiment, including moral fables, romance novella ('Assaulted and Pursued Chastity'), fictionalized treatise ('The She Anchoret'), and the autobiographical memoir, 'A True Relation'" (xi). Substantively, Lilley considers that these experiments with form are linked to the fact that Cavendish's "imagination . . . is most engaged by that which troubles or resists categorization" (xi) and are linked, as well, to the resulting fact that she, like Sei Shōnagon, "has disturbed commentators" (xii).

Forms used by significant numbers of past women political thinkers:

Poetry: Christine de Pizan, *The Long Road of Learning* (1403); Margaret Cavendish, *Poems, and Fancies* (1653); Sor Juana Inés de la Cruz, *First Dream* (1685); Phillis Wheatley, *Poems on Various Subjects, Religious and Moral* (1773); Frances Harper, *Poems on Miscellaneous Subjects* (1854); Warda al-Yaziji, *The Rose Garden* (1867)

Essays: Mary Wollstonecraft, *Thoughts on the Education of Daughters* (1787); Margaret Fuller, *Papers on Literature and Art* (1846); Anna Julia Cooper, *A Voice From the South* (1892); Emma Goldman, *Anarchism and Other Essays* (1910)

Novels: Frances Ellen Watkins Harper, *Iola Leroy* (1892); George Eliot, *Adam Bede* (1859) and *The Mill on the Floss* (1860); Germaine de Staël, *Delphine* (1802) and *Corinne, or Italy* (1807); Harriet E. Adams Wilson, *Our Nig* (1859); Flora Nwapa, *Efuru* (1966)

Letters: Abigail Adams, *The Book of Abigail and John: Selected Letters of the Adams Family, 1762–1784* (published in 1975); Mary Wollstonecraft, *Letters Written During a Short Residence in Sweden, Norway, and Denmark* (1796); Sarah Grimké, *An Epistle to the Clergy of the Southern States* (1836) and *Letters on the Equality of the Sexes and the Condition of Women* (1838); Emma Goldman, *Nowhere at Home: Letters from Exile of Emma Goldman and Alexander Berkman* (1975)

Biographies: Mary Hays, *Female Biography; or, Memoirs of Illustrious and Celebrated Women of All Ages and Countries* (6 vols., 1803); Lucy Parsons and Martin Lacher, *The Life of Albert R. Parsons* (1889); Zainab Fawwaz, *Pearls Scattered Throughout the Women's Quarters* (1894); Hannah Arendt, *Rahel Varnhagen: The Life of a Jewish Woman* (written in 1933, published in 1957); Jane Addams, *My Friend, Julia Lathrop* (1935)

Allegory: Christine de Pizan, *The Book of the City of Ladies* (1405); Aisha Ismat al-Taimuriya, *The Results of Circumstances in Words and Deeds* (1887/8); Olive Schreiner, *Stories, Dreams, and Allegories* (1923)

Autobiography: Harriet Martineau, *Autobiography: With Memorials by Maria Weston Chapman* (1877); Josephine Butler, *An Autobiographical Memoir* (1893); Elizabeth Cady Stanton, *Eighty Years and More* (1898); Emmeline Pankhurst, *My Own Story* (1914); Emma Goldman, *Living My Life* (2 vols., 1931); Charlotte Perkins Gilman, *The Living of Charlotte Perkins Gilman* (1935)

Speeches: Frances Wright, *Course of Popular Lectures* (2 vols., 1829–1836); Lucy Parsons, *The Famous Speeches* (1909); Victoria Woodhull, *Victoria Woodhull Reader* (1974)

Travel books: Nancy Gardener Prince, *A Narrative of the Life and Travels of Mrs. Nancy Prince* (1850); Harriet Martineau, *Retrospect of Western Travel* (1838); Simone de Beauvoir, *America Day by Day* (1948) and *The Long March* (1957)

Plays: Margaret Cavendish, *Plays* (1662); Aphra Behn, *The Amorous Prince* (1671) and *The Rover* (1677); Sor Juana Inés de la Cruz, *The Trials of a Household* (1683) and *The Greater Labyrinth Is Love* (1689); Olympe de Gouges, *Black Slavery; or, The Happy Shipwreck* (1789); Judith Sargent Murray, *The Medium; or, Virtue Triumphant* (1795) and *The Traveller Returned* (1796); Frances Wright, *Altorf* (1822)

Newspapers/Magazines/Journals (as editors or major authors): Emma Goldman, *Mother Earth;* Margaret Fuller, *The Dial,* Charlotte Perkins Gilman, the *Forerunner,* Hind Nawfal, *Al-Fatah;* Amelia Bloomer, *The Lily;* Margaret Sanger, *Woman Rebel;* Frances Wright, *Free Enquirer;* Victoria Woodhull and Tennessee Claflin, *Woodhull and Claflin's Weekly;* Alaíde Foppa, *Fem;* Mary Beard, *The Woman Voter;* Simone de Beauvoir, *Les temps modernes*

Children's literature: Mary Wollstonecraft, *Original Stories* (1791); Lydia Maria Child, *Evenings in New England* (1824)

Dialogue: Margaret Cavendish, *Orations* (1662); Frances Wright, *Athens* (1822).

Advice books: Lydia Maria Child, *The Frugal Housewife* (1829) and *The Mother's Book* (1831); Catharine Macaulay, *Letters on Education* (1790)

In addition to all these sources, Collins suggests looking at "the everyday ideas of Black women" and to "musicians, vocalists, poets, writers, and other artists" as well as "political activists" (15).

This list can be misleading. As the number of names that appear more than once only begins to indicate, many women thinkers wrote in multiple genres. "During the last fifteen or twenty years of her relatively short life

(51 years), [Lily Braun] published a major scholarly work on the political economy of women's labor, a number of lengthy monographs, 120 or so articles ranging from one to about 80 pages, a 2-volume autobiography, and several large works of fiction—novels, a drama, and an opera libretto" (Meyer 1985, xi). Whew.

17. THE OPENING LIST

The opening list in *The Pillow Book* is among its most famous. Sei Shōnagon describes what it is in each season "that is most beautiful." Her list includes the different lights of sun or moon; the colors on specific objects; the precipitation, sounds, acts, and animals (fireflies in summer, crows and geese in autumn) at particular times of day in each season; and emotions associated with them ("how beautiful it is," "more charming still," "one's heart is moved"). She teaches here the appreciation of virtues and beauty in differing contexts. She demonstrates openness to surroundings and exquisite powers of observation. She finds in every season, perhaps in everything, distinctiveness and the positive, even in supposed opposites. Her scenes are full of movement, testimony, processes, rather than frozen moments, and her categories retain a certain fluidity, as when she notes variety within as well as between seasons. In the scenes she paints, the beauty of the world is available to every person, not to only an intellectual or political elite, for it lives in the shapes of clouds and formations of birds. Everyone can recognize the scenes, everyone can learn from them about beauty, difference, change, the connection between heart and eye.

18. THESE APPROACHES

These approaches bear some resemblance to those Sara Ruddick develops a millennium later in "Maternal Thinking (1986), in which she discusses "a mother's *thought*—the intellectual capacities she develops, the judgments she makes, the metaphysical attitudes she assumes, the values she affirms" (369). In particular, one of the interests that she claims governs or is elicited by mothering is an interest in fostering growth. Like Sei Shōnagon's seasons, "a child is itself an 'open structure' whose acts are irregular, unpredictable, often mysterious." Perhaps the world looks different to one who must "expect change [and] change with change" daily and in evolving personalities

(372). As Ruddick describes it, "Change requires a kind of learning in which what one learns cannot be applied exactly, often not even by analogy, to a new situation. If science agrees to take as real the reliable results of *repeatable* experiments, its learning will be different in kind from maternal learning" (372–73). Further, "if we attend to maternal practices, we can develop new ways of studying learning that are appropriate to the changing natures of all people and communities, for it is not only children who change, grow, and need help in growing" (373). Ruddick's book can be linked to Sei Shōnagon's practices and theorizing, with their open structure, connections, and "priz[ing]of the private inner lives of the mind" (372). It may be that both reflect a gendered way of being in the world, that both link one's personal life with intellectual insight, both focus on what moves and changes in their world.

19. THERE IS NO ESSENTIAL CONNECTION

"There is no essential connection . . . between form and sex" (Gardner 2000, 3). There *is*, however, an historical connection. "Women's lives differ systematically and structurally from those of men," with "epistemological consequences," among others (Hartsock 2003, 292). Varying over time and across cultures, the sexual division of labor has wide and deep ramifications, touching our relationships with others, with nature, and with material life. Sei Shōnagon's lists contain variations from her time, including gendered languages, different employment, and different leisure activities, of the sorts of sexual divisions that turn gender into "a world-view structuring experience" (292).

It is empty, if not disingenuous, to say that there have been no women political thinkers because there have been none that wrote in forms used by men of the canon. Not only have some women done just that, so too have many men experimented with form, using some more common to women. But using form as a narrow criterion of whether or not a work constitutes or contributes to theory is a practice that disproportionately discriminates against women, as the long—and still dramatically incomplete—list of women's writings outside the norms of forms shows, and simultaneously against certain models of and insights from philosophy, without justification. The exclusion of certain forms is neither value-neutral nor objective; instead, it "can be traced back to the male bias in . . . the dominant model of moral philosophy" (Gardner 2000, 4, 5).

20. WHAT LISTS CAN CONTRIBUTE

What lists can contribute, in Sei Shōnagon's work as a whole, is as diverse as the subject matter of the lists themselves. A short list, "Different Ways of Speaking," makes visible how language varies by profession, sex, and class. It invites readers to consider the political causes and epistemological consequences of these differences. The list "Depressing Things" does more than point out personal pet peeves; instead, it makes visible poignant moments in life ("A lying-in room when the baby has died"), everyday cruelties ("An ox-driver who hates his oxen"), and contemporary biases ("A scholar whose wife has one girl child after another"). It almost defines disappointment and distress through examples, from personal relationships to political appointments, that open connections and point to parallels between them. If Hobbes gives definitions without many examples to expand or test them, Sei Shōnagon perhaps does the opposite, presenting a range of examples that leaves readers to explore what, for instance, they have in common.

The list "Things That Make One's Heart Beat Faster" contains much variety of both positive and negative examples, leading to questions about the nature of human emotions and mind-body connections. The list comprises examples from the animal world, sensory experiences, and personal relationships. "Unsuitable Things" is about norms specific to people of a certain age or class and shows both the endless minutiae that give voice to such social differences and their presumed importance. Again diverse hierarchies are forefront, allowing inquiry into their sources, functions, and consequences. "Pleasing Things" shows pleasure to be intellectual, emotional and social, mischievous, fleeting and egotistical, and related to other emotions from envy to relief.

Repeatedly, in *The Pillow Book,* the boundaries of accepted form seen in the discipline's "great works" are ignored. Again and again, distinctions between public and private are blurred, and each is used to illuminate the other. The politics of the everyday are incorporated, context is emphasized, diversity is recognized, change is assumed, and connections between the apparently disparate are announced. Sei Shōnagon's *Pillow Book,* long recognized as a literary masterpiece, should be among the works reconsidered by political theorists precisely because of what its form reveals. We should see what we've been missing.

PART 2

DOING POLITICAL THEORY

4

COMMUNITY: MARY WOLLSTONECRAFT AND
ANNA JULIA COOPER

The recent resurgence in political philosophy of interest in communitarianism has, unfortunately, been limited by its general failure to incorporate fully most feminist concerns and research (MacIntyre 1981; Sandel 1982). The enticing possibility of a distinctively feminist communitarianism, on the other hand, has only begun to emerge (Phelan 1991; Weiss and Friedman 1995). But even these nascent developments in feminist communitarianism have paid scant attention to the history of feminist theory. Following the now familiar pattern, one can read most feminist work on community without encountering a single reference to anyone who wrote before the 1970s.[1] We can profit considerably, however, from letting our theoretically inclined foremothers inform our debates; much is sacrificed when we lose our traditions.

In general, consideration of ideas from feminist perspectives is required to accurately represent debates about core concepts in the history of mainstream political thought. Feminist theory also presents unprecedented and exciting opportunities to redefine what political issues should be deemed central in the first place and what it actually means to discuss them thoroughly. That much has already been argued. With regard to the concept of community in particular, historical feminist writings may prove themselves exceptionally invaluable and inspiring. Such works are rife with elaborate arguments about the near impossibility of community in patriarchy, because of, for example, its impoverished sense of common goods and its nearly obsessive emphasis on conflict. They also suggest what liberatory communities might look like, from families to political societies. They challenge

---

1. The only historical figure making more-than-passing repeat appearances is Charlotte Perkins Gilman. Even there, reference is made only to *Herland*, not to her nonfiction work, which is at least equally important to the subject.

ideas about social organization put forth by their more famous brothers and resolutely insist on reevaluating the meaning of, relation between, and importance of ideas such as autonomy and friendship, shared goods and self-interest. They deal more centrally and comprehensively with questions of inclusion, with the public/private distinction, and with a variety of forms of power.

This chapter is but a beginning to understanding the contributions of the history of feminist theory to discussions about community. I look here at communitarian aspects of the work of Mary Wollstonecraft and Anna Julia Cooper, simultaneously focusing sorely needed attention on two particular women thinkers and adding marginalized, if not ignored, historical feminist voices to conversations about this core issue. Wollstonecraft and Cooper may be surprising choices for this undertaking. Wollstonecraft, while relatively well known, is associated with liberalism and individualism rather than communitarianism, while Cooper, unfamiliar even to most feminist theorists, is known primarily as an educator. Each, however, offers us thoughtful and thought-provoking perspectives on community. Too, their thinking on the subject reveals some links between them, a hint of another feminist tradition. Sometimes, looking in unexpected places suggests how pervasive certain ideas and tendencies are. For the most part I deal with Cooper and Wollstonecraft separately and on somewhat differently framed issues related to community, in order to keep their ideas in the larger context of their own work. I reunite them in the conclusion, looking especially for continuities and connections.

COMMUNITARIAN THEMES IN WOLLSTONECRAFT AND COOPER

Clues that Wollstonecraft is relevant to discussions of community begin with the way she frames her most famous work. In the opening dedication to *Rights of Woman*, Wollstonecraft declares her intention: "I plead for my sex," she avows, identifying herself neither as an individual trying to expand her personal opportunities, nor as a philosopher laying out the abstract "rights of man," but a woman consciously and "disinterestedly" writing and acting on behalf of a group to which she belongs, a group whose common goods she identifies with and commits herself to advancing. Wollstonecraft attempts to be inclusive: "Let it be remembered, that for a small number of distinguished women I do not ask a place" (1988, 35). Her dedicatory remarks to Talleyrand also reference certain communitarian aspects of her project: the role of sexual equality in the attainment of *social* goods such as moral and intellectual progress, *political* goods such as patriotism, and *interpersonal* goods such as companionship. From the very outset, then, Wollstonecraft is not limiting her appeal for sexual equality to such traditional liberal ideals as self-interest or individual rights and liberty. Jumping from the initial to the final section of the book, we find Wollstonecraft's "concluding reflections" again emphasizing her social concerns: that women be "truly useful members of society" and that male-female relations be based on friendship and common pursuits (191). Convinced that this supposedly paradigmatic liberal feminist has something to teach us about community, I focus on three intertwined issues in Wollstonecraft's work: the relationship she posits between equality and community, the connections she claims can exist between autonomy and community, and the place of Wollstonecraft in noncommunitarian liberal thought.

Anna Julia Cooper was born of an enslaved mother and probably slave master father in North Carolina in 1859, a century after Wollstonecraft's birth (Hutchinson 1982). She attended St. Augustine Normal School and Collegiate Institute, founded "to educate teachers for the vast number of illiterate freedmen, as well as to prepare candidates for the ministry" (Shockley 1989, 204), and then Oberlin College, the first college to accept white women, in 1833, and blacks, in 1834. She began doctoral studies at Columbia in 1914 and completed them at the Sorbonne at the age of sixty-five, making her the fourth (known) black female Ph.D.[2] She is perhaps most famous for her years as teacher and principal at the only black high school in Washington, D.C., the Washington Colored High School, or the M Street School. An activist, she helped found the Colored Women's League in D.C. and a college for the working class, Frelinghuysen. She left us a trove of papers, editorials, and letters, and in her 1892 collection of essays, *A Voice From the South,* Cooper may be one of the earliest feminist theorists to use the notion of voice as a way of exploring both the difficulties and the possibilities of community.

Like Wollstonecraft, Cooper tells us in her prefatory remarks that she consciously writes from a distinctive standpoint and places herself in a community whose common goods are also hers. Heretofore, she says, "the 'other side' has not been represented by one who 'lives there'" (1988, II). The first

2. Mary Helen Washington lists the previous doctorates as Georgiana Rose Simpson, Eva B. Dykes, and Sadie Tanner Alexander (1988, xxxix).

words of her book provide a stirring example of silencing, of exclusion, of the lack of community that she takes as her starting point and addresses throughout: "In the clash and clatter of our American Conflict, it has been said that the South remains Silent. Like the Sphinx she inspires vociferous disputation, but herself takes little part in the noisy controversy. One muffled strain in the Silent South, a jarring chord and a vague and uncomprehended cadenza has been and still is the Negro. And of that muffled chord, the one mute and voiceless note has been the sadly expectant Black Woman" (I). *A Voice from the South* is about the voices of the silenced. In searching out those perspectives, the means by which they are silenced, the consequences of silencing, and finally the means for regaining voice, Cooper emerges as a theorist of community. Her work contains a deep critique of individualism and constantly appeals to more communitarian concerns, emphasizing women's social influence and responsibilities and stressing the importance of civility, humility, and commitment to helping others. My comments on Cooper convey her portraits of racial and sexual inequality and exclusion, on the one hand, and equality and inclusion, on the other: what the sources of resistance to inclusive community are and what the possibilities are of overcoming them. She, like Wollstonecraft, attempts to be inclusive: "The concept of Equality as it is the genuine product of the idea of inherent value in the individual derived from the essential worth of Humanity must be before all else unquestionably of universal application" (1945, 10).

WOLLSTONECRAFT: EQUALITY AND COMMUNITY

True happiness arose from the friendship and intimacy which can only be enjoyed by equals. . . . Among unequals there can be no society.
—Mary Wollstonecraft, *Thoughts on the Education of Daughters*

"Of particular concern to [Wollstonecraft] was the need to create the possibility for genuinely reciprocal friendships and love relationships between men and women" (Mackenzie 1993, 182). In general, the degree of equality between groups in a society affects the character of relations between those groups and between members of each. In/equality affects the possibilities for self-development of individuals within a group, the opportunities available to them, and the way a group views and treats itself and others. Because the status of the sexes embodies and enforces a whole set of social mores, it affects most aspects of social and political life: who participates in what, why, and how.[3] Inequality for Wollstonecraft (1) makes community between the sexes impossible, (2) hinders community among members of each sex, and (3) damages social and political relations in general. Equality, then, is a means to friendship, to caring relations, to social progress, and to inclusive politics. These are broad claims and ones that directly and boldly contradict those of Wollstonecraft's oft-cited Jean-Jacques Rousseau, who embraces sexual differentiation precisely, though unsuccessfully, as a path to community (Weiss 1993). Community for Wollstonecraft depends upon the existence of equality.

The fact that equality makes *community* possible is considered by Wollstonecraft to be as strong an argument for establishing equality as is the fact that equality makes *self-development* possible. Two centuries after her, the political theorist Jane Mansbridge writes in terms reminiscent of Wollstonecraft: "Equal power is . . . a means to two other ends—maintaining a community of equal respect and promoting personal growth" (1983, ix). In these equations Wollstonecraft acknowledges the complex connections between the personal, the interpersonal, and the political. She goes further than most of her male predecessors in exploring these ties, in appreciating how the political and the personal deeply influence each other. The lack of community is a cost of inequality that Wollstonecraft finds intolerable, but one rendered invisible in many political theories.

"Woman will be either the friend or slave of man" (Wollstonecraft 1988, 35). That inequality prevents or destroys community between the sexes is demonstrated in Wollstonecraft's discussions of contempt and respect, themes that loom large in her thought. Wollstonecraft argues that the condition into which women are forced (5) renders them contemptible. What passes for female virtue—"gentleness, docility" and (my favorite) a "spaniel-like affection" (34)—"is really weakness" (9, 34), for which men feel pity or disrespect.

Contempt is defined in Webster's as "the feeling or actions of a person toward something they consider low, worthless, or beneath notice." It is synonymous with *disrespect, scorn,* and *derision.* Wollstonecraft's argument that men feel and act with contempt for women stresses that the subordination of women rests upon and reinforces the practice of men making of women something "other," something less than fully human. Unfortunately, in practice such inequality is incompatible with friendship, while derision precludes democratic relations.

3. The causal arrows go in multiple, reinforcing directions.

Respect, contempt's opposite, is what Wollstonecraft desires for women: both self-respect (45, 94) and the respect of men (49, 50). She describes herself as "anxious to render my sex more respectable members of society" (10). Again turning to Webster, to respect someone is "to view, treat, or consider [that person] with some degree of courtesy, honor, [or] esteem." *To respect* can also mean "to avoid intruding upon." Wollstonecraft wisely chooses to aim for women's self-respect as well as men's respect for women, limiting the power of men and male standards over women by acknowledging women's rightful power to judge themselves. The practice of men respecting women affects community. With equality, men more easily identify with women, listen to them, consider them, and treat them courteously. From such practices we get images of a community in which self-respecting people both think about and treat others as worthy.

For women to deserve and receive men's respect and self-respect (94), to take back their "lost dignity" (45), to become and to be treated as equals with men, women must be more concerned with being socially useful (22) and less concerned with pleasing and serving men. They must focus less on sensuality and more on developing their rational understandings. Women need to free themselves from their enslavement to men and to love (91). In becoming equal, the sexes would become members of the same community. They would become "companions" (4) linked by "friendship" (6, 8, 29, 50, 73). That is Wollstonecraft's fondest hope.

Although this point is given less attention, Wollstonecraft argues that inequality affects not only female-male relations, but also women's relations with one another, and men's with other men. For example, speaking about mothers and daughters in an unequal world that values reasoning men and pleasing women, Wollstonecraft says: "The mother will be lost in the coquette, and, instead of making friends of her daughters, view them with eyes askance, for they are rivals" (49). She also notes that traditional emphasis on women's dress "gives rise to envy, and contests for trifling superiority" (1995a, 37). To the extent that inequality puts one group at the mercy of another, in this case based on gender, people in the bottom group need to please those above them and will compete with one another to stay in their good favor. In a different manner, those on the top also become competitors, vying for advantage, behaving so as to "support[] their own superiority" (1988, 57). Further, she saw some parenting by men as reduced to "self-love or love for their own name rather than another human being" (Sapiro 1992, 79), an act of the dominant group destructive of community, a lost opportunity for building relationships.

COMMUNITY AND AUTONOMY

Wollstonecraft decries the slavish dependence of women upon men. True to liberal expectations, her goal for women is independence: "Independence I have long considered as the grand blessing of life, the basis of every virtue" (1988, 3; see also 21, 85). But her idea of autonomy is not the individualistic dream of liberals or some communitarian's nightmare. She defines dependence as having "to act according to the will of another fallible being, and submit, right or wrong, to power" (48). For Wollstonecraft, then, independence means not lack of care, connection, or commitment, but the possession of a will that can direct one's own actions, and the ability to converse about, suggest, question, and resist rather than merely submit to other wills: "Her use of *independence* is very similar to the notion of originality in art and imagination used by her friends in the republic of taste. It involves strength of mind, not individualist isolation. This independence is a key to what makes individuals 'socially useful,' and binds them together in their common relationship as human beings" (Sapiro 1992, 214). Wollstonecraft never argues for a lack of "connectedness," nor does she emphasize self-interest, as liberating for either sex. As Sapiro notes, "Far from believing that the sum of self-interests creates community, she believed it created war" (60). What she cares passionately about is that relationships be moral ones, and that requires female independence: "the unfold[ing] of their own faculties and acquisi[tion of] the dignity of conscious virtue" (Wollstonecraft 1988, 26).

In one of Wollstonecraft's early publications, her 1791 *Original Stories from Real Life,* yet other aspects of community's relationship to independence/ autonomy emerge. *Original Stories* is a collection of educational episodes between a tutor and her charges, meant to teach both adults and youngsters. Significantly, the book opens with three chapters on the treatment of animals. The stories in these chapters are full of morals, and it is remarkable how many of those morals have to do with showing children that they share a universe with other creatures of whom they must be considerate. Wollstonecraft wants youth to be trained to think *for* themselves, but not only *of* themselves. Those hearing her stories, like the figures in the tales, are to become thoughtful social actors who see themselves as responsible to others as well as to themselves. Wollstonecraft writes in *Thoughts on the Education of Daughters* that "animals are the first objects which catch their attention; and I think little stories about them would not only amuse but instruct at the same time, and have the best effect in forming the temper and cultivating the good dispositions of the heart" (1995a, 16).

The children are taught in the first story that animals who pose no threat do not deserve to be killed, even if you think them ugly, even if you despise them (1972, 2), even if (like children, incidentally) they are weak and often troublesome (3). They learn to appreciate the relations of animals to one another, to other species, and to God. They come to see that animals suffer, feel affection, and experience enjoyment and should not be interfered with needlessly or merely for human pleasure. To be good is defined as "to avoid hurting any thing; and then, to contrive to give as much pleasure as you can" (3).

These lessons against cruelty, and for appreciation of different species, are to be extended from the animal world to the smaller human one as children develop. Appreciate people, no matter how different from you they seem to be. Respect the meaningful relations they have with others, and realize what they give to the world. Never be cruel. Give pleasure; help to make happy. Perhaps surprisingly, acting this way is what Wollstonecraft explicitly defines as acting rationally (5). Rationality is not associated with either disinterestedness or self-interest but with social virtue, acting sociably. And interestingly, it is from reason, from rationality thus understood, that affections arise (7). For Wollstonecraft, what distinguishes and "exalts" humans are "friendship and devotion." In answering the child's question about how human beings can prove their superiority to other animals, Wollstonecraft's tutor replies, "Be tenderhearted" (8).

Wollstonecraft thus urges upon us the lesson that community and autonomy are not negatively correlated. Given the earlier discussion of respect, it is interesting to note that *to respect* can also mean "to avoid intruding upon." Wollstonecraft's goal of both sexes respecting women not only brings people together but also establishes some limitations upon communal requirements. It is intended that individual integrity, individuality, flourish in Wollstonecraft's community.

WOLLSTONECRAFT AND LIBERALISM

If you have heard of Wollstonecraft you have probably heard her referred to as *the* liberal feminist theorist (Jaggar 1983; Tong 1989). And if you have heard of liberal feminism you have probably heard it referred to as liberalism applied or extended to women: "the overriding goal of liberal feminism always has been the application of liberal principles to women as well as to men" (Jaggar 1983, 35). Liberalism, you have probably heard, is quite indifferent to community at best; it is the political philosophy of the individual, conceived of as egoistic, selfish, and acquisitive (Dietz 1987, 5). It has been said that the "characteristic liberal values" are those "of individual dignity, equality, autonomy and self-fulfillment. Along with these, its ideal society is one which maximizes individual autonomy and in which all individual have an equal opportunity to pursue their own interests as they perceive them" (Jaggar 1983, 39). As John Stuart Mill expresses it, "The only freedom which deserves the name, is that of pursuing our own good in our own way, so long as we do not attempt to deprive others of theirs, or impede their efforts to obtain it" (1989, 16). Liberalism deemphasizes the role of social relationships and human community in constituting individual identity. According to all this, if Wollstonecraft is a liberal feminist, her thoughts on community should be few in number and small in import, peripheral to her political thought.

Yet in what is usually treated as the paradigmatic liberal feminist text in history, we find strong advocacy of autonomy *and* community and find arguments for a positive and dialectical relationship between the two. We find equality defended as necessary for both individual development and community. Independence is defined as a certain kind of relationship, and rationality is tied to concern and affection for others. In all this, Wollstonecraft challenges familiar dualisms and builds bridges between concepts often understood as adversarial. This is not "the application of liberal principles to women as well as to men" (Jaggar 1983, 35).

We have, it seems, three choices: (1) maintain our model of liberal feminism and ignore those parts of Wollstonecraft that fail to conform to it, (2) keep our sketch of liberal feminism intact and place Wollstonecraft elsewhere, or (3) rethink liberal feminism in light of Wollstonecraft. While casting out those parts of Wollstonecraft that stubbornly refuse to accommodate the current conception of liberal feminism seems the most dubious strategy, it is astonishingly common. We tend, I think, to read Wollstonecraft through the liberal lenses provided by Hobbes and Locke, looking for where she agrees with their basic tenets and applies them to women. That search does yield results, but it is a selective search that ultimately distorts both Wollstonecraft and liberalism. In that search, Wollstonecraft is forced by her readers to remain within the confines of the masculine political theory she herself rejected. Gunther-Canada is adamant on this point: Wollstonecraft, she argues, "repeatedly defined her political project as a war of words with the male authors whom she identified as the 'canonized forefathers,' and she rejected the theoretical tradition as falsely universal and inherently patriarchal" (2001, 3).

Instead of ignoring anything in Wollstonecraft that a Locke would not agree with, what if liberalism was defined by Wollstonecraft's version of it? What if we treated her as a founding theorist of liberalism with a competing vision? True, that might make of Hobbes and Locke impossibly inconsistent liberals, but that probably does more justice to them than the standard characterizations of Wollstonecraft do to her.

If Wollstonecraft is a liberal, then we are wrong to assume that liberals see community as of little concern, or as locked in mortal combat with independence.[4] Her independence requires community, and vice versa. If Wollstonecraft is not a liberal, we can more easily take seriously the communitarian (as well as romantic and socialist) aspects of her writings. This is surely an exciting prospect for Wollstonecraft scholars and historians of feminist theory. But one by-product of this revisioning is that we may discover that liberal feminism is something of a curiosity—a theory without a theorist. If it is true that "much of contemporary feminist theory defines itself in reaction against" liberal feminism (Tong 1989, 2), changes in our conception of liberal feminism may alter some contemporary debates, especially by bringing the idea of egalitarian community closer to the center. But if we are not ready to part with the current definition of liberal feminism, we are probably even less prepared to allow thinkers such as Wollstonecraft to redefine liberalism itself. Still, imagine the possibilities.

COOPER: EQUALITY AND COMMUNITY

"Of all the crimes of the universe, exploitation is the quintessence, the sum total of the most monstrous, the most heinous, the most ungodly. Exploitation means using your neighbor for yourself. . . . [It is] the savage expression at the Nth degree of human selfishness, the hoggish principle among men which makes self the center of the universe and stands ready to trample ruthlessly underfoot or greedily devour the entire not-self regardless of right, rhyme or reason" (Cooper, n.d.). Cooper offers us a virtual catalog of forms of silencing, a thread weaving its way through all of her essays. Her examples range from white "Christian men . . . [meeting] at regular intervals for some years to discuss the best method of promoting the welfare and development of colored people in this country," without ever, "strange as it may seem . . . invit[ing] a colored man to take part in their deliberations" (1988, 37) to Mahomet's "mak[ing] no account of woman whatever in his polity" (9–10).

---

4. I am afraid that this is how Fox-Genovese reads her.

Through such stories she points out the patterned deafness and blindness, and the indifference and arrogance, of even most the well-meaning among the privileged. In them Cooper makes visible the hypocrisy that character-izes societies shaped by inequality. She shows the powerful imposing their standards on the marginalized and, from the other side, makes visible the people who are left out of discussions about their own interests. Division takes many forms and wears many guises, from outright exclusion to more veiled but equally insidious varieties of partial inclusion (usually of that por-tion of the subordinated who most resemble the dominant or whose needs the privileged decide merit attention).

Cooper is relentless in confronting her reader with such stories, for much is at stake: society can never fare well in the face of exclusion and preference. Practices of inequality damage or destroy community. Cooper draws a so-cial whole composed of overlapping parts that fail to discuss constructively either their commonalities or their differences. The whole is damaged and even lost as some parts are magnified and glorified, other parts made minis-cule and left wanting. Division and inequality both depend upon a smorgas-bord of social vices, politically destructive mores, including "the pride, the selfishness, the prejudices, the exclusiveness, the bigotry and intolerance, the conceit of self, of race, or of family superiority" (170).

From her examples of partiality and voicelessness Cooper draws pictures of inclusion and community, both implicitly and explicitly. According to her, we need to move from the "paralyzing grip of caste prejudice" (116), narrowness (118), "preconceived notions, blinding prejudices, and shriveling antipathies" (117) to "sympathetic listening . . . receptivity . . . appreciation" (115), "the healthy sympathetic eye" (116), "tolerance," and "charity" (120). One can obtain from Cooper's work a list of virtues essential to community, from courtesy, compassion, and civility to appreciation, open-mindedness, and generosity. Only the practice of such social virtues raises the possibil-ity that difference might be viewed as "an opportunity for broadening and enlarging [one's] own soul" (83).

Cooper thinks limitations upon women and women's influence are de-structive for a community. She argues for "setting free and invigorating the long desired feminine force in the world" by educating women. Giving an example of the potential scope of women's positive influence in the world, she writes:

> You will not find theology consigning infants to lakes of unquenchable
> fires long after women have had a chance to grasp, master, and wield

its dogmas. You will not find science annihilating personality from the government of the Universe and making of God an ungovernable, unintelligible, blind, often destructive physical force; you will not find jurisprudence formulating as an axiom the absurdity that man and wife are one, and that one the man[;] ... you will not find political economists declaring that the only possible adjustment between laborers and capitalists is that of selfishness and rapacity—that each must get all he can and keep all that he gets, while the world cries *laissez faire* and the lawyers explain, "it is the beautiful working of the law of supply and demand;" in fine, you will not find the law of love shut out from the affairs of men after the feminine half of the world's truth is completed. (1988, 57–58)

Our theology, our science, our jurisprudence, and our economic theories are all implicated here, all somehow compromised and distorted because of the silencing of women. Cooper says, "No woman can possibly put herself or her sex outside any of the interests that affect humanity" (143).

To describe the desirable interaction between the masculine and the feminine in the individual and in society, Cooper rejects *counteract* in favor of *complement* and *harmonize*. In rejecting *counteract* she casts out a notion of masculine and feminine as separate and opposed, like counsel for the defense and for the prosecution, or as separate and suspicious, like the branches of a divided government.

In some ways women have been "checks" on men. Cooper herself contrasts "the cold, mathematical, selfishly calculating, so-called practical and unsentimental instinct of the business man" with "the sympathetic warmth and sunshine of good women ... counteracting the selfishness of an acquisitive age" (131). But that is not ideal. A system of counteracting forces has great defects: it is reactive, does not necessarily permanently change either party, and limits women's influence, her ability "to bring a heart power into this money getting, dollar-worshipping civilization; ... to bring a moral force into the utilitarian motives and interests of the time" (131). Such restriction is undesirable, even unacceptable: "In the era now about to dawn, her sentiments must strike the keynote and give the dominant tone" (133). What a change from that "mute and voiceless note" of the "sadly expectant Black Woman" Cooper described earlier.

Viewing the sexes as complements to each other is a much more common perspective historically, and it is not surprising that Cooper employs it. Some ways of defining complementary forces are reminiscent of definitions of counteracting ones, viewing complements as separate, self-contained parts that together make up a whole, as volumes in a set of encyclopedias. But to have things complement each other also implies that each is incomplete— male as well as female, by definition. Cooper seems to be arguing that the world needs what we have come to call masculine and what we have come to call feminine, and we need both "not as inferior and superior, not as better and worse, not as weaker and stronger, but as complements—complements in one necessary and symmetric whole" (60). Further, "both are alike necessary in giving symmetry to the individual" (61) as well as the community. So together, mutually, the two make up what either or both lack alone. This brings us to something that involves the parts ceasing to remain self-contained and becoming part of a new whole, and that is what I think Cooper is aiming at when she brings up another musical term, *harmonize*. To harmonize parts, in a family or in music, is to bring them together in peace and agreement; to have them work for a common end; to add elements to parts to form a new, reconciled, more melodious whole. In Cooper's vision of community between the sexes, they do not stay different and self-contained. They admit of a common purpose as friends, as equals, and their coming together creates a new, more complicated, richer whole. The sexes are not checks on each other, adding a dash of heart for each pinch of acquisitiveness or a portion of compassion for each dose of self-interestedness. Within the individual and within interpersonal and social relationships, people are allowed to become more whole, more integrated, less tied to roles, through their relationships, through community. A fuller self-development, for both sexes, occurs as each blends into some combination of masculine and feminine. Limitation to one or the other is just that—limitation, not development. And the limitation of either sex limits the development of the other (65, 67). Rather than the destruction of bonds between the sexes, such enrichment gives rise to the possibility of true bonds between them. Here, at last, can be communion without suspicion; friendship without misunderstanding; love without jealousy (69). Here, too, women's self-development and the community between the sexes fosters men's self-development:

> Her standards have undoubtedly gone up . . . The question is not now with the woman "How shall I so cramp, stunt, simplify and nullify myself as to make me eligible to the honor of being swallowed up onto some little man?" but the problem, I trow, now rests with the man as to how he can so develop his God-given powers as to reach

the idea of a generation of women who demand the noblest, grandest and best achievements of which he is capable. . . . Nature never meant that the ideals and standards of the world should be dwarfing and minimizing ones, and the men should thank us for requiring of them the richest fruits which they can grow. If it makes them work, all the better for them. (70–71)

Cooper has much to say about the means to the ends of equality and community. An impressive feature of her writings is her determined insistence that the resources of the community be devoted to the education and welfare of women. She notes that women are denied communal resources, ranging from "special stimulus to . . . development" (75) to college admissions (74). In fact, girls even receive "positive discouragements to the higher education" (77). Yet her argument is that "the position of woman in society determines the vital elements of its regeneration and progress" (21), a case she makes for the "society" of African Americans, of all Americans, and for the human race. She goes so far as to say, "There can be no issue more vital and momentous than this of the womanhood of the race" (27). No waiting for her turn here, no putting more "important" causes before this.

Cooper thus calls for "organized effort for the protection and elevation of our girls" (31). She wants "special organizations such as Church sisterhoods and industrial schools . . . devised to meet her pressing needs in the Southland" (43). She asks each member of the race to declare, "I am my Sister's keeper!" (32). Men and women both have roles to play in the elevation of black women. What is required of men, she says, is that they "let their interest and gallantry extend outside the circle of their aesthetic appreciation," while what is required of women is that they be "so sure of their own social footing that they need not fear leaning to lend a hand to a fallen or falling sister" (32–33). From all it is required that "the elevation of their people means more than personal ambition and sordid gain" (35). This sense of obligation toward one's community she expresses in another, beautifully satiric passage: "Not even the senseless vegetable is content to be a mere reservoir. Receiving without giving is an anomaly in nature. Nature's cells are all little workshops for manufacturing sunbeams, the product to be *given out* to earth's inhabitants in warmth, energy, thought, action. Inanimate creation always pays back an equivalent" (46).

Cooper names at least three impediments, or locations of resistance, to equality and community. First, those who are part of an exclusionary com-

munity fear change. As she says with insight and humor about the opening of the first college in American to white women: "It was felt to be an
experiment—a rather dangerous experiment—and was adopted with fear
and trembling by the good fathers, who looked as if they had been caught
secretly mixing explosive compounds and were guiltily expecting every moment to see the foundations under them shaken and rent and their fair super-
structure shattered into fragments" (49).[5] Second, Cooper sees the world of
her day, as many see ours today, as possessed of a "sneaking admiration . . .
for bullies and prize-fighters" that is part of what she calls the dominant
masculine influence (51). Admiration for bullies prevents us from seeing the
need for what she terms "the great mother heart [that can] teach [the world]
to be pitiful, to love mercy, to succor the weak and care for the lowly" (51).
Women's traits are scorned, deemed weak, disallowed. An overhaul of values
is required, because despite the worship of the masculine, "the worship of
the beast" (54), Cooper says, "man-influence, unmollified and unrestrained
by its complementary force, would become . . . dreadful and terrible," de-
vouring (53).

The third source of resistance to racial and sexual equality and community resides with women. While acknowledging the reality of masculine
power, Cooper also discusses feminine power. Her argument is that the
"American woman is responsible for American manners" (86). Here is her
description of trickle-down and -around manners:

> It is pre-eminently an age of organizations. The "leading woman," the
> preacher, the reformer, the organizer "enthuses" her lieutenants and
> captains, the literary women, the thinking women, the strong, ear-
> nest, irresistible women; these in turn touch their myriads of church
> clubs, social clubs, culture clubs, pleasure clubs and charitable clubs,
> till the same lecture has been duly administered to every married man
> in the land (not to speak of sons and brother) from the President in
> the White House to the stone-splitter of the ditches. . . . The atmo-
> sphere of street cars and parks and boulevards, of cafe and hotels and
> steamboats is charged and surcharged with her sentiments and restric-
> tions. . . . The working women of America in whatever station or call-
> ing they may be found, are subjects, officers, or rulers of a strong
> centralized government, and bound together by a system of codes and

5. Cooper later similarly ridicules white women for the stir they made about black women entering their club, sarcastically calling it "an epoch-making crisis" (82) and a "serio-comic dilemma" (84).

countersigns, which, though unwritten, forms a network of perfect subordination and unquestioning obedience as marvelous as that of the Jesuits. (85–86)

Women have power, even in a patriarchy. But women currently wield that power, Cooper contends, in the name of caste (87), or privilege by class and color. Cooper speaks of the blindness of white women who speak of their situation in falsely universal terms (90) and of the feeling of the black woman who is not treated like a white woman, or as a woman at all. "The feeling of slighted womanhood is unlike every other emotion of the soul. . . . Its poignancy . . . is earthly and vulgar, is holier than that of jealousy, deeper than indignation, tenderer than rage" (90–91). Cooper acknowledges the power of women and also places on them responsibility for continuing or ending the degradation of poor women and black women. She transforms women's traditional task. If women are responsible for manners, she says, let women act against caste and prejudice, "bending all [their] energies to thus broadening, humanizing, and civilizing [their] native land" (116). The third obstacle may be obedience to the system.

OVERCOMING

Cooper is *not* advocating an end to gender or racial identity. Quite the contrary. Describing an earlier era in which culture supported slavery, brutality, and aggression, she writes, "Assimilation was horrible to contemplate" (158). Nor does she envision community as some unity without difference or conflict. She puts her own bottom line in italics: *"Equilibrium, not repression among conflicting forces is the condition of natural harmony, of permanent progress, and of universal freedom"* (160). Even this "natural harmony" is conceived in a very particular way. She sees as critical the very communitarian virtues of "compromise and concession, liberality and toleration" (165). But she is also adamant that not all conflict is undesirable or destructive, just as not all absences of conflict represent egalitarian or communitarian victories: "There are two kinds of peace in this world. The one produced by suppression, which is the passivity of death; the other brought about by a proper adjustment of living, acting forces. A nation or an individual may be at peace because all opponents have been killed or crushed; or, nation as well as individual may have found the secret of true harmony in the determination to live and let live. . . . The harmony of a despotism . . . [is] the quiet of a muzzled mouth, the smoldering peace of a volcano crusted over" (149–50).

Cooper has tremendous hopes for the women's movement. She sees there the chance to regain voice and establish community. But its potential can be realized only by means of a thorough commitment to dealing with differences and working for all. "The cause of freedom," Cooper insists, "is not the cause of a race or a sect, a party or a class—it is the cause of human kind [*sic*]. . . . [Woman's] cause is linked with that of every agony that has been dumb—every wrong that needs a voice" (120–22). Cooper knows well the ability of the dominant to divide the oppressed and thus destroy the latter's ability to resist. The dangers of divisions among women is dramatically conveyed by recalling divisions among the enslaved. She tells of a slaveholder who "so insinuated differences and distinctions among [the enslaved], that their personal attachment for him was stronger than for their own brethren and fellow sufferers. . . . [He] pitted mulatto against black, bond against free, house slave against plantation slave, even the slave of one clan against like slave of another clan; till, wholly oblivious of their ability for mutual succor and defense, all became centers of myriad systems of repellent forces, having but one sentiment in common, and that their entire subjection to that master hand" (102).

Community among women is indispensable, as are links with other (often overlapping) oppressed populations: these are necessary, perhaps even sufficient, means to human freedom.

CONCLUDING THOUGHTS

Many of us have discovered that whatever philosophical points divide male philosophers—whether they be existentialist or essentialist, Marxist or capitalist, ancient or modern—their hostility to sexual equality also unites them. To the extent that Wollstonecraft and Cooper are representative of female theorists, it may be the case that the inclusion of women in a richer and more egalitarian community unites women philosophers across their differences. Both consciously try to include not only some women—the rich, the intellectual, the propertied, the white, the native born—but to include them all. Neither does so entirely—lesbians, for example, get short shrift in both—but both contribute to that end and sometimes do so in ways that inform us how to do more. They establish that inclusion as our mandate, a goal without which sexual equality and community are doomed to fail. On this as on other points, a look back at our own feminist history proves productive.

Wollstonecraft and Cooper also agree that various forms of inequality damage the whole social fabric. Their emphasis on the social consequences of inequality enables both to make an extremely persuasive case that the women's movement is a compelling social concern deserving of our common resources.

There is also similarity between Wollstonecraft's use of contempt and respect to characterize first the impoverished present and then the desirable future and Cooper's use of silence and voice. Both sets of terms represent various excluded, silenced, underestimated, and unheeded parties, on one side, and voice, consideration, and respect, on the other. Both even speak of the need to "listen" to the previously muted. And for both, the desirable terms do not so much conjure up a static or detailed picture of utopian community as evoke a process, practices that can create and sustain community and individual integrity. Exclusive communities are dangerous. But ones established securely on processes of listening and consideration seem to them not only safe, but also as good as it gets.

Both Cooper and Wollstonecraft fought hard for education in their own lives, worked in educational institutions of various sorts, and wrote about the importance of education for equality and community. Without education one often cannot find one's voice, or the right words with which to express it, or the courage to speak the words, or the chutzpah to demand the attention of others. They are advocates of education that opens the possibility of individual freedom and contribution to the community. Both offer devastating critiques of bourgeois acquisitiveness based primarily on its social consequences.

Finally, an apparent difference. Cooper seems to give a much more positive evaluation of women's traditional roles, traits, and contributions than does Wollstonecraft. Cooper calls for an expansion of women's traditional sphere and for the integration of women's traits with what have been men's. Men's alone, she declares, would destroy the world. Despite what some commentators say, Wollstonecraft did not accept the traditional male role as ideal, did not idolize what Cooper calls the "bully." A look at Wollstonecraft's *Maria* shows how very much she knows about the damages wreaked by patriarchal bullies, as do numerous passages in *Rights of Woman.* But

Wollstonecraft does call women in their traditional roles "useless," and their pursuits "trivial": advocates of inequality "render women more artificial, weak characters, than they would otherwise have been; and, consequently, more useless members of society. . . . [They are] thrown out of a useful station by the unnatural distinctions established in civil life" (1988, 22, 24).

While there is some difference between the two theorists on this point, something less than a gulf separates them. Wollstonecraft is sometimes doing no more than saying that an uneducated woman is relatively useless, given what an educated woman, even in a traditional role, can contribute, and that women have been forced out of conversations and away from actions that were of greater import even to them than those they were allowed. Finally, even Cooper finds it necessary to transform women's traditional role before it can work its revolutionary magic.

Both see elevation of women as elevation of men. So what they ask for is not a situation where the positions of the sexes are merely reversed, where the elevated one keeps the other down. Women's virtues help here.

In 1983 Nancy Hartsock wrote, "The public world constructed by the *eros* of citizen-warriors took the form of competition for dominance and resulted in the creation of a community of men based on dualism and contradiction. . . . A community structured by forms of *eros* that express women's experience might take quite different form" (210). Hartsock explores what she calls "an alternative tradition" in women's writings about power. I believe that there is also a "tradition" of feminist thinking about community. Calling such theorizing a tradition implies that it has a past, that there is something distinctive about it, and that it offers alternatives to malestream thinking on the subject. Wollstonecraft and Cooper present evidence of this tradition. We should continue the process of gathering such ideas.

> We are not independent. Let's admit it, and if it's any comfort to know it, neither is anybody else. Independence is all a big bluff.
> —Anna Cooper, *A Voice from the South*

5

REVOLUTION: DECLARATION OF SENTIMENTS AT SENECA FALLS

On July 14, 1848, the *Seneca County Courier* published a small, unsigned notice announcing an upcoming convention "to discuss the social, civil, and religious condition and rights of women."[1] A mere eight days later a crowd of about three hundred people arrived in Seneca Falls, New York, marking "a pivotal point in the history of women in the modern world" (Bernhard and Fox-Genovese 1995, ix). The Declaration of Sentiments at Seneca Falls, which was passed at that convention, has been lauded as the "most famous document in the history of feminism" (Lindgren and Taub 1993, 23) and said to have provided "a road map for... the women's rights movement for decades to come" (Sigerman 1994, 36). Despite the highly significant status frequently awarded it, however, to this day "the first female legal text in U.S. history" (Hoff 1991, 138) has, remarkably, received virtually no serious analysis as political creed or theory.

The most obvious explanation for inattention to the Declaration of Sentiments is the assumption that because it uses the form of the 1776 Declaration of Independence, Sentiments is a kind of minor corrective to the brilliant but modesty flawed original: "certain guarantees [were] added to its basic principles" (Foner 1976, 5), which themselves, the story goes, rightly remained unaltered—indeed, remained celebrated.[2] Further, "alternative" declarations such as Sentiments, whether by labor groups, women, indigenous

---

1. In Judith Wellman's *The Road to Seneca Falls,* the lack of individual signatures is associated with a deliberate desire "to be recognized not for themselves as individuals but as representatives of local citizens" (2004, 189). The notice was published in other papers and publicized through Friends' meetings and informal networks.

2. It is worth noting that if "imitation" was a consistent basis for neglecting political documents, Independence itself would be considerably less fascinating to scholars. It was influenced by previous formal declarations from the kingdom of Scotland's 1320 Declaration of Arbroath and the 1581 Dutch republic's Oath of Abjuration to Virginia's 1776 Declaration of Rights, and by political philosophers from John Locke to Thomas Paine. Jefferson even wrote that the purpose of the document was "not to

peoples, or abolitionists, are understood as political strategy rather than political theory: using a preexisting framework, they make certain needs more
manifest, and ongoing struggles more legitimate. Alternative declarations are
understood as pleas for consistency of principle rather than opportunities for
rethinking principles, as demands for the extension of rights to more groups
rather than reconsideration of what rights belong to whom or how they
can be realized in daily life. In the end, like most political work by women,
whether treatise, tract, or travel memoir, declarations like that issued in 1848
are assumed to be atheoretical and unoriginal even when, as here, very little
serious examination of the work precedes such judgment.

The small literature on Sentiments generally supports these readings of
the document, thereby inadvertently contributing to continued neglect of
it. Matilda Joslyn Gage, official secretary at Seneca Falls, went so far as to
consider Sentiments' resort to "masculine productions" a "humiliating fact,"
mandated by the short length of time in which to prepare a document (three
days before the convention) and its authors' lack of experience organizing a
convention (Gage 2004, 2). More commonly, however, scholars argue that
explicit strategy rather than desperation and inexperience were involved in
the decision to make use of Independence. According to Linda Kerber, for
example, using the language of the 1776 document usefully demonstrated
"that the women's demands were no more or less radical than the American
Revolution had been," since they "were in fact an implicit fulfillment of the
commitments already made" (1987, 3). Similarly, Sigerman asserts that by
borrowing from its esteemed predecessor, its authors prudently "hoped to
provide their cause with the same moral and political justifications that had
inspired the American Revolution" (1994, 34), and Anderson refers to their
practical desire to "seize[] the moral high ground for women by identifying them with the rebellious American colonists" (2000, 168–69).[3] These
"strategic" explanations establish the political framework for Sentiments as
wholly within that set by Independence. As one commentator summarizes
the relationship between the two, "the Declaration of Independence was so
perfectly tailored to their needs that in 1848 the first women's rights convention in history adopted a manifesto that *was* the Declaration, with a few

---

find out new principles, or new arguments, never before thought of . . . but to place before mankind
the common sense of the subject, in terms so plain and firm as to command their assent, and to justify
ourselves in the independent stand we are compelled to take." One might even see Sentiments as less
able than Independence to rely upon old arguments—its cause was even more politically novel, more
marginal (Wills 1978).

3. Whether or not any strategy could make "the claims of the Seneca Falls women as self-evident
as the other truths," it certainly did not greatly "deflect hostility" (Kerber 1987, 115), as hostile published reactions to the Seneca Falls gathering show.

appropriate changes in wording" (Kraditor 1968, 16). I argue, however, for a more theoretically substantial and radical understanding of its essential character and contribution: most basically, Sentiments simply cannot be understood as an "extension" to women of the rights Independence grants to men, or even as calling for the same kind of revolution.[4]

If we begin with a focus on the formal differences alone, Sentiments' departures from Independence are numerous.[5] First, there are insertions of phrases such as "and women" to such passages as "all men are created equal." These alterations make gender inequities and exclusions in the original document easily visible. Second, arguments originally targeted at England's power over the colonies are reframed and directed at a new villain: men's power over women. This change boldly introduces patriarchy as an illegitimate form of government; throughout, Sentiments will refer to male domination in employment, family, culture, and politics as usurpations of power that deny women both their rights and their happiness. Third, there is in the "grievances" section—the list of "wrongs" prompting and justifying rebellion—an imitation of form with a complete reworking of material—not a single original grievance transfers over. This wholly novel material establishes new standards of what it means to have a free and equal citizenry—a democratic society, not just a democratic state. Finally, Sentiments adds a closing section, "resolutions," for which there is no parallel in the original. It lays out principles and policies that sustain equality, prioritizing women's happiness, challenging norms of masculine behavior, treating equality as an individual and social good, describing the nature of oppression, and calling on both women and men to be agents of political and moral change. Interestingly, the two new sections actually constitute the majority of the document. Justifying inattention to Sentiments because of its supposed lack of originality, then, fails to explain why even its sizable differences from Independence have gone unstudied. "When compared word-for-word with the Declaration of Independence, only 152 of the 1,071 words in the original were duplicated exactly in 1848" (Hoff 1991, 443n45). Alone and together, these departures make abundantly clear that something new is afoot.

There is convincing evidence that some of the participants themselves also understood the ideas of Sentiments as giving voice to something

---

4. I do not mean to dismiss summarily the political potential of extending rights; however, that is not what is happening in this document, and it *is* more radical than that.

5. This really useful framework begins with points made by Kingdom (1991) in her analysis of Olympe de Gouges's "Declaration of the Rights of Woman and Citizen," and then takes some different turns.

unprecedented. Sentiments sets up a political future by calling for more meetings: "We hope this Convention will be followed by a series of Conventions, embracing every part of the country." This hope was realized as the first of these took place a mere two weeks later, and many more were held over the following decade. In the 1850 convention in Worcester, Paulina Davis described the revolution they envisioned: "The reformation which we purpose, in its utmost scope, is radical and universal. It is not the mere perfecting of a progress already in motion, a detail of some established plan, but it is an epochal movement—the emancipation of a class, the redemption of half the world, and a conforming re-organization of all social, political, and industrial interests and institutions. Moreover, it is a movement without example among the enterprises of associated reformations, for it has no purpose of arming the oppressed against the oppressor, or of separating the parties, or of setting up independence, or of severing the relations of either" (Proceedings 2006, 4). That is, it has none of the same purposes as Independence. The penultimate sentence of Thomas Jefferson's document contains the following resolution: "We do assert and declare these colonies to be free and independent states, and that as free and independent states, they have full power to levy war, conclude peace, contract alliances, establish commerce, and to do all other acts and things which independent states may of right do." Unlike Paulina Davis and Sentiments, Jefferson's resolution indeed describes the goal as separation and the establishment of a new, independent state, and in defining the various powers of a new state it emphasizes that which continues to dominate politics in the United States: war and peace, international relations, and commerce. By contrast, Sentiments ends with eleven resolutions that lay out a different goal—happiness for women as well as men—and emphasizes quite different powers of the state and of individuals. In what follows I explore what, precisely, Davis and others saw as "radical" in Sentiments that we have lost track of. What "interests and institutions" are reorganized, and guided by what principles? I use the themes of equality, the state, the political, and happiness to explore the distinctiveness of the Declaration of Sentiments, integrating the particulars throughout.

EQUALITY

When, in the course of human events, it becomes necessary . . .
for one people to dissolve the political bands which have connected them with
*   another, and to assume among the powers of the earth, the separate and*
*   equal station . . .*

for one portion of the family of man to assume among the people of the earth
a position different from that which they have hitherto occupied. . . .

The opening indicates that the equality concern of Sentiments is at variance with that found in Independence. The latter asserts that independent nations, such as England and the emerging United States, are equals in being equally sovereign over their people and in possessing identical political powers (again, emphasizing war and peace, international relations, and commerce). The Americans, the document essentially claims, are politically mature, "ready for full self-government" (E. Morgan 1976, 67).

The opening of Independence refers to "one people" asserting its separate and equal existence, while Sentiments speaks of "one portion of the family of man" wanting a different position in that family. In his reference to "one people," Carl Becker notes, "Jefferson endeavored to make it appear that the people of the colonies were thoroughly united in wishing to 'institute new government' in place of the government of the king" (1958, 9). What is striking in comparison is Sentiments' spotlight on a previously unrecognized internal *dis*unity. The Seneca Falls proclamation refers to a whole that is more universal than that appealed to in Independence: not "a people," which refers to a limited political association, but the whole human family. Unlike the "one people," this "family" is not united, despite assertions to the contrary, especially by male heads of households. The constituents of "one portion"—women—are presenting themselves simultaneously as an integral part of humanity and as a separable political part challenging the status quo. Dramatically, this assertion makes of women a distinct political group, one not automatically represented by or in agreement with the heads of their households. Sentiments' demand, then, is not about equality among nations and each nation's right to be self-governing; rather, it concerns equality between groups of people that are not even divided by private property lines, no less national borders. From the outset, its concern is more about democratic societies than about national sovereignty.

All men are created equal.
All men and women are created equal.

The second sentence includes an assertion of equality. But between whom, and on what grounds? Saying that all men are created equal supports the idea that every citizen has an equal right to be part of an independent political community and rejects the idea that some communities get to be self-governing while others are inhabited by colonized half-citizens of a state with limited political rights and powers. The subject of Independence is not relations between citizens of one country, but between citizens of two countries. Sentiments does not extend this principle to residents of more nations, but shifts it to another plane: the political relations between individuals and groups of individuals, regardless entirely of national boundaries.

While many men had reasonable hope that they would gain politically and economically from independence, the fact that it would mean very little in women's lives reveals the limited nature of Independence's concern and scope. Women would not gain political or civil rights when the colonies became states, and there would be no change in their social or economic status; instead, the state that had power over them would change hands, and they would have no more part in drafting its new Constitution than they had had in drafting Independence. More important, the power that men had over women was completely unabated; if anything, it was now in the hands of even more empowered individuals with the blessing of a newly legitimized government. It would take Sentiments to show what freedom and equality for women as well as men and nations might begin to look like.

All further references to equality exist only in Sentiments—Independence is finished with the subject. The very fact that the former raises it at least another six times shows how much more central it is to the "revolution" advocated, as well as how substantive the Resolutions are.

> *Resolved, That woman is man's equal—was intended to be so by the Creator, and the highest good of the race demands that she should be recognized as such.*

This resolution, even more than the phrase "all men and women are created equal," is the clearest, most unmistakable expression of gender equality. It states that equality does not end with creation, with all having been *created* equal, for still today "woman *is* man's equal." Instead of linking equality to individual choice, as it does elsewhere (in referring to women, rather than men or laws, determining women's station, for example), this resolution focuses on equality as a social good, and on the compatibility of equality with divine ordinance. More commonly, sexual equality was seen as contrary to God's will, and women's subordination, rather than her equality, was justified by its supposed contribution to the common good. With equality understood as a social good, to deny the equality of the sexes is to harm the human race: *"Equality of human rights results necessarily from the fact of the identity of the race in capabilities and responsibilities.... Being invested... with the same capabilities, and the same consciousness of responsibility for their exercise, it is demonstrably the right and duty of woman, equally with man, to promote every righteous cause by every righteous means.*"

Sentiments' advocacy of equal rights results from and contributes to a broad reassessment of woman's and man's natures: their abilities, goals, obligations, realm of action, and political role. Woman and man, according to the resolutions, have the same capabilities and, interestingly, the same "consciousness of responsibility for their exercise." This unfamiliar wording not only makes possession of abilities important, but also emphasizes exercise of them, use of them, in an individually self-aware and socially responsible manner. Equality is not an abstract right but seen in concrete actions; it is not only something we are born to but also something that we live with; not only something given to us but also something we use to give back. A world in which both sexes cannot *use* their capacities is one in which people cannot act responsibly, or morally; that is, a world in which both can not use their capacities is itself immoral. Here ideas about equality are linked to standards of legitimate political community: "*The same amount of virtue, delicacy, and refinement of behavior that is required of woman in the social state, should also be required of man, and the same transgressions should be visited with equal severity on both man and woman.*" The equal moral character and moral obligations of both sexes is a major theme of Sentiments. Both sexes are capable of virtue, both are to be held accountable for unjust and unrefined behavior, both have duties "to participate . . . in teaching" morals and religion "in private and in public."

Sentiments calls for a single code of morality for all, a unified standard of virtue and vice. The problems with the double standard are threefold: first, the practice of allowing women to commit certain crimes with impunity reinforces an unequal model of marriage in which women do not act based on their own consciences and decisions but are dictated to by and merely obey their husbands. That which seems like a "boon" for women—being able to commit crimes without repercussion—is in fact a disadvantage, linked to having a domestic master and being considered in all contexts as "morally, an irresponsible being." Second, the "different code[s] of morals for men and women" generally operate to limit what women can do both when followed ("good women don't") and if broken ("bad women shouldn't") and forgive men the same trespasses. That is, the moral codes shrink only women's opportunities and actions, thus contributing to inequality. Third, when such vices are "deemed of little account in man," are "tolerated," we in fact actively encourage them. "Boys will be boys" is used to explain and justify certain destructive activities from fighting to drinking, for example. Yet these acts are often especially harmful to women and children, associated as they are with sexual and domestic violence, unfulfilled responsibilities, and poverty. Sentiments focuses on the behavior of men as well as women and bravely asserts that the standards of behavior for men should often be raised to those of women, rather than women being allowed as much destructive leeway as men. This early document does not accept the male norm as unproblematic in political or personal life, a position that explains many of its important departures from Independence.

Reassessed natures lead to reconceived relationships and opportunities, public and private. Given their equality of capabilities and responsibilities, neither sex is rightly master of the other. Therefore, woman should not promise obedience in wedding vows, and men should possess no "power to deprive her of her liberty [or] to administer chastisement." Her equal, he has no right to her property or her wages. Able, virtuous, educable women, like their male counterparts, should have access to every profession, including those bringing "wealth and distinction." Sentiments singles out as examples of injustice that "as a teacher of theology, medicine, or law, she is not known." Perhaps most broadly of all, man, possessing the same conscience and religious sentiments as woman, does not decide for her what shall be her "sphere of action."

Equality is not only about policies and processes of government or about relations between nations. There is in Sentiments a group of grievances that concerns political rights, but others extend equality concerns to employment opportunities, family relations, social mores, religion, and education. Together they show how women are consigned, in one institution after another, from church to courtroom, to "a subordinate position," one not equally fully human, and how this connects to their systematic oppression.

THE STATE

If women are to be equal citizens to men, certain things are required of the state. The state must grant equal legal rights, from suffrage to property. Lawmakers must listen to women's voices. Laws must recognize women's equal moral authority and equal moral responsibility. Laws must limit the power of some individuals over others, including limiting the power of husbands over wives. If Sentiments was transformed into the language of the Bill of Rights, it would say such things as

> no state can declare or act as if either sex is superior to the other; therefore, the state shall guarantee equal protection of the laws on the basis of sex, including the right to vote, to own property, and to divorce;

no state shall deny or tolerate denial of equal educational opportunity;

no state shall deny or tolerate the denial of equal employment opportunity, including occupational freedom of choice and equal pay for equal work; and

no state shall condone religious institutions' closing the ministry to women, or forbidding women the teaching of theology, or limiting women's participation in any way.

While both documents contain a list of grievances, it is especially noteworthy that there is absolutely no overlap between them. What that means is that a government that satisfies all the demands and standards laid out in the Declaration of Independence is still not, according to the Declaration of Sentiments, a legitimate government. It means that Independence took little notice of sexual equality, or of issues of special concern to women as citizens, as employees, as students, as wives, as mothers, or as individual personalities. It deems a government legitimate that allows and contributes to women's subordination, as long as other requirements are met, such as holding regular elections and maintaining a separation of powers between the branches of government.

While the policies and processes of the state are not its only concern, they are a major focus of Sentiments, which both grants certain powers to the state and limits them. The fundamental limits are, as in Independence, the restriction of power so that government is not tyrannical, but tyranny is understood differently in the two documents. The grievances in Independence and Sentiments are the evidence to support their general charges of tyranny. Many of them in Independence concern breaches of divisions of power. Regarding the legislative branch, Houses were "dissolved . . . for opposing" the king, who was also charged with "preventing elections of new legislatures" and refusing to give "his Assent to Laws." With regard to the judiciary, he obstructed the establishment of judiciary powers and "made Judges dependent on his will alone" for tenure and salary. He interfered with state executive power, forbidding "Governors to pass Laws of . . . pressing importance," and mishandled his own executive powers, keeping standing armies in peacetime. Citizens of the colonies were denied basic rights: denied, the document reads, trial by jury, for example. In general terms, legitimate government was destroyed: the king attempted to introduce "absolute rule into these colonies"; he failed to provide security, himself "waging War against us"; and he governed without the consent essential to legitimate rule.

Independence is completely focused on government. In general terms, it considers whether consent has been properly given for certain acts, and whether the forms of colonial government are preserved. More specifically, it raises questions about the division and separation of powers, that is, about the independence and authority of each branch and each level of government. Tyranny, therefore, is defined as breaches of these matters: one branch or level of government stepping outside its bounds, taking over or obstructing another. Individual rights appear only in "depriving us in many cases, of the benefits of Trial by Jury," an exception that is used primarily to provide evidence for corruption of the judiciary.

By contrast, Sentiments looks at individual rights to vote, to own property, to choose an occupation, and to obtain an education. It also concerns itself with civil society, including family relations and standards of morality and virtue, and speaks of nongovernmental institutions such as religious organizations. At perhaps its political peak, it talks not only of individual laws and policies but also of their joint operations and general assumptions, and of the interaction between the political, the civil, and the personal. Sentiments addresses the role of entities other than government in creating domination, while also highlighting government complicity. While it agrees with Independence that government has acted tyrannically, Sentiments extends its analysis beyond one branch exercising power belonging to another, because fixing that would leave untouched women's subordination and second-class citizenship.

THE POLITICAL

The only possible mention in Independence of the private realm is in the complaints of "quartering large bodies of armed troops among us" and sending "swarms of Officers . . . to harass our People, and eat out their substance." By contrast, a whole group of grievances in Sentiments concerns women's relative status in the home, especially her relationship with her husband. Under the doctrine of coverture, a married woman is, "in the eye of the law, civilly dead." A husband owns his wife's property and even has a right to wages she earns. A wife "is compelled to promise obedience to her husband," and the law grants him "power to deprive her of her liberty, and to administer chastisement." The grounds for divorce are limited and, should divorce be granted, custody of the children likely belongs to the father. The sum of these specifics is captured in powerful political language:

"Her husband . . . becoming, to all intents and purposes, her master." Like the king, he has usurped powers not belonging to him, but different powers with different consequences. He is part of the illegitimate patriarchy, inappropriately governing women's lives, exercising control over their property, their liberty, and their happiness. Sentiments does not limit its understanding of illegitimate power to that which can be held by the state, and it does not allow the state to be silent or conspiratorial where nonstate actors are involved in oppression.

This difference in the sphere deemed political is captured in the titles of the two documents. Had it been nothing but an extension of the original, the attendees at Seneca Falls might have entitled theirs "The Declaration of Women's Independence." Instead, significantly, they chose the word *sentiments*. In Sentiments, "revolution" is about more than, other than, government; in fact, because of the understanding that Sentiments develops about connections between rules and feelings, government and mores, a revolution limited to government could not support itself.

"Sentiments" has a political history. In general, a *sentiment* is defined as "an attitude, thought or judgment prompted by feeling." It points out the interaction between opinion and emotion; the two are not opponents, but collaborators. Politically, this changed relationship reveals that institutions and practices are not maintained or altered by argument alone.

David Hume (1711–76) argued that sentiment, like reason, is about the general rather than the particular and asserted that both can be disinterested and stable. Unlike reason, however, he saw sentiments influencing action, explaining their prominence in the realm of politics. They connect to an understanding not merely of self-interest but of what benefits and hurts larger groups, including society as a whole. Their basis is sympathy, and they apply to artificial as well as natural virtues and vices.

Mary Wollstonecraft's 1792 *Rights of Woman* concludes with a call for "a REVOLUTION in female manners" (1988, 192). She, too, is concerned with what is injurious and beneficial collectively. Sentiments are, she thinks, learned, and they change. They are not only evolving but also corruptible. In fact, sexual inequality teaches us to value not real virtue but traits that degrade women and, ultimately, society. Movements for sexual equality have to reckon with the content and power of corrupted sentiments, and to create and sustain different moral judgments about sexual vice and virtue.

Probably the most prominent recent precedent to Seneca Falls was the 1833 treatise also named Declaration of Sentiments, which served as a creed for the American Anti-Slavery Society. The 1848 document shared ground with the 1833 one, rather than with the 1776 one, in focusing on "the condition" of a sizable group of people and on the role both of law and "treat[ment] by their fellow-beings" in this state of affairs. Put another way, the Anti-Slavery Society saw slavery as "a base overthrow of the very foundations of the social compact," referring to the establishment of government, and as "a complete extinction of all the relations, endearments, and obligations of mankind," referring broadly to civil society. It implicated not only the federal and state governments, and not only slaveholders, but every citizen of free states who "enable[s slaveholders] to perpetuate [their] oppression." It set "emancipation" "and the elimination of artificial barriers to self-fulfillment" as the goal and called for both "moral and political action." It is, I believe, because of its attention to both spheres, rather than to the narrowly governmental, that *sentiments* is a fitting word for the title in 1848 as in 1833, one that encompasses not only legal judgments but also popular attitudes, that speaks to the spirit and not only the mind. William Lloyd Garrison, who led the society, and the Garrisonians were frequently considered " 'fanatics' because they had repudiated all religious and governmental institutions as hopelessly corrupted by slavery" (McKivigan and Harrold 2003, 6). Given that analysis, they had to look beyond government for solutions. Independence understood the problem and the solution to be narrower. As a consequence of the expanded understanding of the political, not only law, but "any custom or authority adverse" to sexual equality, "whether modern or wearing the hoary sanction of antiquity," is an example of "corrupt customs" and "perverted application of the Scriptures" that are declared harmful, tyrannical, and against God's will.

HAPPINESS

Now to what may be the real goal of both documents: happiness. But whose happiness? Understood as what? Achieved how? The word *happiness* appears twice in Independence, which Sentiments largely repeats. It adds another three references to happiness and, related, one to being "satisfied." *"We hold these truths to be self-evident, that all men [Sentiments: and women] are created equal, that they are endowed by their Creator with certain unalienable Rights, that among these are Life, Liberty, and the pursuit of Happiness."* Even the shared references to happiness unexpectedly carry different meanings. The pursuit of happiness is, in Sentiments as in Independence, declared to be an unalienable right. In fact, "approximately two-thirds of the state constitutions adopted by the American people from the beginning of their independence to the beginning of the twentieth century have solemnly stated or guaranteed a right to happiness, or to pursue happiness, or to pursue and obtain happiness, or to pursue and obtain happiness and safety, or to pursue happiness in some other connection" (K. B. Jones 1953, 26). In its famous alteration, Sentiments asserts that women, too, have a right to pursue their own happiness. It certainly cannot be assumed that such an assertion is part of Independence, both because of the gendered language asserting the pursuit of happiness to be a right of "all men" and because the status quo with which Sentiments' view of women's happiness contrasts was *not* considered tyranny by Independence's authors. Women's happiness was not understood by them in the same individualist terms as was men's, and the relationship between the sexes was not subjected to political analysis. Happiness for women was pursued indirectly through fulfilling one's obligations to family, making husbands and children happy, not by developing one's distinctive talents or following one's particular dreams, not by participating in political life or pursuing a trade or profession. In fact, a woman following such paths was likely to be considered unnatural, unmarriageable, irreligious, unpatriotic, and, therefore, decidedly unhappy. A man's happiness might be the result of certain kinds of independence (political and economic, for example) and accomplishment outside the family (education, religion, and business) but hers was not. In explicitly asserting that women have a right to pursue their own happiness, Sentiments challenges what Independence accepts, broadening opportunities for women and reenvisioning family life and, incidentally, giving government more for which to be accountable: *"That whenever any Form of Government becomes destructive of these ends, it is the Right of the People [Sentiments: the right of those who suffer from it] to alter or to abolish it [Sentiments: to refuse allegiance to it], and to institute [Sentiments: to insist upon the institution of a] new Government, laying its foundation on such principles and organizing its powers in such form, as to them shall seem most likely to effect their Safety and Happiness."* Because a government can make rights *more* secure, people consent to be governed in the first place; thus, a government that violates inalienable rights is a tyranny, while one that adds nothing to the security of rights is useless, also legitimately to be resisted. While it follows Independence in stating that the happiness of the people, like their security, is to be a standard for legitimate government, Sentiments alters the content by making the safety and happiness of women as well as of men a criterion by which effective government is measured. Recalling the earlier point about disunity, Sentiments also differs in empowering "those who suffer" rather than "the people," placing the right to rebel in their hands, not allowing those who do not suffer to overrule them. Further, the right recognized in Independence is to alter or abolish government, while in Sentiments it is to refuse allegiance. Even the disenfranchised can refuse allegiance and can insist upon the institution of new government even when they cannot themselves institute it because of exclusion from political institutions and practices. The less powerful are not powerless, Sentiments seems to be asserting, but their position *is* politically different, which Independence takes no notice of. After these two somewhat shared references, Independence does not use the word *happiness* again. *"He has so framed the laws of divorce, as to what shall be the proper causes of divorce; in case of separation, to whom the guardianship of the children shall be given; as to be wholly regardless of the happiness of women."* In Sentiments *happiness* appears next as a standard by which to judge not only government in general, but also particular laws; specifically, divorce and custody laws are held up as examples of tyrannical governance because they do not take account of women's happiness. The language is important: those laws are "wholly regardless of the happiness of women." Sentiments is not asserting that the laws have to be made only or even primarily with women's happiness in mind, but is stating that to take no regard of it is essentially to sacrifice women's well-being for some other ends. In Independence a government that sacrifices and disregards the happiness of the people in general is tyrannical; in Sentiments one whose specific policies sacrifice the happiness of a distinct segment of the population is also a tyrannical government. Sentiments might be seen in this instance as adding a standard for legitimate government to that established in Independence; further, though, it is also implicitly raising questions about who constitutes "the people" whose happiness is being considered, about what actually contributes to the happiness of different people, about the connection between the well-being of smaller populations and communities and the well-being of the entire citizenry, and about the government's obligations to identifiable groups of citizens rather than only to the more abstract whole. Each of these constitutes a significant addition.

Following the grievances, the resolutions begin with a reference to William Blackstone on natural law: *"Whereas, The great precept of nature is conceded to be, that 'man shall pursue his own true and substantial happiness.' Blackstone in his Commentaries remarks, that this law of Nature being coeval with mankind, and dictated by God himself, is of course superior in obligation to any other. It is binding over all the globe, in all countries and at all times; no human laws are of any validity if contrary to this, and such of them as are valid, derive all their force, and all their validity, and all their authority, mediately and immediately, from this original."* Continuing with a "strategic" interpretation of Sentiments, Hoff claims that the "paraphrase from Blackstone's infamous Commentaries . . . allowed these women to present their resolutions in 'higher-law' rhetoric that placed them above the secular and theistic practices that they wanted changed" (1991, 139). While true, the "paraphrasing" merits more analysis as it signals substantive departures on the subject of happiness. Sentiments' statement combines several quotes from Blackstone's *Commentaries on the Laws of England,* all part of his discussion of the law of nature. At issue for him is whether everyone can or will know the "abstracted rules and precepts" that constitute the laws of nature by "due exertion of right reason." Blackstone asserts that, fortunately, the Creator has "so inseparably interwoven the laws of eternal justice with the happiness of each individual, that the latter cannot be attained but by observing the former; and, if the former be punctually obeyed, it cannot but induce the latter." Following the laws of nature contributes to happiness; attaining happiness means having observed the laws of nature. Blackstone emphasizes that the "rule of right" can be learned and obeyed by rightly pursuing happiness, rather than through "a chain of metaphysical disquisitions," which perhaps suggests that individual happiness can be a means to universal justice.

Sentiments subtly shifts Blackstone's focus. It emphasizes the overriding importance and validity of women's pursuit of their own true happiness, as individually defined, rather than the relationship of happiness to natural law. Women's happiness is said to be the law of nature, God's will, universally applicable, and a standard by which to judge every particular human law. Women's happiness is not to be sacrificed for the supposed well-being of her family or her community, it is not identical with the happiness of her husband or children, it is not determined by any law or person other than herself, and it is not limited to what she can obtain in her traditional role. Perhaps this stance is one that contributes to the document's "radical" character, not only in 1848 but still today: *"That such laws as conflict, in any way, with the true and substantial happiness of woman, are contrary to the great precept of nature, and of no validity."* The first resolution following the reference to Blackstone does not quote Blackstone exactly; the main difference is the inclusion of "in any way" to Blackstone's phrase "no human laws are of any validity, if contrary to this." To say that any law is invalid that conflicts in any way with the happiness of woman is to make absolutely clear that women's happiness cannot be sacrificed for any higher good—it *is* the highest good, as is man's happiness. Further, this resolution moves happiness from a general and abstract idea to a concrete test for any and all individual laws. As a test of specific laws, women's happiness is at less risk of being "forgotten," to use Abigail Adams's notion, an imaginative transformation of Blackstone's check on "right reason" into a consciousness-raising device. Such a device is required when governmental practices actively work against women's happiness, establishing laws, consciously or not, in conflict with it. The interpretation I am suggesting here means that the document sees women as individuals, whole persons, politically identical to men, separable from husbands, children, and families: *"That the women of this country ought to be enlightened in regard to the laws under which they live, that they may no longer publish their degradation by declaring themselves satisfied with their present position, nor their ignorance, by asserting that they have all the rights they want."*

Although it uses the word *satisfied* rather than *happy,* I include a sixth reference that seems to me to be in the same category. The motive for this passage, as for several others, is to respond to popular arguments against women's rights. One argument surely is that women are satisfied with the status quo. Sentiments has just urged us to see women's happiness as a most important standard for both individuals and laws. How can women's assertion of their own happiness be reconciled with calls for change, if change is justified by its contribution to women's happiness? Sentiments proposes an explanation for women's "satisfaction" that adds to the indictment against rather than to the vindication of inequality. To be satisfied with being subordinated might mean that women do not know "the laws under which they live," so that they wrongly think "they have all the rights they want" when they in fact do not, a problem relatively easily attended to by education. Or, their satisfaction with inequality may be the result of not wanting enough—the rights they have are sufficient for the desires they have. Or, they may suffer from such "degradation" that they think they are in an inferior position because they belong there. Understanding the internalization of oppression, Sentiments mourns that "he has endeavored, in every way that he could to destroy her confidence in her own powers, to lessen her self-respect, and to make her willing to lead a dependent and abject life."

The idea that inequality shapes our very desires is a deeper problem than, say, that inequality limits our opportunities. It links politics and psychology, connects the internal with the external. Such an analysis means that change in the external alone will never bring about equality. It makes added sense of using Blackstone, given his reference to "true" happiness, which implies the possibility of individual misperception or political misdirection, and contributes to the enlargement of the political considered earlier.

Altogether, Sentiments establishes that women, as well as men, rightly pursue their own happiness, as individually determined. Women's happiness is not only a valid end but, like men's, also has supreme status as the most imposing obligation. According to Sentiments, not only in the United States, but across the globe, every individual's true happiness is the will of God, the precept of nature, the test of any law's validity and authority. Any political community that fails to recognize these facts is "at war with mankind."

CONCLUSIONS

Sentiments contains a different understanding of human nature (including "women's versus men's nature" and the poles of human happiness and degradation). From this redefinition of the nature of woman and man emerges a reassessment of familial relationships (marriage, parenthood) and consideration of women's needs and potential in new roles and arenas (employment, education, politics, religion) where their participation was previously banned or restricted. What emerges next is a definition of oppressive political power broad enough to encompass men's unjust power over women and, on the other hand, a deeper conception of democratic relations both extending to supposedly nonpolitical institutions and practices and expanding the scope of participants. Not only is the political less contained, the interaction between spheres and arenas (public and private, legal and cultural, religious and political) is newly emphasized. Also resulting is a multifaceted sense of what equality means (and what it requires of individuals and the state), divergent from what is seen in Independence. Overall, in "challenging traditional norms about women's place in the family, society, and the polity, the women of Seneca Falls were implicitly—and often explicitly—calling into question the fundamental principles of social life" (Bernhard and Fox-Genovese 1995, 14).

Sentiments is richer than most suspect, for most have read it, understandably, less on its own terms than from a perspective learned from Independence. Nonetheless, it is incomprehensible as a minor fix to its more famous brother. It does not accept the rights that Independence's males possess as a legitimate model for the rights that all people should possess. It is not content with the brief attention to equality in what have become its most famous words: "All men are created equal." It does not accept the narrow terms of revolution from Independence, for the governmental is inadequate to make or sustain political change, and the truly unequal can still be silenced. It is less concerned with the boundaries of various states, because it takes a surprisingly international stance toward sexual equality (Anderson 2000), and less concerned with the boundaries around every branch and level of government, and between each citizen and the others, for such lines also cause problems, and distract us, and give short shrift to our connections and communities. The fact that the two documents do not share a single grievance in the face of what both term tyranny is most revealing of the distance between them.

The final paragraph of Sentiments is unlike anything found in Independence. Independence ends by saying that "for the support of this Declaration, with a firm reliance on the Protection of Divine Providence, we mutually pledge to each other our Lives, our Fortunes and our sacred Honor." By contrast, Sentiments sets out to accomplish "the great work" it describes by first acknowledging yet another obstacle: "We anticipate no small amount of misconception, misrepresentation, and ridicule." Some people objected to the independence of the colonies, but even they did not generally find it a laughable suggestion. There is, however, something incredible about women's freedom, something humorous about sexual equality. Saying the sexes shall be equal is less like saying two nations shall be equal than that two species shall be. Sentiments' prediction, which turned out to be utterly correct, is itself evidence of women's degradation. Stanton's opening address at the Seneca Falls meeting also dedicated its last and lengthy paragraph to the subject. Women need "to buckle on the armor that can best resist the keenest weapons of the enemy—contempt and ridicule." Stanton foresaw not reasoned arguments for and against women's rights, but an emotional battle for which women must be prepared. Ironically, the move away from intellectual argument is not a result of the limits of women's intellectual ability but caused by the nature of the opposition: "bigotry and prejudice" characterize the opposition, "entrenched" and "fortified" by "custom and authority." Interestingly, the colonies resorted to force to conquer arguments, while women largely stuck to the pen and the law to combat irrationality.

The organizers of the Seneca Falls convention had expected criticism, but perhaps even they were unprepared for the torrent of sarcasm and ridicule that rolled in upon them in the following few weeks. In New York and Philadelphia, newspapers extolled the virtues of traditional women and condemned the newly declared advocates of women's rights as heretics, radicals, and old maids. The Seneca Falls convention and the Declaration of Sentiments were dismissed as the work of unnatural women (Bernhard and Fox-Genovese 1995, 11).

The character and strength of the opposition is more support for my basic argument. The revolution called for in 1848 was in fact different from and more revolutionary than that advocated or even imagined in 1776. The separation from England certainly challenged many ideas about states and citizens, obligations and rights, legitimacy and necessity. But much of what it left safely intact was precisely what was taken up anew in 1848. The equality of the sexes challenged ideas and practices about life lived in the private sphere as well as in the public; it focused as much on our obligations as human beings as on our duties as citizens; it asked tough questions about the freedom and independence of citizens as well as of states, and even about what tasks "independent states may of right do." It redefined oppression, unapologetically took the side of the oppressed, and was uncompromising in demanding that the world change to accommodate women's freedom rather than that women compromise their happiness lest they impose upon the world. Its use of Independence was more than strategic—it laid out substantively what ideas and institutions it was *re*considering. It was not so much claiming that to be consistent with its own ideas Independence should have mentioned women, but saying that the kinds of questions asked in 1776 needed to be *brought up again*—that clearly we had not got it all right. Such are the realities that demand a revolution in sentiments.

Sentiments deserves to be studied more. There are numerous angles in need of examination; a detailed analysis could contribute to our understanding of, for example, what inclusive politics require. Second, just as Independence "is written in the lost language of the Enlightenment" (Wills 1978, xiv), Sentiments reflects a different but neglected aspect of the Enlightenment, found in writings by women thinkers of the time such as Olympe de Gouges and Marie-Madeleine Jodin. Finally, Sentiments should be studied as an early declaration of sexual equality that has been followed by dozens of others. Even in Rochester, two weeks later, participants "reworked a number of the earlier claims to make them more radical and inclusive," for example, "adding female 'industrial' rights to their agenda" (Anderson 1998, 170). That evolution of statements about what is wrong, how it can be fixed, and where we should be headed could be so revealing. Declarations are, after all, unique combinations of theory and policy, descriptive and normative politics, reason and sentiment, past, present, and future.

APPENDIX

DECLARATION OF SENTIMENTS

When, in the course of human events, it becomes necessary for one portion of the family of man to assume among the people of the earth a position different from that which they have hitherto occupied, but one to which the laws of nature and of nature's God entitle them, a decent respect to the opinions of mankind requires that they should declare the causes that impel them to such a course.

We hold these truths to be self-evident: that all men and women are created equal; that they are endowed by their Creator with certain inalienable rights; that among these are life, liberty, and the pursuit of happiness; that to secure these rights governments are instituted, deriving their just powers from the consent of the governed. Whenever any form of Government becomes destructive of these ends, it is the right of those who suffer from it to refuse allegiance to it, and to insist upon the institution of a new government, laying its foundation on such principles, and organizing its powers in such form as to them shall seem most likely to effect their safety and happiness. Prudence, indeed, will dictate that governments long established should not be changed for light and transient causes; and accordingly, all experience hath shown that mankind are more disposed to suffer, while evils are sufferable, than to right themselves by abolishing the forms to which they are accustomed. But when a long train of abuses and usurpations, pursuing invariably the same object, evinces a design to reduce them under absolute despotism, it is their duty to throw off such government, and to provide new guards for their future security. Such has been the patient sufferance of the women under this government, and such is now the necessity which constrains them to demand the equal station to which they are entitled.

The history of mankind is a history of repeated injuries and usurpations on the part of man toward woman, having in direct object the establishment of an absolute tyranny over her. To prove this, let facts be submitted to a candid world.

He has never permitted her to exercise her inalienable right to the elective franchise.

He has compelled her to submit to laws, in the formation of which she had no voice.

He has withheld from her rights which are given to the most ignorant and degraded men—both natives and foreigners.

Having deprived her of this first right of a citizen, the elective franchise, thereby leaving her without representation in the halls of legislation, he has oppressed her on all sides.

He has made her, if married, in the eye of the law, civilly dead.

He has taken from her all right in property, even to the wages she earns.

He has made her, morally, an irresponsible being, as she can commit many crimes with impunity, provided they be done in the presence of her husband. In the covenant of marriage, she is compelled to promise obedience to her husband, he becoming, to all intents and purposes, her master—the law giving him power to deprive her of her liberty, and to administer chastisement.

He has so framed the laws of divorce, as to what shall be the proper causes of divorce; in case of separation, to whom the guardianship of the children shall be given; as to be wholly regardless of the happiness of women—the law, in all cases, going upon the false supposition of the supremacy of man, and giving all power into his hands.

After depriving her of all rights as a married woman, if single and the owner of property, he has taxed her to support a government which recognizes her only when her property can be made profitable to it.

He has monopolized nearly all the profitable employments, and from those she is permitted to follow, she receives but a scanty remuneration.

He closes against her all the avenues to wealth and distinction, which he considers most honorable to himself. As a teacher of theology, medicine, or law, she is not known.

He has denied her the facilities for obtaining a thorough education—all colleges being closed against her.

He allows her in Church as well as State, but a subordinate position, claiming Apostolic authority for her exclusion from the ministry, and, with some exceptions, from any public participation in the affairs of the Church.

He has created a false public sentiment, by giving to the world a different code of morals for men and women, by which moral delinquencies which exclude women from society, are not only tolerated but deemed of little account in man.

He has usurped the prerogative of Jehovah himself, claiming it as his right to assign for her a sphere of action, when that belongs to her conscience and her God.

He has endeavored, in every way that he could to destroy her confidence in her own powers, to lessen her self-respect, and to make her willing to lead a dependent and abject life.

Now, in view of this entire disfranchisement of one-half the people of this country, their social and religious degradation,—in view of the unjust laws above mentioned, and because women do feel themselves aggrieved, oppressed, and fraudulently deprived of their most sacred rights, we insist that they have immediate admission to all the rights and privileges which belong to them as citizens of these United States.

In entering upon the great work before us, we anticipate no small amount of misconception, misrepresentation, and ridicule; but we shall use every instrumentality within our power to effect our object. We shall employ agents, circulate tracts, petition the State and national Legislatures, and endeavor to enlist the pulpit and the press in our behalf. We hope this Convention will be followed by a series of Conventions, embracing every part of the country.

Firmly relying upon the final triumph of the Right and the True, we do this day affix our signatures to this declaration.

RESOLUTIONS

Whereas, the great precept of nature is conceded to be, "that man shall pursue his own true and substantial happiness," Blackstone, in his Commentaries, remarks, that this law of Nature being coeval with mankind, and dictated by God himself, is of course superior in obligation to any other. It is binding over all the globe, in all countries, and at all times; no human laws are of any validity if contrary to this, and such of them as are valid, derive all their force, and all their validity, and all their authority, mediately and immediately, from this original; Therefore,

Resolved, That such laws as conflict, in any way, with the true and substantial happiness of woman, are contrary to the great precept of nature, and of no validity; for this is superior in obligation to any other.

Resolved, That all laws which prevent woman from occupying such a station in society as her conscience shall dictate, or which place her in a position inferior to that of man, are contrary to the great precept of nature, and therefore of no force or authority.

Resolved, That woman is man's equal—was intended to be so by the Creator, and the highest good of the race demands that she should be recognized as such.

Resolved, That the women of this country ought to be enlightened in regard to the laws under which they live, that they may no longer publish their degradation, by declaring themselves satisfied with their present position, nor their ignorance, by asserting that they have all the rights they want.

Resolved, That inasmuch as man, while claiming for himself intellectual superiority, does accord to woman moral superiority, it is pre-eminently his duty to encourage her to speak, and teach, as she has an opportunity, in all religious assemblies.

Resolved, That the same amount of virtue, delicacy, and refinement of behavior, that is required of woman in the social state, should also be required of man, and the same transgressions should be visited with equal severity on both man and woman.

Resolved, That the objection of indelicacy and impropriety, which is so often brought against woman when she addresses a public audience, comes with a very ill grace from those who encourage, by their attendance, her appearance on the stage, in the concert, or in the feats of the circus.

Resolved, That woman has too long rested satisfied in the circumscribed limits which corrupt customs and a perverted application of the Scriptures have marked out for her, and that it is time she should move in the enlarged sphere which her great Creator has assigned her.

Resolved, That it is the duty of the women of this country to secure to themselves their sacred right to the elective franchise.

Resolved, That the equality of human rights results necessarily from the fact of the identity of the race in capabilities and responsibilities.

Resolved, therefore, That, being invested by the Creator with the same capabilities, and the same consciousness of responsibility for their exercise, it is demonstrably the right and duty of woman, equally with man, to promote every righteous cause, by every righteous means; and especially in regard to the great subjects of morals and religion, it is self-evidently her right to participate with her brother in teaching them, both in private and in public, by writing and by speaking, by any instrumentalities proper to be used, and in any assemblies proper to be held; and this being a self-evident truth, growing out of the divinely implanted principles of human nature, any custom or authority adverse to it, whether modern or wearing the hoary sanction of antiquity, is to be regarded as self-evident falsehood, and at war with the interests of mankind.

[At an evening session] Lucretia Mott offered and spoke to the following resolution:

Resolved, That the speedy success of our cause depends upon the zealous and untiring efforts of both men and women, for the overthrow of the monopoly of the pulpit, and for the securing to woman an equal participation with men in the various trades, professions and commerce.

The Resolution was adopted.

6

CHILDHOOD: EMMA GOLDMAN

Stop me if this sounds familiar. Within a given academic discipline—in this particular case the field of political theory—a large segment of the population is rarely written about in any particular depth, or even at any great length. When they are written about, they are not really the direct or main subject of political inquiry, and they are not being treated as primary political actors, but are merely mentioned, often as representatives of some undesirable quality. The words are penned by people who by institutional design and cultural practice have relationships with them that are hierarchical, and who exclude them from many practices deemed important or even distinctly human. They appear as a fairly homogenous group, not receiving the subtle attention required to differentiate between them by, say, age or class. They rarely speak in their own voices.

The sort of pattern described above is, of course, familiar, because feminist theorists have so thoroughly documented and thoughtfully analyzed the canon's treatment of women. In this chapter I consider another group that fits this unfortunate description: children. The plight of children in political theory's canon indeed resembles that of women, as I will briefly discuss, sometimes for identical reasons. Arguably, the consideration the two groups receive is not only analogous, but also interrelated. But perhaps if we look in some new places—such as Emma Goldman's writings—we can find political theory's more "legitimate" children.

Our neglect of the young in political theorizing is a costly oversight. It deprives us of their insights, lets us avoid truly difficult political questions about power and democracy, and allows institutions involved most deeply in children's lives to escape certain kinds of oversight and critique. "The relation of the State to the child is little thought of, much less understood" (Gilman 2003, 278). Children often have direct relationships to the political community, visible in such matters as "juvenile justice" and child soldiers, and indirect relations to the state, seen in education, workplace, and family policies. Children participate in civil society through youth groups (and more) and are prepared for citizenship through families, schools, and religious institutions. It therefore seems not only appropriate but critical for political theorists to approach children and childhood with the queries similar to those posed about other subjects. The innumerable understudied questions include, In what respects is it possible and desirable for the young to be part of political life, and what are the various consequences of admitting or excluding them? How much freedom can and should children have? What does it mean that childhood is characterized as a period both of unmatched freedom for the young and of nearly unparalleled obedience to adults? Does a society's commitment to equality have any relevance to children—people who are often used to explain the very nature of hierarchical relationships, who lack precisely those rights used to determine equal status, whether that means, in various societies, the right to vote, the right to make contracts, or possession of personal freedom? What does childhood reveal about the nature and limits and potential of a "democratic" society, when children's voices are consistently discounted or ignored, in arenas from courtrooms to classrooms?

A BIT OF HISTORY

Let me introduce you to a few of the children who exist in the history of canonical political thought.[1] In Aristotle we meet creatures essentially defined by the fact that "the faculty of deliberation . . . *if* children . . . possess it," they possess "only in an immature form" (1975, 35; emphasis added). Because of their "youth and immaturity," they are ruled by "the head of the household," and the relation between child and father is "like that of a monarch over subjects" (32). These youthful humans assumedly feel affection toward their father-king, for Aristotle asserts both that "the male parent is . . . entitled [to] . . . the[ir] affection" (33) and that "youth never resents being governed" (316). Aristotle writes that "the goodness of children . . . makes a[] difference to the goodness of the polis. . . . It must make a difference [since] . . . children grow up to be partners in the government of the

---

1. I choose Aristotle and Hobbes simply to show two very different and common ways political theorists think about children, and two that contrast well with Goldman. There are other models, more and less troubling.

state" (37–38). Their education, therefore, "should prepare the way for the occupations of later years" (329).

Thomas Hobbes, too, calls his children "reasonable creatures" only "for the *possibility* apparent of having the use of reason in time to come" (1994, 26; emphasis added). He calls "childish" those adults ignorant of science (26) and those who confuse custom for justice (61). Hobbes's children "rely principally on helps external" (32), clearly an undesirable, because vulnerable, status to him. Adults lock up their goods because of children (77). Children cause some fundamental but unacknowledged problems in Hobbes's contractual thinking: he says children are subjects of their parents "from the child's consent, either express or by other sufficient arguments declared" (128), but also that "over . . . children . . . there is no law . . . because they had never power to make any covenant or to understand the consequences thereof" (77), and yet again that they are subjects by "natural force," because "a man maketh his children to submit themselves and their children to his government, as being able to destroy them if they refuse" (109–10). Regardless, children should be obedient and thankful to parents, for otherwise there would not "be any reason why any man should desire to have children, or take the care to nourish and instruct them, if they were afterwards to have no other benefit from them than from other men" (224). Because of their distinctive and somehow similar situation, "children and madmen are excused from offences against the law natural" (198). Unlike Aristotle's children, Hobbes's are by nature under "the dominion [of] . . . the mother" (129).

These two examples alone reveal some interesting tendencies in the political analysis of children. Children are defined by what they lack in comparison with (some) adults, and adults are consequently ridiculed for acting childishly. Various forms of dominion over children are held to be justified (which only sometimes meet the general standards for legitimate political authority), yet children are expected to respond to their rulers not only with obedience but also with affection and gratitude.

In this chapter, instead of writing more about "what men have said" about children, I write about "what women have said," or at least what one particular woman has said. Turning to Emma Goldman for this project may seem surprising. She had no biological children. She did not campaign directly for children, as did other political thinkers and activists of her time, such as Jane Addams, and children were the main subject of relatively few of her essays. But she is, in fact, a very interesting case study. As she works for and writes about numerous other causes, I will ultimately argue, she fully and consistently incorporates children into her thinking. Her analysis of them offers deep challenges to the ideas of Hobbes and Aristotle sketched above. What compels both that attention to children and those challenges, I will also argue, is her anarchist feminism, which makes visible and questionable the authority used against children, the effects of traditional families upon them, and the numerous means employed to socialize them into conformity, obedience, and passivity.

Goldman treats children's lives as relevant to analysis and evaluation of political, economic, military, and familial institutions and practices. She talks about children not only as political subjects, but as political actors; considers them not as immature adults, but as individuals in their own right; asks not what the state needs of them when they are grown, but what kind of society they need in order to grow; and focuses not on what rights parents have over children, but on what children need from parents. In the end, her anarchist feminism and her concern about children's lack of liberty are integrated and integral parts of her political theory.

CHILDREN IN THE LANDSCAPE

Goldman mentions children in nearly everything she wrote, which itself is uncommon—perhaps even unprecedented—in the history of political thought. Children were always present in her landscape. Whether she was writing about prostitution or patriotism, employment or education, marriage or morality, syndicalism or the state, the relevance of these topics to children, and of children to these topics, comes through repeatedly. Critically, the mention that children get is not merely in passing, but actually affects the substance of her argument. For example, in writing about prostitution, Goldman sees child prostitution as an intrinsic part of the institution. Her acknowledgment of that aspect of the practice allows her to connect prostitution not only to economic realities, which is her take on the subject with which we are perhaps most familiar, but also to issues such as sex education, double standards on sexual activity, and child-rearing practices. Because she wrestles with the existence of the child prostitute, her analysis of prostitution ends up being much fuller, reckoning with complex relationships between seemingly discrete social practices. The same might be said of her analysis of patriotism, which is richer for addressing how governments manipulate both children and childish adults into sacrificing for the state and seeing their own as superior to other states. It can also be said, to make clear the pattern, of her analysis of the family, which considers, among many other things, the costs to children of overworked parents, of family traditions, and of loveless marriages. Goldman does not just mention children in passing, then. She seems to stop and talk with them, and they influence what she consequently says.

In what follows I am guided by consideration of the following questions: What does Goldman see as the nature of a child? How do her children and their environments interact? How much attention do differences between children get from her? In what ways are and are not her children actual and potential political actors? What might constitute a more ideal childhood to Goldman, and what would be necessary to make it possible? In the end, what does a distinctively feminist anarchist perspective have to teach us about children?

THE NATURE OF THE CHILD

Children are often defined in comparison with adults, much as women get defined in comparison with men, and the comparisons tend, unsurprisingly, to reflect unfavorably upon children and women, in ways that are subsequently used to justify excluding them from aspects of the adult/male world. They are not rational enough, or sufficiently morally developed, or experienced enough, it is variously said, to be given voice, choice, control, or power in families, governments, jobs, or schools. Goldman, however, is less concerned with measuring children against the adult to see what the former lack, and more interested in knowing what is distinctive about children so that we meet their needs and allow them to flourish. It is her feminist anarchism that gives her this particular perspective on children: even the most benign nonanarchists are more attentive to what society and the state need children to be shaped into than they are to what individual children are and can become, and most nonfeminists are less attuned than she is to the effects of power in supposedly nonpolitical arenas such as families and schools upon what is called one's "nature."

I use two main strategies for getting at what Goldman thinks is the nature of a child. I look, of course, at her writings where children receive the most attention. I also search through her essays to find the kinds of people and things with which children are grouped, the analogies and metaphors Goldman makes that involve children, and the qualities that she calls "childlike."

The analogies Goldman makes involving children contain some revelations about her conceptualization of the young. Starting with a reference to the youngest—babies—she explains people's lack of sustained attention to the evil of prostitution by saying, "Only when human sorrows are turned into a toy with glaring colors will baby people become interested—for a while at least. The people are a very fickle baby that must have new toys every day" (Goldman 1972, 144). Here babies are portrayed as distractible, as interested in amusement and easily entertained, but not for long. She asserts that people and governments know and manipulate this in both adults and children: "The powers that have for centuries been engaged in enslaving the masses . . . know that the people at large are like children. . . . And the more gorgeously the toy is dressed, the louder the colors, the more it will appeal to the million-headed child. . . . An army and navy represent the people's toys" (1969, 135). This appeal explains why governments spend money on military parades, "fireworks, theatre parties, and revelries" (136). Goldman's children are impressionable and manipulable, for better and worse.

Goldman calls Americans "naive . . . crude and immature in matters of international importance" (1972, 64). She considers whether this is "merely a sign of youth" and, in doing so, reveals two interesting aspects of children. First, she notes that "it is indeed beautiful to possess a young mind, fresh to receive and perceive" (64–65), giving dignity to a youthful stage of life and acknowledging its admirable open-mindedness and perceptiveness. Second, however, she says that "unfortunately the American mind seems never to grow, to mature and crystallize its view" (65). Here she reminds us that youth is a stage, not the end of development, of what people can become, and that it is a stage that can be characterized by an "indefinite, uncertain mind . . . [holding] contradictory ideas . . . a sort of intellectual hash" (65). "Childlike naivety" (1969, 127) apparently has its place and its benefits, but beyond those bounds, which are not merely of age, it is potentially limiting and even dangerous.

Goldman says of the "ignorant mass" that "its reasons are like those of a child," by which she means, "it makes no pretense of knowledge or tolerance [and acts] by mere impulse" (48). On the other hand, Goldman also refers to something as having "a childlike nature" when it is "sweet and tender, unsophisticated and generous" (148). Positively, again, she admires Santo Caserio, who explains his actions in a childlike manner, whose "reasons for the act are set forth in so simple [and] dignified [a] . . . manner" (1972, 225). She calls savage revenge "child's play" in order to reveal by comparison the horrors of civilized revenge seen in prisons (1969, 119). In these examples, Goldman's children are relatively harmless and straightforward.

Delineating those things and people with which Goldman pairs children reveals yet more of her viewpoint on the young. References to "defenceless women and innocent infants" (104) and to "a drowning child or a crippled woman" (1972, 37) seem to place both women and children in the all-too-familiar position of helpless, endangered dependents. Yet in the first instance cited above Goldman is employing this tactic to condemn political tyranny. King Umberto, she recounts, had ordered the shooting of women and children during a bread riot. In this instance they were not acting helplessly at all, but rebelliously and in concert. In the second instance above she is referencing people's natural sociability. She attributes certain positive acts and attributes to "intellect or temperament" rather than to government regulations, saying they "could never have been induced by government any more than the spirit which impels a man to save a drowning child or a crippled woman from a burning building" (37). Pairing "children and cotton slaves" (1969, 129) as illegitimate sources of wealth, Goldman also portrays the child as an economic actor, and an especially exploitable one. Still, like those today who speak about women and children who are injured and killed in wars as casualties seen as somehow essentially different from men who are injured and killed in war, using children, and appealing to common sentiments about children, to demonstrate the depths of political corruption is a practice that always entails the risk of reinforcing those common stereotypes about them even if it also reveals hypocrisy among those claiming to protect children. Goldman's children in these examples are vulnerable to political and economic oppression, but in the absence of corruption, also somehow potentially relatively easy recipients of care.

The images Goldman uses to show the damage done to children are potent, and they again speak to the child's nature. A first set of images contains her criticism of those who do not recognize the humanity of the child. She complains that children are "kneaded like dough" and "moulded according to the whims and fancies of those about" them (1972, 107). Too often a child, capable of so much more, is "treated as a mere machine or as a mere parrot" (107). She compares the fate of a girl being prepared for marriage to that of "the mute beast fattened for slaughter" (1969, 230). A child is raised as if it were "inanimate matter for parents and guardians, whose authority alone gives it shape and form." Goldman's children are, most emphatically, fully human; in practice, however, they are wrongly silenced and wastefully underestimated.

In a second set of images, plant analogies abound. We erroneously treat the child as a "delicate human plant [kept] in a hothouse atmosphere, where it can neither breathe nor grow freely" (1972, 109). She contrasts the "young delicate tree that is being clipped and cut by the gardener in order to give it an artificial form" with the truly well-reared child who, "allowed to grow in nature and freedom," can reach "majestic height" and "beauty" (112). We should look at a child as a "budding and sprouting personality" (122). Our practices, however, result in "absolute death and decay to the bud in the making" (113). In these plant metaphors, the nature of the child comes across as hardy, in need of space, and containing within itself much of what it needs to mature, even as it is susceptible to the often-unhealthy manipulations of others. Like a plant that can be "overprotected" to death—overwatered, kept from the sun, and so on—a child's "good" can be wrongly determined to its detriment, from a wide assortment of motives.

Looking at what Goldman says about the nature of children when they are the main subject of her essays yields results that are consistent with and further develop the ideas already touched upon in the analogies and metaphors. First, Goldman's approach is built upon the notion that children can be driven from within to develop, as the plant analogies hinted at. In order to support "the natural growth of the child," we have to allow it "to grow from within" (107) rather than stifling it from without and gradually destroying "its latent qualities and traits" (109). Hence Goldman characterizes education as properly "a process of drawing out, not of driving in; it aims at the possibility that the child should be left free to develop spontaneously" (120). The "individual tendencies" of a child are revealed "in its play, in its questions, in its association with people and things" (108). Goldman's children may be malleable, but they are not Lockean blank slates. On the other hand, while they enter the world with unique sets of tendencies and traits, those do not necessarily unfold entirely on their own or in all social settings.

At times Goldman sounds like Rousseau expounding on negative education: don't "mold," don't "knead," don't "stifle," don't "cramp," don't "force," and don't "interfere."[2] She brings the same anarchist perspective to bear on schools as on prisons and, in fact, finds that against children we routinely use varieties of force that overlap to a frightening degree with those we employ against prisoners (and in neither case, according to Goldman, does this improve the individuals or benefit their communities, however passionately some might contend otherwise). While Goldman sometimes portrays children as helpless in familiar ways, she is unusual in the factors she cites as those from which they need help: for example, she writes, "Unless the

2. See Rousseau's *Émile*. The extent to which his educational scheme is in fact "negative" is often exaggerated, for there is quite a "positive" program endorsed.

young be rescued from that mind[-] and soul-destroying institution, the bourgeois school, social evils will continue to exist" (1969, 148). Her "negative" approach necessarily sees in children a natural desire to learn and develop: "It is reasonable to assume that the child is intensely interested in the things which concern its life" (1972, 121).[3]

Second, Goldman's theory depends upon a view of children that says they are not dangerous or destructive. She asserts that belief in the necessity of authority, whether governmental or parental, religious or educational, has "at its base . . . the doctrine that man is evil, vicious, and too incompetent to know what is good for him" (90). She characterizes children in such ways as to make it "safe" to allow them to develop without force and interference. They have "large, wondering, innocent eyes . . . [that wish] to behold the wonders of the world" (108). They have an "original sense of judgment" (111). Importantly, the child "has no traditions to overcome. Its mind is not burdened with set ideas, its heart has not grown cold with class and caste distinctions" (1969, 148). If we are to allow children to flourish, we need to "destroy the cruel, unjust, and criminal stigma imposed on the innocent young" (1972, 149). Even punishment is unnecessary and undesirable, "since the child is thereby led to suppose that punishment is something to be imposed upon him from without, by a person more powerful, instead of being a natural and unavoidable reaction and result of his own acts" (121).[4]

Third, Goldman insists that we recognize the humanity of the child. A child is a person, not a thing, whose thoughts and feelings deserve respect. Her main complaint about schools is that they have "such little regard for [a child's] personal liberty and originality of thought" (118). Like an adult, Goldman's child "is bent on going its own way, since it is composed of the same nerves, muscles and blood, even as those who assume to direct its destiny" (112). Children are more than potentially rational adults, blessed instead with a range of intellectual abilities: they are "ready to receive and assimilate" (120), can know themselves and their relations to others, can express themselves, use judgment and initiative, and work from both experience and imagination (121). They even have some advantages over adults. Not only, put negatively, are they "very vivid . . . not yet having been pounded into uniformity," but, put positively, "their experience will inevitably contain much more originality, as well as beauty" (121). Above all, then,

---

3. This is a view that even "brave" liberals such as John Stuart Mill are willing to apply only to adults. See J. S. Mill 1978, 9.

4. This is a viewpoint similar to that found in Charlotte Perkins Gilman's 1900 *Concerning Children,* especially in chapter 2, "The Effect of Minding on the Mind" (Gilman 2003).

"the child [is] to be considered as an individuality," rather than "as an object to be moulded according to the whims and fancies of those about it" (107).

DIFFERENCES BETWEEN CHILDREN

While I have been talking about the nature of the child in general, I do not want to overlook the fact that Goldman makes some distinctions between children of different ages, of various classes, and on the basis of sex. Such distinctions are consistent with what she says about the nature of childhood and also again reveal a more-than-passing interest in children. In this greater attention to them, Goldman's analysis is increasingly political, an idea that is the subject of the subsequent section of this chapter.

Before regarding the stages of childhood, Goldman studies the familial environment into which children are born. In terms of cultural norms, we are unfortunately born to those who see "the child [as] merely part of themselves" (1972, 111). So-called sexual morality leads many to become "incessant breeder[s] of hapless children" (129). Rather than have to partake in "the indiscriminate breeding of children," she acknowledges that a woman "desires fewer and better children, begotten and reared in love and through free choice" (166). We have lost the fact that it could be "her most glorious privilege, the right to give birth to a child" (140). What we would wish for is that "love begets life [and] no child is deserted, or hungry, or famished for the want of affection" (166). Sexual norms, economics, and family traditions conspire to create a setting in which children are not always wanted, loved, able to be cared for, or treated as fully human. Fascinatingly, insightfully, Goldman acknowledges the desirability of parents' "grow[ing] with the child" (167)[5] and asserts that children need "the love and devotion of each human about him, man as well as woman" (138).

Tragically, from "earliest infancy," Goldman asserts, "every effort is being made to cramp human emotion and originality of thought in the individual into a strait-jacket" (108). The lessons can, from the outset, sometimes differ by sex. "From infancy, almost, the average girl is told that marriage is her ultimate goal" (161). Seeming to address boys, she says that "from early infancy, the mind of the child is poisoned with blood-curdling stories about the Germans, the French, the Italians, etc. When the child has reached

---

5. This feature is one noted by Sara Ruddick and developed many decades later in "Maternal Thinking" (1980).

manhood, he is thoroughly saturated with the belief that he is chosen by the Lord himself to defend *his* country" (1969, 129). It makes a certain sense to Goldman that "the method of breaking man's will must begin at a very early age; that is, with the child, because at that time the human mind is most pliable" (1972, 116). It is probably not going too far to say that for all children—though in a variety of ways and toward some different ends—this "breaking" is currently the defining element of childhood.

The middle ages of childhood get attention on economic grounds. She refers to "middle-class girls . . . thrust into life's jungle at an early age" (129). It is obvious in reading Goldman that she has seen "mere children, work[ing] in crowded, overheated rooms ten to twelve hours daily" (150), as well as many of those "thousands of women and girls [driven] into prostitution (144), and mourns the "numberless little children ground into gold dust" (132). Of those aspiring to be professionals she says, "The years of their youth are swallowed up in the acquisition of a profession" (179). Sex-differentiated lessons also persist into adolescence, especially on matters related to sexuality. It is true that in general "the young [are kept] in absolute ignorance on sex matters," but at the point of adolescence we teach that "the boy may follow the call of the wild; that is to say, that the boy may, as soon as his sex nature asserts itself, satisfy that nature; but our moralists are scandalized at the very thought that the nature of a girl should assert itself" (149).

What Goldman's attention to differences between children shows is that they are reared to become particular kinds of adults, prepared to participate in certain kinds of institutions. What children want or can do hardly matters. Their differential treatment by class and sex shows fates to be predetermined.

"POLITICIZING" CHILDREN

In some ways Goldman provides a model for the kinds of questions political theorists should be asking about children. For a political thinker to ask such questions requires that children be deemed relevant to politics and that they be deemed relevant not only because they will one day become adults, but because even as children they are fully human. When Goldman "politicizes" children she understands them to be affected deeply by politics, to have social awareness, to be gauges of the legitimacy of social practices, to have claims to liberty, and to be ones whose needs should help to shape their environments. Her understanding of the nature of the child supports her ideas about their place in the social and political world.

Goldman's children are far from politically oblivious. Reflecting back on her own childhood, she says, "Since my earliest recollection of my youth in Russia I have rebelled against orthodoxy in every form." And look how many forms of orthodoxy the young Goldman recognized: "I could never bear to witness harshness whether on the part of our parents to us or in their dealings with the servants. I was outraged over the official brutality practised on the peasants in our neighborhood. I wept bitter tears when the young men were conscripted into the army and torn from homes and hearths. . . . I was indignant when I discovered that love between young people of Jewish and Gentile origin was considered the crime of crimes, and the birth of an illegitimate child the most depraved immorality" (1972, 386–87). Speaking again to children's consciousness, Goldman declares that prostitution is "an institution, known almost to every child" (143). A thinking being, even the impressionable child can see when "the lives of their parents are in contradiction to the ideas they represent" (114). Goldman's children are aware of and sensitive to injustice. They are not so unthinking as to be oblivious to hypocrisy, or so self-centered as to be blind to inequality, or so impressionable as to accept proffered explanations for abuses heaped on others or themselves without question.

Like adults, Goldman's children are dramatically affected by their environments. Economically, because parents are overworked and underpaid, "the home has been left to the care of the little ones" (1969, 89). Politically, patriotism requires parents to "sacrific[e] their own children" (133). Economics thrust "middle-class girls . . . into life's jungle at an early age" (1972, 129). Moral codes "condemn[] woman to the position of a celibate, a prostitute, or a reckless, incessant breeder of hapless children" (129). Because laws do not solve problems, child labor laws prevail in states where child exploitation flourishes (1969, 64). Familial norms mean that parents "make their children pay for the outrage perpetrated upon them by their parents . . . by traditions and habits" (1972, 124). As these examples show, children's lives are deeply affected by all their surroundings—economic, governmental, educational, familial, and cultural—both directly and through the effects on their parents.

It is in part because of their consequences for children that Goldman criticizes certain institutions. For example, her condemnation of marriage is based in part on its effects upon children, and on this subject her writing becomes quite passionate: "The sham, the hypocrisy of it! Marriage protecting the child, yet thousands of children destitute and homeless. Marriage protecting the child, yet orphan asylums and reformatories overcrowded, the

SPCC keeping busy in rescuing the little victims from 'loving' parents. . . . Oh, the mockery of it!" (1972, 164). Similarly, her criticism of schools is based on what they do to children. What she opposes is the "legal trickery, spiritual debasement and systematic indoctrination of the servile spirit, which process is known as 'education'" (89). And these various institutions do not operate in isolation but conspire against the development of the free individual: "The majority for centuries [have been] drilled in State worship, trained in discipline and obedience and subdued by the awe of authority in the home, the school, the church and the press" (93).

We saw earlier that both Aristotle and Hobbes, despite their dramatically different political and philosophical perspectives, easily justify authority over children and demand obedience from them. Yet when Goldman talks about the pain and loss of constant external interference in one's life, she looks in part to children, who are most obviously subject to widely accepted constraints. It is in writing on education, on children, that she says: "Discipline and restraint—are they not back of all the evils in the world? Slavery, submission, poverty, all misery, all social iniquities result from discipline and restraint" (Goldman 1969, 165). Children, like adults, have claims to liberty. Failure to respect those claims has a number of sources, including a misunderstanding of the abilities and nature of the child and lack of liberty in the lives of adults. Goldman's analysis of the effects of obedience and discipline lead her to question the structure of the family and the school. This is a tremendously important point: Goldman understands children to be affected by politics, broadly understood, but also, and consequently, to be a critical gauge by which to measure the legitimacy of various institutions. Their needs ultimately help her envision anarchist alternatives.

Finally, then, these sensitive and aware youngsters with claims to liberty, who are being deeply and negatively affected by certain practices, should help shape alternatives to the status quo. Goldman is not averse to education, only to certain forms of it. Like other political theorists, she stresses its importance: "It is through the channel of the child that the development of the mature man must go" (1972, 107). Unfortunately, what we create through great and lifelong effort is "a patient work slave, professional automaton, tax-paying citizen, or righteous moralist" (108).

A different education is needed to create "a well-rounded individuality" (108). What Goldman endorses is an education whose "scope . . . is truly phenomenal, including sex hygiene, the care of women during pregnancy and confinement, the care of home and children . . . every branch of human knowledge" (75). She applauds Faure's approach: "He took the children out into the open . . . showed them the splendor of the sunset, the brilliancy of the starry heavens, the awe-inspiring wonder of the mountains and seas . . . explained to them in his simple, direct way the law of growth, of development, of the interrelation of all life. . . . He prepared them to succor the poor . . . taught them the humiliation, the degradation, the awfulness of poverty . . . the dignity and importance of all creative efforts, which alone sustain life and build character" (1969, 162). She is absolutely insistent that a child can and should be "directing his own efforts and choosing the branches of knowledge which he desires to study" (1972, 120), because children are fit to use their own judgment and initiative (121). The authority over children exercised in schools is criticized on exactly the same grounds as adult obedience to government and religion; more, they are necessary to each other. In Goldman's anarchist schools, there would be "no coercion" (120) of children, just as there would be none of adults where anarchism prevails.

It is, of course, not enough to change schooling—in fact, one could not truly change schools to align them with an anarchist spirit and *not* change the world outside the school with which it is connected. In a more ideal childhood, the various environments in which a child grows up would work together: "Only when the material needs, the hygiene of the home, and intellectual environment are harmonious, can the child grow into a healthy, free being" (1969, 151). The familial environment would change: "A child born in freedom needs the love and devotion of each human being about him, man as well as woman" (1972, 138). Like teachers, parents would nurture the individuality of the child. Sex would be a topic of "intelligent discussion" (125). We would learn about and tend to a child's soul as we do now the child's physical well-being (112).

CONCLUDING THOUGHTS

Those of us who have spent a good deal of time in the company of children may look at childhood as anarchic in the negative sense of the word, for children certainly bring in their wake all kinds of disorder, as well as in the positive sense, for children have an endless capacity for experimentation. But we also know that those anarchic possibilities are not looked upon kindly, and much of adult interaction with children seems bent on stamping them out. I think it is precisely that aspect of childhood that brings Goldman back to the subject in so much of what she wrote.

Turning children into neither angels nor devils, Emma Goldman reveals to us a unique anarchist feminist perspective on children. While recognizing that there are different stages of childhood, and that children do differ in some ways from adults, her political philosophy nonetheless applies with equal force to adults and youngsters. She makes crimes against children visible in her essays; one might even say that her political ideas are as shaped by the injustices done to children as they are informed by those visited upon adults. Her positive ideas about freedom and individuality have concrete consequences for the lives of children, just as they do for adults, and demand the reshaping of educational, political, and economic practices. Goldman truly integrated children into her political theory, no small or common accomplishment.

Goldman has much to teach us about children and about how to incorporate children's lives into political thought. She uses the same principles to reveal and to judge what children do and what is done to children as those she uses with adults. She examines the environments in which children spend their time with the same critical eye she casts upon those that influence the lives of adults, but without losing the child's-eye view of them, and without losing sight of the special vulnerabilities or gifts of childhood. Goldman's study of children gives her a deeper understanding of adults, of what they have endured and might regain. It gives her a more complete picture of the social environment.

Children whose liberty and individuality is respected have knowledge and experiences that enable them to be free and unique adults and to see and resist infringements upon their freedom or their personality. Treated with respect; nurtured; freed from oppressive schools, families, and workplaces, Goldman's children get to be children without being condescended to. Her challenges to us might be that we respect and learn from the natural anarchy that is childhood, that we adapt to the needs of the young, help develop their potential, and be willing to learn from their distinct perspective.

These are Emma Goldman's children. In comparison to them, Hobbes's and Aristotle's children look like victims of neglect in theory and abuse in practice. Goldman's consideration of children is not always presented with enough detail—her discussion of curriculum changes, for example, makes questionably easy distinctions between the teaching of facts and interpretations of theory—or with enough attention to the needs of very different children—those with "weak natures" (1972, 115), for instance. But her ideas are invaluable and surpass those of most of her male predecessors. She should be commended for wrestling with the whole child—a being with emotional, sexual, social, and intellectual needs and desires. We should find, as she does, reason to be hopeful about the possibilities for change; and interestingly, some of that hope is to be found in the "very refreshing and encouraging psychological forces" (115) evident in children.

We live in a world that thinks Emma Goldman is wrong about children. Many abuses of children get understood as such fairly easily: for example, we are saddened by young children who are put to work or made to bear arms and by those who are sexually exploited or denied an education. But if Goldman is right, then our mistreatment of them includes not only child labor, but also the way we train children for labor. If Goldman is right, our problems include not only sexual abuse, but also denial of sex education, of sexual freedom, and of sexual choice. If Goldman is correct, we need to address not only lack of access to education, but also education that takes from children much of what makes life worth living—creativity, individuality, and experimentation. If Goldman has captured things correctly, we are wrong not only for sending children to war, but also for training them in the nationalism and patriotism that will justify and garner their support for future wars.

In the United States today there are a few educational experiments that give tremendous choice to children about what and how they learn, just as there are alternate families in which children are heard and are not reared to prove their parents' worth. If we take Goldman's political theory more seriously, greater attention should be paid to such schools and such families. But I fear that trends are taking us farther from Goldman's ideals. Standardized testing is all the rage and is incompatible with individualized education, "alternative education" has come to mean ever more rigid classrooms for "problem" students, and our public high schools are required to allow the military to set up recruitment tables.

If Emma Goldman is right, we are committing great injustices against our youth. For the world to treat children with the dignity they deserve will require revolutionary changes. Informed by Goldman, among others, we can make moves in that direction with a deeper sense of them as actors, thinkers, and innovators and with an understanding of them as fully human rather than potentially complete. We can view and interact with children as determining factors of our societies, rather than adapters to it, and as individuals, not undifferentiated members of a homogenous group. I think she *is* essentially right about children.

7

POWER: MARY ASTELL

But to what study shall we apply ourselves? . . . When they would express a particular Esteem for a Woman's Sense, they recommend History; . . . tho' it may be of Use to the Men who govern Affairs, to know how their Fore-fathers Acted, yet what is this to us, who have nothing to do with such Business? . . . How will this help our Conduct, or excite in us a generous Emulation? Since the men being the historians, they seldom condescend to record the great and good Actions of Women; and when they take notice of them, 'tis with this wise Remark, That such Women acted above their Sex.[1]

—Mary Astell, *A Serious Proposal to the Ladies for the Advancement of Their True and Greatest Interest*

As Mary Astell (1666–1731) herself might well have predicted, it is unlikely that political philosophers reading this have even heard of her. She is included in but a single general political theory textbook (Waters 2000). Her writings have been collected and published only twice, and not in their entirety. Until 2005, the sole book published on her was a biography (Perry 1986). Only in the last few years have more academic articles been written on her philosophical and political ideas than can be counted on one's fingers.

Astell is, however, not a woman who acted "above [her] sex" (Astell 1986c, 201) but one who wrote on a range of subjects with a sensitivity and responsiveness to its limitations, challenges, and insights. Arguably, she should be considered a formidable political thinker, despite the unfortunate fact that those men who have written history have yet to "take notice of" her (201). In just those few studies of her now available, intriguing arguments are emerging that she is "a forerunner of [David] Hume" (Duran 2000, 150), that she provided "not only the first but perhaps also the most sustained contemporary critique of [John] Locke's *Two Treatises*" (Springborg 1995, 629), that she "combined Christian faith with a sophisticated rationalist construction in a

---

1. Just as Astell's quote foretold, a 1731 obituary said of her that she demonstrated a "Turn of Genius above what is usual in her own Sex," confusing being female with being limited (see Kinnaird 1983, 31).

system that paralleled [René] Descartes's 'Discourse on Method'" (Smith 1982, 119), and that she "generated the concept of *patriarchy*... that we have come to use and accept as a reality today" (Spender 1982, 51). There is adequate indication, then, of breadth, of engagement with canonical figures over core political ideas, of influence, and of originality to justify serious attention being paid to her. I argue here that through her analysis of power, she also provides a valuable and relatively early example of more gender-inclusive political theorizing than was offered by virtually all her philosophical male predecessors.

Astell, like most women of her time, lacked formal education. Nonetheless, she studied subjects from French and theology to logic and philosophy, and she saw some advantages (as well as the more obvious disadvantages) to this independent education. First, and ironically, she notes that "thro' Want of learning... she was ignorant of the *Natural Inferiority* of our Sex" (1996b, 9), an "ignorance" that allowed her to avoid common "masculine" mistakes in her thinking. Second, her situation not only pointed her away from certain erroneous assumptions but also provided her a worthy critical perspective and allowed her more easily to pursue new ideas: "'Women and Children... do not dare to judge without examination, and they bring all the attention they are capable of to what they reade. Whereas... the Learned... will not take the trouble of examining what is contrary to their receiv'd Doctrines'" (1996b, 22).[2] An intellectual not born into nobility or wealth, Astell had the tremendous good fortune to associate with a group of thinkers that included several other women—perhaps most notably Lady Mary Wortley Montagu and Elizabeth Elstob—and also knew and was known to such celebrated male writers as Daniel Defoe and Bishop Berkeley. She had her work published in her lifetime, sometimes in several editions, but like other women intellectuals, she was first widely read, debated, and imitated, and then satirized, plagiarized, and finally written out of mainstream political theory. Her list of published literary, religious, and political writings includes the 1694 *A Serious Proposal to the Ladies for the Advancement of Their True and Greatest Interest;* the 1695 *Letters Concerning the Love of God;* the 1700 *Some Reflections upon Marriage; Moderation Truly Stated, A Fair Way with the Dissenters and Their Patrons,* and *An Impartial Enquiry into the Causes of Rebellion and Civil War in this Kingdom,* all published in 1704; and the 1705 *The Christian Religion, as Profess'd by a Daughter of the Church of England.* Taking issue with noted literary, political, and religious

2. Astell is here translating and transforming Nicolas Malebranche's 1678 *De la recherche de la verité* (see Springborg 1996, 21–22n).

thinkers, Astell's writing is not only logical and persuasive, as one would expect, but often wonderfully witty and refreshingly sarcastic, as well.

In contemporary feminist theory it is often said of the "classic theorists of political philosophy" that "their subject matter reflects male concerns, deals with male activity and male ambitions and is *directed away from* issues involving, or of concern to, women. As a consequence, women themselves do not appear as actors in the realm of social and political thought. Where she is present, woman is either a partial figure engaged in activities which can easily be described by direct analogy to men . . . or she is an ideological construction of the male theorist's imagination. . . . What is missing from social and political theory is . . . Women qua women. What women are, do and can become are not the central concerns of male-stream theory nor are they considered appropriate concerns for such theory" (B. Thiele 1986, 30).

The intriguing question this well-founded charge leaves us with is, What does political theory look like when women *are* among its "central concerns" and speak in their own voices? There are, I imagine, numerous ways to make the diversity of women's lives a more fully integral part of various political philosophies. Astell long ago contributed to this enterprise, reminding us that history offers so much more than models of exclusionary, patriarchal social theorizing. Reading her works, one encounters examples of what it means to include women when (1) defining the problems of politics, (2) defining the boundaries of politics, and (3) analyzing particular political ideas. These three exemplary strategic alternatives to malestream theory provide the framework for this chapter.

The two works of Astell's I rely upon most here are *Some Reflections upon Marriage* (1996b) and *A Serious Proposal to the Ladies* (1986b). *A Serious Proposal*, Astell's first published work, advocates a "Religious Retirement," or female academy, where women could retreat, worship, learn, teach, and in general lead the intellectual life to which they had a right and for which they had the ability. In this piece she makes "important points about the nature of human knowledge and human cognitive faculties . . . [and] link[s] the development of our rational faculties with the practical action that is necessary for our salvation" (Atherton 1994, 98). *Reflections upon Marriage,* published six years later, contains Astell's response to the divorce of the duke and duchess of Mazarin, a public case complete with elements of monetary wealth, wasted potential, sexual scandal, and probable abuse. *Reflections* treats the reader not only to "a satire of the manners and mores governing early eighteenth-century marriage" (Springborg 1996, 3), but also to "one of the earliest critiques of the cornerstones of early modern political theory" (Springborg 1995, 631). Especially important here, both works plainly display the political and philosophical character and intentions of their author: Astell's analysis of marriage uses and reconsiders such central political notions as obligation, obedience, consent, liberty, and tyranny, and her study of education is tied to political thoughts on human happiness, custom, and epistemology. Astell's "educational" *Serious Proposal,* then, is no less a political and philosophical tract than is John Dewey's *Democracy and Education* (1916) or Sor Juana Inés de la Cruz's 1691 *Reply to Sor Philothea* (1987),[3] and her *Reflections,* with its focus on mores and relationships, is perhaps in a category that includes Jean-Jacques Rousseau's *Julie* (1761) and E. Pauline Johnson's *A Red Girl's Reasoning* (1893).[4]

In addition, I use Thomas Hobbes to make visible by contrast some important elements of Astell's political theory. It is true that on those few occasions when she has been studied, she has been looked at as a critic of Locke rather than of Hobbes, probably because "Locke is Astell's consistent target" (Springborg 1995, 625): she "disagreed with Locke's *Two Treatises* . . . on the question of political prerogative, as she disagreed with him on everything else" (Perry 1986, 170). Nonetheless, both common ground and differences between Hobbes and Astell make comparing the two especially fascinating and illuminating. Hobbes and Astell write only some fifty years apart, both are English, and both often use English political experiences as their subject. In their outlook on humans as naturally appetitive, ambitious, and vain, they closely resemble each other. They look with equal alarm at resistance, disobedience, and revolution as threats to the state, and both avidly support monarchy. Both argue creatively and at great length for their often unorthodox ideas' compatibility with traditional religious prescriptions. Astell was even familiar with Hobbes.[5] They did, however, lead radically different lives, in large part as a result of gender, and without question Astell rejects the contractarian approach to politics that Hobbes makes central

---

3. Carroll describes this 1691 work as "embodying a spirited, eloquent, learned, and carefully reasoned defense of women and intellectual freedom" (2000, 84). A complete English translation, side by side the original Spanish, by Margaret Sayers Peden (1987) is also available.

4. Johnson is also named Tekahionwake. Discussing a marriage, the story simultaneously explores racism, love, change, and oppression.

5. Ruth Perry notes that "the writers [Astell] took seriously in her own work were, predictably, Hobbes and Locke and [Third Earl of] Shaftesbury, as well as [Daniel] Defoe and [Charles] D'Avenant. She devoted hundreds of pages to her responses to their points" (1986, 8). Perry herself devotes little attention to Astell's critique of Hobbes, even as compared with the other four figures she mentions.

(Springborg 1996).[6] She, however, makes primary in her theorizing topics of little concern to Hobbes, especially ones related to family and education.

Hobbes provides a useful backdrop for introducing Astell onto the stage because while the setting is similar for the two of them, the contrasts between their stories help to show precisely where women get speaking parts in Astell that they lack in malestream theory, of which Hobbes is a fair example. Hobbes is not a straw person here, but a formidable and enlightening point of comparison. Imagining the two performing together, we may also see the utility of expanding the range of conversations in which Astell is considered a legitimate, contributing participant. Emerging with feminist sensibilities, she casts more women, and it may be that her script avoids certain inconsistencies and omissions that she enables us to see in Hobbes. At best, then, comparing Astell with the more familiar Hobbes enables each to shed light on the other.

Hobbes has been the subject of a number of contemporary feminist critiques. His views on human nature have been considered masculine, his contractual view of parenting deemed inadequate, and his inclusion of women in the social contract proved meager (Stephano 1983; Held 1987; Pateman 1988). Desiring neither to diminish nor to directly address these, I am interested only in how reading Hobbes helps us read Astell, and in what *she* has to say about a Hobbesean politics. I am not trying to offer a new or unsettling interpretation of Hobbes, either, and indeed often rely on the most uncontroversial ones, since that best suits my purpose of helping us to focus on Astell's political theory.

It has been argued by C. B. Macpherson that Hobbes "exposed the lineaments of power more clearly than anyone had done since Machiavelli, more systematically than anyone had ever done, and than most have done since" (1968, 9). But I might suggest that Astell "exposed the lineaments of power more clearly than anyone had done since" Christine de Pizan (see, for example, Blumenfeld-Kosinski 1997a), for she "reconceptualised . . . the conventional cultural view of the world . . . from the perspective of women who must daily deal with male power" (Spender 1982, 51).[7]

---

6. Hobbes, like Astell, was influenced early on by an uncle, but Hobbes's uncle sent him to Oxford at the age of fourteen rather than educating him himself or leaving him on his own. For most of the rest of his life Hobbes had ready access to libraries, influential people, and travel. He served as a tutor to the eldest son of William Cavendish, Earl of Devonshire. As C. B. Macpherson has said, Oxford put Hobbes "up one rung on the social ladder," while his position with Cavendish in a noble household "opened a still higher world to him" (1968, 15). Among those whom Hobbes knew and by whom he was influenced were Francis Bacon, René Descartes, and Galileo Galilei.

7. My point here is twofold: to reopen questions of comparison by enlarging the pool of those considered, and to challenge the male as the measure by using women as markers.

MAKING WOMEN'S LIVES VISIBLE: DEFINING THE PROBLEMS
OF POLITICS

Not uncommonly, philosophers convey their political vision by depicting an
ideal, legitimate, or best practical political community, as Plato does in his
Republic (1974) and Charlotte Perkins Gilman does in *Herland* (1998; originally published in 1915 as a series in Gilman's magazine, *The Forerunner*).
But political theories are also deeply informed by visions of evil, corruption,
impotence, or oppression, as is Mary Wollstonecraft's *Maria* (1975; the text
was still being written at the time of her death in 1797) and George Orwell's
1984 (1992). It is obvious that predicaments described in the latter work help
define the problems politics is established to address, but even those not
writing dystopias use scenes of corruption and destruction for such a purpose and are inspired by them to put pen to paper. As R. S. Peters notes, for
example, Hobbes's *Leviathan* "attempted a systematic answer *to the problems*
posed by the far-reaching social changes of the sixteenth and seventeenth
centuries. . . . [Hobbes] found himself in a country where peace and security were constantly in jeopardy" (1962, 7; emphasis added). Further, even
"utopian thinking turns out to be connected with critical reflection" (Plattel
1972, 6). It is, then, essential to locate in a political theory what problems
are said to demand the attention of the political system, the predicaments
that in fact are often used to explain the need for and the legitimacy of a
political system. Where is the discontent or disregard, the danger or the
damage, the disenchantment or the disempowerment? Studying the "dystopian" aspect of Astell and Hobbes, we can discern how, from the outset,
Astell includes women's lives in defining the problems for politics in a way
Hobbes does not.

Each describes a situation that each terms "miserable." Hobbes famously
writes of such a condition:

> Whatsoever therefore is consequent to a time of war, where every man
> is enemy to every man; the same is consequent to the time, wherein
> men live without other security, than what their own strength, and
> their own invention shall furnish them withal. In such condition, there
> is no place for industry; because the fruit thereof is uncertain: and
> consequently no culture of the earth; no navigation, nor use of the
> commodities that may be imported by sea; no commodious building;
> no instruments of moving, and removing, such things as require much
> force; no knowledge of the face of the earth; no account of time; no

arts; no letters; no society; and which is worst of all, continual fear, and danger of violent death; and the life of man, solitary, poor, nasty, brutish, and short. (1994, 76)

This bleak scenario is not confined to a prepolitical period but extends to any situation in which people are without effective sovereign authority, including civil war in the most developed of nations and, to an extent, even conditions in merely "imperfectly sovereign states" (Macpherson 1962, 20). Hobbes warns potential rebels: "The state of man can never be without some incommodity or other; and . . . the greatest, that in any form of government can possibly happen to the people in general, is scarce sensible in respect of the miseries, and horrible calamities, that accompany a civil war, or that dissolute condition of masterless men" (1994, 117).

Although he denies that our nature entails any ultimate human good (57), Hobbes easily imagines the ultimate misery, describing it in unforgettable terms and images. War is a plague both in itself and for the general consequences and conditions that it imposes: "All such calamities as may be avoided by human industry arise from war" (Hobbes, cited in Macpherson 1968, 9). Lack of effective authority is Hobbes's culprit; hence, restrictions on the actions of individuals via the establishment of strong sovereign power— "a common power to keep them in awe"—is his response to it (1994, 109). He emphasizes the human proclivity to become so completely and narrowly consumed with self-preservation and self-interest as to cause and justify the most abhorrent acts in war, but, with that air of scientific certainty often found among his contemporaries, he does not doubt the human capacity to establish effective political restraints. His focus, consequently, is upon governmental structures and political practices that most reliably counter threats to the emergence or maintenance of a commonwealth at peace with its political neighbors and, especially, at peace with itself.

In contrast with Hobbes's portrait, Astell's "miserable condition" is envisioned as follows: "To be yok'd for Life to a disagreeable Person and Temper; to have Folly and Ignorance tyrannize over Wit and Sense; to be contradicted in every thing one does or says, and born down not by Reason but Authority; to be denied one's most innocent desires, for no other cause but the Will and Pleasure of an absolute Lord and Master, whose Follies a Woman with all her Prudence cannot hide, and whose Commands she cannot but despise at the same time she obeys them; is a misery none can have a just Idea of, but those who have felt it" (1996b, 33–34). This depressing picture alone cannot convey the chilling depths of the problem, any more than a snapshot of one individual stealing goods from another captures Hobbes's dreary natural condition, for both require certain settings. Astell provides the following context: "Men are possess'd of all Places of Power, Trust and Profit, they make laws and exercise the Magistracy, not only the sharpest Sword, but even all the Swords and Blunderbusses are theirs, which by the strongest Logic in the World, gives them the best title to every thing they please to claim as their Prerogative; who shall contend with them? Immemorial Prescription is on their side in these parts of the World, Antient Tradition and Modern Usage! Our Fathers have all along both Taught and Practis'd Superiority over the weaker Sex" (1996b, 29).[8] Using language familiar on the political scene (but not famous until uttered by Rousseau), Astell asks: "*If all Men are born free,* how is it that all Women are born slaves? as they must be if the being subjected to the *inconstant, uncertain, unknown, arbitrary Will of Men, be the perfect Condition of Slavery?*" (1996b, 18–19).

For Astell, *too much power and authority*—economic, military, intellectual, religious, cultural, political, and legal—in the hands of undeserving men is the culprit. More warranted and limited power for them, and more empowerment for women and government, are her responses to it: "Single Medicines are too weak to cure such complicated Distempers, they require a full Dispensatory" (1986b, 149). She recognizes the human susceptibility to tyranny and submission, but does not doubt the capacity to establish effective political restraints on the illegitimate possession or exercise of power and to educate power holders in virtue. Her focus, consequently, is upon structures and practices that prevent, limit, or end the unjustified and injurious subordination of some part of the population to another part, of some individuals to others, of women to men.

While it might initially seem an unusual approach, I think that in comparing Hobbes's and Astell's "miserable conditions" we can see an instance of a political theory becoming more or less exclusionary and partial in defining the very concerns of politics, in its expression of whose lives—with their possibilities and difficulties—will be better represented in what will be the realm of politics. There is surely overlap and similarity between the two dark visions. Several of the critical assumptions about human nature that make Hobbes's natural condition believable are also used by Astell to explain the causes of unnecessary injustices committed against women in

---

8. I find this argument strikingly similar to an early one from the most recent wave of the women's movement, that of Kate Millett's *Sexual Politics* (1969).

marriage. She, too, refers to "boundless Appetites" (1996a, 195). She, too, thinks we desire power over others, which includes being esteemed by them: "Such is the vanity of Humane nature that nothing pleases like an intire Subjection" (1996b, 61). And it is also true that Astell's portrayal of misery, like Hobbes's, is unavoidable without a strong sovereign.[9] But we can also see in these comparative portrayals of darkness that while the problems Hobbes names are mostly considered by Astell, those arising from or visible because of the subordinate political status of women are reckoned with only by Astell. I would argue that we find in Hobbes, then, an example of a political theory that "reflects male concerns," and in Astell an effort to make "what women are, do and can become . . . appropriate concerns" for political philosophy (B. Thiele 1986, 30).

First, looking back on their compelling descriptions of human misery, Hobbes and Astell both raise questions such as, What is (in)security and what are its causes? What are the tragic consequences of instability, for the individual and the race, and what might the benefits of security be? and How can we use more than our individual resources to find safety? But Astell's description of misery leads to further inquiries: How does enslavement differ from obedience to legitimate rule? How does the power of one individual over another compare with the power of a political ruler over subjects? What constitutes the range of consequences of subordination for the oppressed and the oppressor? How do political arrangements affect relations in the household? and What does it mean to be silenced? Introducing distinctions, relationships, and outcomes that Hobbes either knowingly rejects or unintentionally ignores, these added inquiries are more than agreeable supplements to a solid structure; instead, they reveal a cracked foundation and the need for a revised design—for a broader and deeper sense of the very items constituting the political structure.

Second, for both writers, it is the inadequacy of personal relationships that proves problematical and dystopian, but in exploring this we begin to see, as well, where the two part ways. Astell's miserable condition is most obviously a corrupt relationship, based on all the wrong motives. The paradigmatic undesirable model is one in which the one designated "inferior" has no voice, no presence: her words and actions are "contradicted," her desires are "denied," and she must obey what she rightly despises (1996b, 33–34). The "superior" in this relationship is allowed relatively free rein for his

---

9. In fact, Astell's rather Hobbesean comfort with strong monarchical authority confuses commentators who mistake her for a liberal based on her advocacy of sexual equality (see Perry 1990).

follies, ignorance, disagreeableness, and tyranny, and the positions of both are firmly reinforced by social and political norms and practices (1996b, 33–34, 29). The inequality between them can have the most dire consequences for the dominated, including physical violence used against them with impunity.[10] At the root of all the ills in Hobbes's miserable condition is also the absence of trustworthy relationships. This absence mandates virtually total self-reliance, limiting what any individual or group can accomplish and restricting how secure one's life and possessions can be. Absent trustworthy alliances, individuals become insecure, fearful, endangered, and finally entangled in the hopeless dynamics of war.

For Hobbes, lacking enforcement of laws and contracts, separate-and-equal individuals cannot trust anyone, reducing the power of each and precluding the existence of a stable or coherent group. Diffidence rightly and universally reigns, because no state exists to terrorize people into acting in trustworthy ways. Astell's negative condition, however, is the result *not* of equality and individual distrust but of an *inequality* that *should* leave the less empowered suspicious but often does not,[11] and in which the state is complicitous. The contrasts are rather stark: he has problematized equality, she inequality; he sees the state as the solution, while she cannot wholly agree, for it is also part of the problem. Perhaps most critically, he imagines one condition in which everyone is rightly distrustful and another—civil society—in which there are grounds for the establishment of trust, while she demonstrates how women's justifiable distrust of male power *in* a civil society with effective law enforcement can be redirected or invalidated without being resolved, much to women's injury. Finally, he worries only about "masterless men" (Hobbes 1994, 117), while she also mourns the unhappy fate of a woman subjected to "an absolute . . . Master" (Astell 1996b, 33). The range of relationships seen as something for politics to concern itself with is broader in Astell, in part because her analysis of the dynamics of those relationships is considerably more subtle. Simply but startlingly, women's problems, as explicated by Astell, are not part of politics as described by Hobbes.

Third, political power for both Hobbes and Astell is an instrument for keeping people in line. As such, for Hobbes it is desirable, because people

10. Astell says domestic violence is a "Brutality" she refuses to confuse with "that Love and Worship he promised in his Matrimonial Oath" (1996b, 8–9).

11. I find Astell's discussion of this to be quite profound and blunt. She concludes, "Can a woman then be too much upon her Guard? Can her prudence and Foresight, her early Caution, be reckon'd unnecessary suspicion, or ill-bred Reserve, by any but those whose Designs they prevent, and whose Interest it is to declaim against them?" (1996b, 66).

without a common power end up warring. Astell, despite her Hobbesean belief in absolute monarchy, still manages to confront and challenge the bases for the subordination of women. Importantly, most of this can be read as an attack not on the political power of the monarch but on the inegalitarian political culture, whose influence extends much farther. Astell need not be speaking of the monarch at all when she discusses how power is used to "Authorize" prejudice against women (1996b, 7) and to justify sexual inequality as "a Self-Evident and Fundamental Truth" (1996b, 9). The power that concerns her extends to "Arbitrary Power... in Families" (1996b, 17) and to custom, forcefully characterized as "that merciless torrent that carries all before it" (1986b, 147), which together "put Women, generally speaking, into a state of Subjection" (1996b, 10). Here as elsewhere she speaks not only to lawmakers, but also to priests, philosophers, educators, husbands, historians, and others. Hobbes, too, addresses "what opinions and doctrines are averse, and what conducing, to peace" (1994, 113). While "what conduces to peace" can be interpreted broadly, as is it by Astell, Hobbes's examples of "seditious doctrines" (1994, 212) focus exclusively on those that challenge the need for or the rightness of strong sovereign power, whether on the grounds of conscience, religion, or politics. His focus renders realities such as sexual inequality invisible.

Hobbes's political theory, then, marks fewer forms and practices of power as the concern of politics. Consequently, he does not problematize sexual inequality, does not include it as part of what can make life miserable, does not see there the dreadful nastiness, brutishness, and potential for violence that he devotes himself to correcting elsewhere. A political theory is only likely to offer effective, systematic remedies to what it deems politically relevant, to what it calls problems subject to political solutions. A Hobbesean political "order," then, can easily be compatible with sexual inequality, while Astell can still criticize the political "disorder" Hobbes's state incorporates.

KEEPING WOMEN'S LIVES VISIBLE: DEFINING THE BOUNDARIES
OF POLITICS

In the previous section I explored how women's lives do not really inform Hobbes's core understanding of the problems politics should address, as they do for Astell. Now, using as an illustration the subject of insecurity—a predicament both Hobbes and Astell *do* think belongs on the agenda of

politics—we see the two theorists draw different boundaries around the
political. As they define and confront insecurity they necessarily reveal something of what resources politics has at its disposal and what aspects of a
problem get deemed political. Because she includes women in her political
thought, Astell uses a broadened sense of the political, while Hobbes nar-
rows the boundaries in a way that allows the exclusion of issues arising from
sexual inequality.

Perhaps no idea is more closely associated with Hobbes than is security,
and rightly so. The desire to be secure plays a large role in his political theory:
it explains the preemptive strikes that destine the natural condition to be one
of war, provides a compelling motive for leaving the natural condition, helps
determine the specific terms of the social contract, explains the dependable
willingness to abide by those terms in civil society, and exists as the only
legitimate basis for disobedience. Hobbes asserts that "the motive and end
for which this renouncing and transferring of right is introduced, is nothing else but the security of a man's person, in his life and in the means of so
preserving life as not to be weary of it" (1994, 82). Establishing security is the
objective—it is the answer to Hobbes's miserable condition, to the experience of de facto powerlessness in a context where anything goes. The sovereign, the "soul" of the commonwealth, is the means to security. Absent the
state, individuals simply do not have adequate effective power to satisfy their
desires, insufficient trust between individuals does not allow them to cooperate for mutual satisfaction, and no common power prevents anyone from
injuring another. Empowering the sovereign, the *only* suggested remedy, sets
up the conditions of security that allow people to satisfy their individual
desires; that is, empowering the sovereign simultaneously empowers the citizens, furnishing "the means to obtain some future apparent good" (50).

Astell concurs with Hobbes on the significance of security. She, too, in-
vestigates the causes of civil war, and she, too, sees the desire for security as
reliable grounds for obedience to the state: "Hopes to gain more, or at least
to secure what one has, will always be a handle by which Humane Nature
may be mov'd" (1996a, 195). But despite Hobbes's belief that his powerful
state establishes the longed-for security, Astell finds that women—half the
population—are still at risk there. Peering into the household as she checks
on the security of the citizenry, Astell finds something astonishing: another
Hobbesean state of nature. Within what Hobbes calls civil society, not all
individuals, it turns out, can look to the sovereign for safety from one another. Given that "the obligation of subjects to the sovereign is understood

to last as long, and no longer, than the power lasteth by which he is able to protect them" (Hobbes 1994, 144), inattention to gender may unwittingly invite into the commonwealth the potential for revolt Hobbes sought to eliminate. Sexual inequality may return us all to the state of nature, if, as Astell says is possible, though undesirable, it "provokes the Oppress'd to throw off even a Lawful Yoke that sits too heavy" (1996b, 78).

Astell analyzes how the insecurity of women within the household shares two essential and ultimately decisively destructive features with Hobbes's natural condition, one related to contracts and one to rights. First, Hobbes writes: "If a covenant be made wherein neither of the parties perform presently, but trust one another, in the condition of mere nature . . . he that performeth first has no assurance the other will perform after" (1994, 84). Astell undoubtedly agrees with the disturbing consequences of the absence of reliable covenants, but carries Hobbes's political analysis across the domestic threshold, applying it to "Covenants betwixt Husband and Wife" (Astell 1996b, 52). She notices that *within* Hobbes's civil estate, "a Man enters into Articles very readily before Marriage, and so he may, for he performs no more of them afterwards than he thinks fit" (1996b, 51). That is, like individuals in the natural condition, the wife in Astell's view of supposedly civil society has "no assurance the [husband] will perform" as he promises, with equally disturbing consequences. Further, while Hobbes remarks that "in a civil estate . . . there is a power set up to constrain those that would otherwise violate their faith" (1994, 5), Astell demonstrates that the state does not require that a husband do what he promises, whether his promise is about her property or his fidelity, her happiness or his authority.

Hobbes vehemently insists that contracts will be broken in the state of nature "because the bonds of words are too weak to bridle men's ambition, avarice, anger, and other passions" (1994, 84). Such breaches are exactly what Astell witnesses in marriage, precisely because "Woman has in truth no security but the Man's Honour and Good-nature" (1996b, 51), and "where can one find an Instance that this is any security? There are very many indeed which shew it is none" (69). As a predictable result of the institutional framework of unequal marriage, "there have been but too many instances of Husbands that by wheedling or threatning their Wives, by seeming Kindness or cruel Usage, have perswaded or forc'd them out of what has been settled on them" (51). Too, as a foreseeable result, "perhaps Husbands . . . claim their Right oftner and more Imperiously than either Discretion or good Manners will justifie" (53–54).

A second parallel between Astell's analysis of marriage and Hobbes's description of the natural condition involves the scope of individual rights. The rights that individuals possess in a Hobbesean state of nature ultimately cause their unhappiness: "As long as this natural right of every man to everything endureth, there can be no security to any man" (Hobbes 1994, 80). Therefore, such counterproductive rights are what they must forfeit in order to establish peace. "The only way to erect such a common power as may be able to defend them from the invasion of foreigners and the injuries of one another, and thereby to secure them in such sort as that by their own industry, and by the fruits of the earth, they may nourish themselves and live contentedly, is . . . if every man should say to every man *I authorize and give up my right of governing myself. . . [and] thou give up thy right*" (109). What Astell discloses is that the subordination of women rests on men *not*, in fact, actually surrendering their rights of nature. The consequences of this for women, as well as for the social contract itself, are potentially staggering.

Astell explains that while it is true that "a Husband can't deprive a Wife of Life without being responsible to the Law," it is also true that "he may however do what is much more grievous to a generous Mind, render Life miserable, for which she has no Redress, scarce Pity which is afforded to every other Complainant. It being thought a Wife's Duty to suffer everything without Complaint" (1996b, 18). Astell's language seems to encourage readers to link these domestic abuses to a miserable Hobbesean state of nature: she says of "he who would have every one submit to his Humours" that "he's not fit for a Husband, scarce fit for Society, but ought to be turn'd out of the Herd to live by himself" (37). That is, he is living by the rules of the state of nature, not by the strictures of civil society. Despite the Hobbesean social contract, men still have rights to women's bodies and to women's property—still have the rights of the state of nature, as defined by Hobbes: "In such a condition every man has a right to everything, even to one another's body" (Hobbes 1994, 80). Women, it appears, have about the same degree of security in civil marriage that all individuals have in the natural state: next to none. The dismal failure of even the strongest state to protect fully half of its adult citizens is perhaps what Astell has in mind in referring to certain "Truths which no Man wou'd say."

If the power of private citizens over one another presents no discernable threat to the sovereign's authority, it is immaterial to Hobbes, with no regard to whether those with more power are many or few, a stable or a shifting group, systematically advantaged or just individually well endowed, beneficent rulers or oppressive tyrants. In fact, consistent with his overall project, women's resistance to tyranny could appear to Hobbes to be more of a plague than the inequality they resist, were it to entail a threat to the civil "peace."[12] Such is a possible consequence of narrowly defining the political.

Matters worsen when Hobbes turns to the domestic realm for examples not of inequality of rights or unenforced contracts, not of tyranny or injustice or vice, but of liberty. To those who see the Leviathan crushing liberty, he makes the following claim: "Seeing there is no commonwealth in the world wherein there be rules enough set down for the regulating of all the actions and words of men (as being a thing impossible), it followeth necessarily that in all kinds of actions by the laws praetermitted men have the liberty of doing what their own reasons shall suggest for the most profitable to themselves" (1994, 138). The state can and thus will regulate some actions only. Where the state is silent the liberty of the individual resides. In some matters the state must speak; for example, it is "annexed to the sovereignty" to prescribe the rules of property, and of punishment (114, 115). But other things are not so attached, and in those areas the sovereign may or may not prescribe, as it chooses. Hobbes marks out as possible arenas of individual liberty the freedoms to "contract with one another; to choose their own abode, their own diet, their own trade of life, and institute their children as they themselves think fit" (138). In such matters, the sovereign may be silent. But *precisely* where Hobbes says liberty may reside, Astell finds quite unfree women. For example, when Astell looks at freedom to "contract with one another" she knows it does not mean the same thing for both sexes because (1) the marriage contract grants radically unequal power to the parties— "she has by much the harder bargain . . . because she puts her self entirely into her Husband's Power"—and (2) the arrangement is not even equally freely chosen: "A Woman indeed can't properly be said to Choose, all that is allow'd her, is to Refuse or Accept what is offer'd" (1996b, 46, 43). Similarly, Hobbes may see potential liberty where one can "choose their own abode," but Astell wonders about the free choice of abode for that woman "who is Sold, or any otherwise betray'd into mercenary Hands, to one who is in all, or most respects unequal to her" (1996b, 50). Women in the times of Hobbes and Astell clearly are not free to choose "their own trade of life,"

---

12. This is not an unfamiliar political phenomenon: for example, the enforcers of what counted as "peace" in the United States once considered civil rights activists, rather than segregationists, the problem.

because most trades, and the education they require, are forbidden them. Whatever examples Hobbes offers, he seems at most to be speaking about freedom that Astell sees only men exercising, to be including only men's lives when deciding where to draw lines around the political. Astell actually represents women in considering these matters, and women of different fortunes, at that.

To further demonstrate the rightful discretion of the sovereign, and thus the potential liberty of the individual, Hobbes mentions sex-based laws regulating marriage: "Liberty is in some places more, and in some less. . . . In some places of the world men have the liberty of many wives; in other places such liberty is not allowed" (1994, 143). Ignoring all gender-differentiated aspects and effects of policies regarding polygamy, Hobbes makes the claim that where such liberty exists, individual will rather than the sovereign's will prevails: whether or not one chooses multiple wives will be a matter of personal preference, a question of whether one feels an appetite for or an aversion to such an arrangement. The sovereign would be uninterested in one's decision. But again, it is precisely in such matters that Astell says "the Will and Pleasure" of men take precedence over the will and pleasure of women, and over the reason of both. Where the sovereign ends its rule over women, the rule of men over women can take over. Both sexes are subject to the political sovereign. But men retain the rights and freedom of the state of nature in the household. Where the sovereign is silent, women may be silenced.[13]

Domestic tyranny was a political problem that Astell—not Hobbes—set out to address. Having removed it from the list of concerns, Hobbes worsens matters by rather casually turning to the domestic realm for positive examples of liberty to parade about in defense of his politics. The fact that the examples apply to only half the adults goes unmentioned. The boundaries of Hobbesean politics, based on the lives of men more than women, can be drawn at the front gate of the private household, making women's insecurity and unfreedom within it irrelevant. Inside Hobbes's civil state, a state in which there is no civil war and in which laws are generally obeyed, there are

---

13. Some may think that any sovereign who allows such inequality would be deemed corrupt or illegitimate by Hobbes as well as Astell. Hobbes, however, does not spend much time on illegitimate regimes other than those that have insufficient power, just as he does not address inequality within the state as a problem, though he notes its existence. Too, in Hobbes's owns examples, he points out the liberty in situations in which men dominate women, which seems to imply some acceptance of the scenario (1994, 143). Further, even if women would be *entitled* to rebel by Hobbes's standards, he fails to address how the nature of women's subordination renders that most unlikely, and therefore of little actual consequence.

as many pockets of the original condition as there are private households. If Astell is right, then Hobbes stopped before society was really civil.

HEARING WOMEN'S VOICES: ANGLES ON EQUALITY

Astell, I have argued, inserts problems more incident to women's lives into politics and actually looks at women's lives when trying to address political matters. An expeditious examination of the issue of equality, long considered a core concept in political thought, shows how Astell begins to interject more voices and perspectives—female ones—into a political conversation than does a theorist such as Hobbes.

Hobbes asserts that "as to strength of body, the weakest has strength enough to kill the strongest, either by secret machination, or by confederacy with others, that are in the same danger with himself" (1994, 74). Rather than agree with this seemingly admirably egalitarian stance, Astell echoes without argument the more familiar view that "Women are acknowledg'd to have least Bodily strength" (1996b, 15). Similarly, on the question of mental powers, Hobbes writes: "And as to the faculties of the mind . . . I find yet a greater equality amongst men, than that of strength" (1994, 74–75). Astell, on the other hand, surprisingly attests to "the Superiority and Pre-eminence of the Men" (1996b, 28). Neither starting with assumptions of equality, however, nor arguing for the original political irrelevance of inequality compels Hobbes to be an advocate of equality, sexual or otherwise. Astell, adding to political thought some female voices, becomes the much more thoughtful analyst of equality.

Hobbes notes that mental superiority belongs to only "the very few . . . [and] but in few things" and that general "prudence is but experience; which equal time, equally bestows on all men, in those things they equally apply themselves unto" (1994, 74–75). He offers as evidence of equality individuals' satisfaction with their abilities, even their presumably erroneous belief that there are not "many so wise as themselves," for "there is not ordinarily a greater sign of the equal distribution of anything than that every man is contented with his share" (1994, 75). But Astell points to a most interesting political phenomenon. When the Hobbesean observation that "the *value* or WORTH of a man is . . . so much as would be given for the use of his power" (Hobbes 1994, 51) is combined with the Astellean insight that "a Man [cannot] respect his Wife when he has a contemptible Opinion of her and her Sex" (Astell 1996b, 57), then what Astell finds is not universal comfort with or arrogance about one's wisdom but a situation in which women "think as humbly of themselves as their Master can wish, with respect to the other Sex" (1996b, 29). She in fact finds women to be "preposterously humble" (1986b, 141). The unfortunate consequence of women being a subordinated class is that "We value *them* too much, and our *selves* too little" (1986b, 141). Hobbes considered as conclusive evidence too small a range of examples. Once again, we see exactly where in Hobbes "women's lives and thoughts and works have been obscured or erased by the men who control the cultural tools for noting and recording such things" (Spelman 1988, 161).

Like Hobbes, Astell knows that cunning can compensate for relative physical weakness: "Those who have least Force, or Cunning to supply it, will have the Disadvantage" (1996b, 15). In fact, such cunning, rather than women's strength or their reason, has been deemed the appropriate means for women to use to accomplish their ends, and Astell alone is aware of the *costs* of this, not just the benefits. She neither asserts that equality exists, then, nor sees all means to accomplishing one's ends as equal. Hobbes is right when he cautions that "some have attributed the dominion to the man only, as being of the more excellent sex; they misreckon in it. For there is not always that difference of strength, or prudence between the man and the woman, as that the right can be determined without war" (1994, 152). But he only uses this statement for, and only raises it in the context of, sustaining his vision of the natural condition of war; it is not a starting point for analyzing causes, consequences, or cures for inequality.

Because of the entry of women's voices, Astell is led to reassess the relevance of inequality in physical strength. She departs from Hobbes in arguing that (male) might does not equal (male) right; because might, or "Superior Power," is not correlated with "Understanding" (Astell 1996b, 16), it establishes no basis for any right to rule, over a spouse or a community. Again departing from Hobbes, and representing subordinated and silenced women, she argues that rule over any weaker group "is in pure kindness to them and for their Quiet and Security, as well as for the Exercise of their Virtue" (15). She also emphasizes that in general "the Relation between the two sexes is mutual, and the Dependance Reciprocal" (1996b, 13), with any advantage or superiority in one area reconceived as something balanced by advantage in another; interdependence, not domination, is the envisioned framework.

Astell does more than just assert, as Hobbes does, that there is relative intellectual equality between the sexes. A more thorough writer on the subject, she first explains the origin of superior male intelligence in education: all we can conclude from past practices, Astell sarcastically insists, is that "after many years of Study and Experience they become Wise and Learned, and Women are not Born so!" (1996b, 28). And while Hobbes looks to experience as an equalizer, Astell sees that men and women do *not* "equally apply themselves" to the same tasks in a gendered society.

But Astell goes beyond a standard account of intellectual inequality as rooted in unequal educational practices. She also questions whether we can in fact simply call male intelligence "superior." Her "feminism" does not assume that the male model is unproblematical. One way she questions it is by calling logically dubious arguments "Masculine Understandings" (9). Another is by including among male "accomplishments" some quite disastrous events: "Have not all the great Actions that have been perform'd in the World been done by Men? Have not they founded Empires and overturn'd them? Do not they make Laws and continually repeal and amend them? Their vast Minds lay Kingdoms wastes. . . . They make Worlds and ruine them, form Systems of universal nature and dispute eternally about them; their Pen gives worth to the most trifling Controversie" (61). Astell also challenges the correlation of maleness and intelligence by making the point, as perhaps the central argument against unequal marriage, that to obey the husband often means for the wife to accept "a crooked Rule to regulate her Actions" (50). In sum, she says, "a wise man and a Husband are not Terms convertible" (62).

Astell does not stop with challenging the association of intelligence with maleness but proceeds to establish positive female association with wisdom. Citing biblical figures, for example, she mentions the "superior Understanding" displayed by Sampson's mother, "Abigail's wise conduct," and the "good Judgment" exercised by the Queen of Sheba (24).

The earlier charge against malestream theory was that its "subject matter reflects male concerns, deals with male activity and male ambitions and is *directed away from* issues involving, or of concern to, women" (B. Thiele 1986, 30). Perhaps Astell can be seen as saying to Hobbes that in his treatment of equality he ignores the existence of certain forms of inequality and fails to assess their causes or their costs. The silenced woman of Astell's dystopia could not find voice in Hobbes's Leviathan. The scope of Astell's politics is broader, her account of equality more comprehensive.

AUTHORITY AND CONSISTENCY

Astell is seen as someone who both revealed the problems in marriage and supported that institution: the "paradoxical tension of her position" (Duran

2000, 148) is that she held "a simultaneous belief in authority and recognition of its incompatibility with justice in domestic life" (Perry 1986, 165). Hilda Smith, noting that Astell is at least "less self-contradictory than . . . the duchess of Newcastle," nonetheless remarks that Astell "was inconsistent in her own way. The conflict within Astell's feminism revolved around the axis of church, state, and women's subordinate status" (1982, 115, 117). Such problems do seem to jump off the page as one reads Astell. But I would like to raise for more consideration in this context that Astell (1) consistently criticizes various forms of authority, (2) argues for the legitimacy of new forms of authority, and (3) tries for some degree of reconciliation based on much redefinition.

Throughout *Reflections upon Marriage* (1996b) Astell offers criticisms of obedience to authority and can never rightly be said to be someone who merely advocates submission to all powers that be. The book opens with a presentation of its design: to "Correct some Abuses, which are not the less because Power and Prescriptions seem to Authorize them" (1996b, 7). At least some power can be said to be abused, and should be corrected. Not all authority *is* to be obeyed: "'Tis a very great Fault to regard rather who it is that Speaks, than what is Spoken; and . . . to submit to Authority, when we should only yield to Reason" (1996b, 7). Reason as an authority can overrule other forms of authority. This is not so troublesome a position. "A meer Obedience, such as is paid only to Authority, and not out of Love and a sense of the Justice and Reasonableness of the Command, will be of an uncertain Tenure" (50). Obedience to authority per se is not necessarily compatible with the political stability that she, like Hobbes, so desires, and it is that stability that consistently pulls together certain otherwise seemingly contradictory ideas.

Astell criticizes the authority of tradition when she disagrees with those who "Marry without any thought at all, further than that it is the Custom of the World" (43), for such acts corrupt the institution of marriage rather than contribute to its stability. Even parental authority is questionable on these grounds: one shouldn't marry because "their kind parents and Guardians chuse as they think convenient" (43). She challenges the authority of custom: "The Right can no more be prov'd from the Fact, than the Predominancy of Vice can justife it" (10). She challenges the authority of interpretations of scripture: "Scripture is not always on their side who make parade of it, and thro' their skill in languages and the Tricks of the Schools, wrest it from its genuine sense to their own Inventions" (14). This is quite a broad list of questionable authorities.

Astell also establishes new authorities, including granting women, for example, the "Natural Right of Judging for her self" (1996b, 10). *This* is an authority to be obeyed! She says that in writing *Reflections,* "she neither advis'd with Friends, nor turn'd over Antient or Modern Authors, nor prudently submitted to the Correction of such as are, or such as *think* they are good Judges" (8). She rejects the "masculine understandings" she so pointedly ridicules and relies upon her own genius. This reliance contrasts beautifully with women's supposed lack "of that Superior Genius which Men as men lay claim to" (9).

Before endorsing obedience to authority, Astell hopes to change the mores of those in power. When, for example, men redefine their self-interest so that a "good wife" is not a servant or a plaything but an educated and equal companion, and when women value *only* those men who are "Wise and Good" (79–80), as well as themselves, then a woman can be virtuous and secure while following her husband's rule.

Other similar points might be made, all of which at least complicate the charges of inconsistency. The charges themselves, even were they proved correct, do not necessarily justify dismissing Astell's contributions to political thought. We might even be so generous as to end up with the type of verdicts that are rendered regarding authors such as Jean-Jacques Rousseau, whose inconsistencies are attributed to his understanding of the tragic nature of life, or Marx, for whom we distinguish between his early and late theorizing.

CONCLUDING THOUGHTS

We can consider Astell or anyone else "included" as a political philosopher when we find her on our syllabi and in our philosophy textbooks, and when she is interpreted and debated about and argued over and looked at from multiple perspectives by scholars across disciplines. Interested writers might note that "there is tantalizingly little current scholarship" on Astell, leaving "vast room for further study" (Waters 2000, 11).

What thinkers such as Astell have to offer is not a "parallel" or independent history of theorizing; instead, we need to understand that they and their more celebrated brothers have long been in conversation, borrowing from, building upon, stealing from, and debating with each other. We cannot fully understand either "tradition" without the other. In the most recent wave of feminist movement, academic feminists have put canonical thinkers through a whole new series of examinations. It appears, however, that some of the criticisms that have emerged are not new at all. Just as Wollstonecraft is still among the most profound critics of Rousseau, offering arguments we are still coming to appreciate, so Astell gave us a head start on Hobbes that we still have the opportunity to learn from.

Further, Astell, like other women theorists through the centuries, is more than a "critic" in the supposedly derogatory sense of being a "mere" commentator upon or evaluator of another's work. She is a critic in the way that Locke or Rousseau are critics of Hobbes. That is to say, Astell is a contending voice in the very defining and shaping of modern political thought. As a consequence, is impossible to say without qualification such things as that modern thought ignores patriarchy as a form of political power, or excludes women from its concept of the human, or sacrifices the private to the public, or defines freedom based on a male standard. Now we can make those charges against only *some* modern thinkers. What we call modern political thought can and must be reconceptualized: "What is transmitted from generation to generation is not only the stories, but the very power of transmission" (Minh-ha 1989, 134).

8

EQUALITY: QUILTED VOICES

feminism: 1: the theory of the political, economic, and social equality of the sexes
2: organized activity on behalf of women's rights and interests

While perhaps no concept seems as inherently linked to feminism as equality, as most dictionary definitions demonstrate, examination of historical feminist views on the subject is relatively rare. It seems fitting to close this book by beginning to bring together feminist theorizing on this defining topic. It also seems appropriate to end by attempting to (dis)cover common themes, rather than points of contention. More attention is generally paid to different schools of feminist thought—to disagreement—than to common ground among feminists, and surely we need knowledge of both. I argue, through a variety of excerpts from the history of feminist thought, that here again are hints of traditions of feminist theorizing across the centuries. When assembled, the individual voices become, variously, bodies of similar, overlapping, or connected concerns and not only divergent views that accord with assorted feminisms or competing nonfeminist political schools of thought.

As the current canon reveals, the fact that ideas constitute a tradition does not itself mean they are necessarily of ongoing usefulness, no less perennial truths: "We cannot do without traditions, but our concept of tradition is necessarily and inescapably reflexive. My critique of the canon is thus not that it is an invented tradition—it could hardly be anything else—but that it is an unreflexive invented tradition that is no longer adequate to our history and our present concerns" (Stuurman 2000, 165). To turn to patterns of thought in feminist theory is to give due weight to problems, ideas, questions, and concerns that our predecessors have deemed of special and recurring interest and importance. The examples below only set the stage for open-minded inquiry into the possibility that such views might continue

to be relevant and enlightening, worth learning and teaching, a basis for reclaiming our history and building upon it an ever more promising political
future. Always we should be mindful of the important fact that the presence
of a tradition does not indicate lack of variety and even dissent, nor does it
imply a desire merely to rest on our laurels.

The subject of equality is clearly treated as a core theme by both feminist
and canonical political thinkers. As demonstrated in other chapters, feminist theory does not merely mirror mainstream theory in the questions it
asks, the stances it takes, the justifications it employs, the issues and actors
it considers political, or the importance it ascribes to various forms of political participation and institutions. Including feminism in the conversation
about political ideas potentially expands not only the number of participants but also the number of vantage points, contributing to a history of
political ideas that is built upon a broader range of visions and concerns.
"To put forward a radically different frame of reference for explaining the
world (and seeing the world through the eyes of those who are oppressed
rather than through the eyes of those who do the oppressing *does* make
a radical difference) is to enter the realm of the unknown, the invisible"
(Spender 1982, 7).

While I am not focusing on differences between theorists, the authors I
include represent a range of time frames and political frameworks, affilia-
tions and positions, and some do very much disagree with one another. In
fact, while "feminism is often defined as a commitment to social equality
between men and women . . . the concept of equality is itself a focus of feminist controversy" (Jaggar 1994, 13). Ultimately, the aim is to recover more
perspectives from our history, though I imagine that they will continue to
overlap in additional patterns even as they depart from what is presented
here. "Our first urgency . . . built into our situation and our method, is to
be engaged with the greatest possible range of perceivers, of theorizers. . . .
The World, According to Women, has never been anything but an anthology,
a collection of tales unified, like any yarn, only by successively overlapping
threads held together by friction, not riveted by logic" (Frye 1992, 70–71).

LOOKING BACK(WARDS)

One of the most persistently difficult challenges in writing about any topic
in feminist political theory is allowing feminist ideas to establish the framework for the discussion. Few of us in academia did *not* read the canonical

figures of our disciplines as part of our professional training, and just as few *did* read even the female "greats," the so-called exceptional women, whose names never made or were erased from most "required reading" lists. Consequently, we tend to see the issues, the landscape, as we have learned them from nonfeminists. While it is true that "Western feminists have drawn on the nonfeminist traditions of thinking about equality in our reflections on sex equality," it is also true that "many have found that nonfeminist conceptions of equality are inadequate to comprehend the variety of ways in which male privilege over women is expressed" (Jaggar 1994, 13). Wanting almost desperately for feminists to define the terms of the debates, I begin with the briefest glimpse of nonfeminist thinking on equality, just enough indication of the contrasts to invite a greater appreciation of feminist theory: "Just as in the traditional canon, the concepts of liberty and equality [in a revised canon] will be among the key notions of the history of political thought. However . . . a critical approach is called for, one which will pay special attention to the exclusions and tacit limitations of the discourses of liberty and equality. . . . The history of political thought would thus include the construction of a genuine 'history of equality'" (Stuurman 2000, 162).

In a volume that attempts to "pay[] more attention than is customary to the great questions underlying the theory and practice of government," Tinder's popular political theory textbook uses the following queries to give a sense of the "perennial questions" of the history of political theory on the subject of equality (2003, vii):

Are human beings unequal in essence?
If some human beings are essentially superior to all others, how and by whom can they be identified?
If human beings are essentially equal, are all conventional inequalities wrong?
If all conventional inequalities were abolished, could liberty survive?
If all conventional inequalities were abolished, would estrangement disappear?

Tinder's goal is not to provide a comprehensive perspective on equality; nonetheless, there is a politics to the choices he makes. Among my concerns, Tinder's list does not require attention to any particular forms of (in)equality, including sexual inequality. It leaves unexamined the very terms of the debate, such as *essences* and *superiority*, and distinctions such as conventional versus natural inequality. It links equality only to liberty and estrangement.

By contrast, here is my initial list of the sorts of questions raised by feminist thinkers on the subject of equality. The themes I discuss later in this chapter develop several of them.

What exactly is a nature or essence? Is there some nature all women and men share? Is this the source of their equality?

Are there sex-differentiated natures? If so, do these constitute "essential" or "accidental" differences? Historically, how have the natures of the sexes been described differently? Evaluated differently? What have been some of the political consequences of this?

Is either human nature or the nature of some humans fixed? If so, in what aspects? If not, what causes change? (When) Are (what) changes desirable?

In what respects are people to be compared? What similarities and differences are to be deemed least and most relevant? Do differences of kind and of degree both matter? What counts as evidence of (in)equality?

Is human life directed toward any particular ends that enable us to speak of a more or less "fully human" existence? Who decides and on what basis? Is this idea linked to questions of worth, of equality? If so, what forces encourage or thwart such development? What implications does this have for social organization?

How valid is the "nature-nurture" distinction? How do the two cooperate? What happens when they conflict? Are questions of conventional inequality different from those about natural inequality?

How does one form of (in)equality influence another? That is, what are the differences and connections between natural (in)equality, social (in)equality, political (in)equality, economic (in)equality, racial (in)equality, and sexual (in)equality?

What social forces sustain and challenge (in)equality?

How does inequality affect theorizing about equality?

When and why is equality a desirable ideal? Who benefits from what forms of it, who does not, and in what ways?

Are some forms of inequality acceptable? If yes, which ones, on what grounds, and on what occasions? How many forms of inequality can be eliminated? Should be? Likely will be? How much of our fund of social resources should we direct to maintaining or compensating for or erasing inequalities?

Is a claim to equal citizenship linked with any particular traits, rights, and obligations? Who should participate in government? Are various forms of participation equally available to all citizens? Does voluntary nonparticipation carry the same costs and benefits (to individuals and society) as compulsory nonparticipation?

How does equality interact with other social and political goods, which may include community, enlightenment, participation, autonomy, liberty, justice, friendship, virtue, progress, or a combination of these?

Perhaps the largest problems in the history of political theorizing on gender equality are presented in brief in Stanley Benn's essay surveying general philosophical thought on equality.

> Plato preached the political equality of the sexes, Aristotle that of all free citizens; nevertheless, both laid more stress on not treating unequals equally than on any general conception of equality. Aristotle believed that some men were slaves by nature, Plato that some souls were not merely capable of higher development than others but more valuable on that account. The political egalitarianism of Pericles' Athens, described by Thucydides, was concerned only with the equality of Athenian citizens and excluded slaves and foreigners. . . . Medieval social theory was, on the whole, antiegalitarian, deeming hierarchy to be natural both to society and to the whole universal order. (Benn 1967, 39)

As Benn lays out, the dominant traditions in political theorizing on equality (1) were more concerned with the proper recognition and institutionalization of inequality than of equality; (2) often accepted radical forms of inequality; (3) justified political inequality on grounds ranging from group differences to the nature of the universe; (4) considered hierarchy the essence of communal "order"; and (5) provided models of equality between some that presumed and were based on the inferiority and exclusion of others, often with unexplored consequences.

By contrast, feminist analysis is at least initially suspicious of both inequality and explanations and justifications for it. It emphasizes the consequences of inequality of power, consequences that range from the epistemological (who knows what; what counts as knowledge; and how does power affect perception, for example) and the personal (what choices are "realistic"; how much safety and happiness one experiences) to the customary (what traditions are celebrated, which erased; and what justificatory stories are influential) and the political (who has what rights; whose voices count more). In theorizing about equality it focuses on the complexity, messiness, and centrality of interactions, whether between the public and private or oppressions based on different characteristics. It appears from the outset to be unwilling to look at factors and facets in isolation and to be committed to digging beyond the familiarly persuasive (such as that women's subordination serves the common good), even when the conventional seems to "advantage" women (namely, claims of women's superior moral goodness, or women's protection as the intended product of inequality). What follows are ten themes about equality that resurface over the centuries. They are representative but not comprehensive, and they only begin to draw on the seemingly inexhaustible but nearly untapped material available.

1. The standard history of political theory will prove to be an inadequate basis for feminist thinking about equality, for at least two reasons.

a. First, it has been written by the privileged, whose power has distorted both their self-perception and their perception of others.

Writing in 1706, Mary Astell declares, "Superiors indeed are too apt to forget the common Privileges of Mankind; that their Inferiors share with them the greatest Benefits, and are as capable as themselves of enjoying the supreme Good. . . . From his own Elevation he looks down on them as void of Understanding, and full of Ignorance and Passion, so that Folly and a Woman are equivalent Terms with him. . . . A Husband indeed is thought by both Sexes so very valuable, that scarce a man who can keep himself clean and make a Bow, but thinks he is good enough to pretend . . . to any Woman" (1986c, 110, 111, 119). Astell suggests that just as "winners write history," so have the privileged authored our influential political treatises, which rarely call for them to cede their power. "Forgetting" the humanity of entire segments of the population—the majority, even—may be a predictable consequence of political "superiority" that disqualifies the unselfconscious privileged from certain tasks of political philosophy. In 1829 determined democrat Frances Wright, lecturer, activist, leader, and author, also points to some of the epistemological consequences of unequal power: "Those who arrogate power usually think themselves superior de facto and de jure" (1973, 108). Wright's claim, too, is that the social fact of inequality leads the dominant to assume that the inequality is defensible, that they have a legitimate claim to superiority.

Famed transcendentalist thinker Margaret Fuller, writing in 1843, introduces a related limitation on theorizing by the privileged: "Men do *not* look at both sides, and women must leave off asking them and being influenced by them. . . . Their minds are so encumbered by tradition" (1971, 121, 172). The standpoints of women, who are less steeped in tradition via education, and less vested it in via politics, are essential contributions in the conversation that forms political philosophy, Fuller contends. M. Carey Thomas, president of Bryn Mawr College from 1894 to 1922, insists that men's assumptions about women have nothing to do with what women are really like; instead, and importantly, they are evidence of the distorting effects of power. In a speech given in 1908, she said: "Now we know that it is not we, but the man who believes such things about us, who is himself pathological, blinded by neurotic mists of sex, unable to see that women form one-half of the kindly race of normal, healthy human creatures in the world" (1968, 91). In Thomas, the distorting effects of male power take on the characteristics of a disease, one that affects the ability to *see* the subjects about whom one is theorizing.

Finally, Suzanne LaFollette, founder and editor of *New Freeman* and author of a libertarian feminist classic, *Concerning Women,* declares in 1926: "It seems also to be characteristic of the dominant sex . . . to regard itself as humanity, and the other sex as a class of somewhat lower beings created by Providence for its convenience and enjoyment; just as it is characteristic of a dominant class, such as an aristocracy, to regard the lower classes as being created solely for the purpose of supporting its power and doing its will" (1973, 542). Taking patriarchy seriously as a form of governance, LaFollette can use insights from the study of one variety of inequality to learn about another. Power dynamics between the sexes have epistemological effects similar to those of other institutionalized inequalities, she argues, emphasizing the creation of otherness.

b. A related reason why the dominant traditions will prove inadequate is that political theorists have failed to consult or to hear the "others."

If "inferiors" are viewed as "abnormal" and, in Astell's words above, "void of Understanding," they are not likely to be valued consultants on philosophical and political questions. Author of a book of advice to princes a century before Machiavelli, Christine de Pizan became aware of this failure to communicate when she saw the contrast between what had been written about women by the great theorists and poets, on the one hand, and her self-knowledge and the testimony of other women, on the other. As she wrote about it in 1405: "Thinking deeply about these matters, I began to examine my character and conduct as a natural woman and, similarly,

I considered other women whose company I frequently kept, princesses, great ladies, women of the middle and lower classes, who had graciously told me of their most private and intimate thoughts, hoping that I could judge impartially and in good conscience whether the testimony of so many notable men could be true. To the best of my knowledge, no matter how long I confronted or dissected the problem, I could not see or realize how their claims could be true when compared to the natural behavior and character of women" (1982, 4). Unfortunately, men did not cease writing about women even though they were without the knowledge of women that Pizan and her sisters possessed. Inequality affects both the ability and desire to converse and the access to certain information one is likely to be granted (Scott 1990).[1]

Anna Julia Cooper's landmark 1892 *A Voice From the South*, as discussed in an earlier chapter, portrays numerous forms of silencing. When she compares what "has been said [about] . . . the South" in all the "noisy [and] . . . vociferous disputation . . . [it] inspires" with the "mute and voiceless . . . Black woman" (1988, I and II), she highlights beautifully the ironic contrast between Black women of the South as the subject of "controversy" with their absence among the speakers on the subject. Here, again, part of what is being documented is theorizing about women that is oblivious to the testimony of women themselves. Sexual inequality results in political theory built on ignorance about women. More recently, Lugones and Spelman add: "For it matters to us what is said about us, who says it, and to whom it is said: having the opportunity to talk about one's life, to give an account of it, to interpret it, is integral to leading that life rather than being led through it; hence our distrust of the male monopoly over accounts of women's lives. To put the same point slightly differently, part of human life, human living, is talking about it, and we can be sure that being silenced in one's own account of one's life is a kind of amputation that signals oppression" (1986, 20). The "male monopoly over accounts of women's lives" is problematic because those accounts require and are built upon the silence of women, the silencing of their own accounts. The vacuum silencing creates is a political space that is then filled with stories that ultimately support the monopoly itself.

1. These effects may be part of what Astell is referring to when she mentions "much" evidence about sex equality "to the contrary" of what is claimed in patriarchal theory (1986b, 71) and can explain Wollstonecraft's criticism of Rousseau's account of youngsters as not based on accurate information: "I have, probably, had an opportunity of observing more girls in their infancy than J. J. Rousseau" (1988, 43).

The persistence of certain themes is undeniable: the erroneous, predictable association of political superiority with intellectual superiority; intellectual superiority as a justification for silencing others; silencing masked by an "already full chorus"; the noise of the chorus as a cause of grave and costly distortion and error; erroneous claims used to justify inequality. As Cooper concludes, the subordinated are "little understood and seldom consulted. . . . The 'other side' has not been represented by one who 'lives there' " (1988, I, II).

"Others" have been spoken for and they have been spoken about. Rarely have they been spoken with and listened to thoughtfully. Rarely has their own speech been decisive to outsiders. Nonetheless, their silencing has not been complete. When subordinated groups have written, they have not been read, translated, or studied; when they have spoken others have not heard, or worked hard enough to understand. But so many of their stories and their papers, their visions and their evidence are still out there, still waiting to be read or heard, studied and learned from, and more are told or rediscovered every day. Voices have been silenced, but not eradicated.

Overall, because inequality has epistemological consequences, investigation into sexual inequality is a necessary starting point in the quest for knowledge. For all these thinkers, men's failure to "see" women constitutes both evidence for the existence of male privilege and part of the critique of it.

2. The same unequal power that distorts thinking about equality also contributes to the creation of real differences between people.

One aspect of this argument is that women's "inferiorities" (and men's advantages) are the consequence rather than the cause of the sexual division of labor. Mary Astell, in 1696: "Instead of inquiring why all Women are not wise and good, we have reason to wonder that there are any so. Were the Men as much neglected, and as little care taken to cultivate and improve them, perhaps they wou'd be so far from surpassing those whom they now dispise. . . . Women are from their very Infancy debar'd those Advantages, with the want of which they are afterwards reproached, and nursed up in those Vices which will hereafter be upbraided to them" (1986b, 142–43). Astell, like many feminists, focuses on a particular paradox: the intentional social creation of creatures who are then despised, especially by those with most influence on the blueprints. She refers to the critical role played by the dedication of social resources to benefit those stubbornly called "naturally" better. Emma Willard brings in the factor of sexual segregation as well as the persistence of the idea of "natural" superiority. Founder of the Troy Female Seminary, the first college-level school for women in the United States, Willard asks in 1819: "When the youth of the two sexes has been spent so differently, is it strange, or is nature at fault, if more mature age has brought such a difference of character?" (1968, 80).

Harriet Taylor Mill (to whom John Stuart Mill gave credit for coauthoring *On Liberty*, but whose name he did not include on the book's title page) gives a specific example of the kind of created difference Willard mentions: "Whether nature made a difference in the nature of men and women or not, it seems now that all men, with the exception of a few lofty minded, are sensualists more or less. Women on the contrary are quite exempt from this trait, however it may appear otherwise in the cases of some. It seems strange that it should be so . . . or it may not be so   it may be only that the habits of freedom and low indulgence in which boys grow up and the contrary notion of what is called purity in girls may have produced the appearance of different natures in the two sexes" (1998, 21–22). More famously, John Stuart Mill discussed how little we know about men's or women's natures: "I deny that anyone knows, or can know, the nature of the two sexes, as long as they have only been seen in their present relation to one another. . . . What is now called the nature of women is an eminently artificial thing— the result of forced repression in some directions, unnatural stimulation in others. It may be asserted without scruple, that no other class of dependents have had their character so entirely distorted from its natural proportions by their relation with their masters" (1988, 22). Inequality itself—women's "relation with their masters"—*creates* sexual "character." Mill turns "different educations" into the more politically powerful "forced repression" and "unnatural stimulation."

Anna Julia Cooper continues the focus on social resources, hinting at an even wider range of factors: "The atmosphere, the standards, the requirements of our little world do not afford any special stimulus to female development" (1988, 75). Simone de Beauvoir, author not only of the epochal *The Second Sex* but also of critically acclaimed metaphysical novels, notes that "these questions are not new." Centuries later, she continues Astell's inquiry: "Our task is to discover how the nature of woman has been affected throughout the course of history; we are concerned to find out what humanity has made of the human female. . . . The concept of femininity is artificially shaped by custom and fashion, it is imposed upon each woman from without" (1989, xxi). "Femininity" appears in Beauvoir as both shaped by custom and itself shaping women. "Imposition" makes a mockery of the language of "choice."

More recently, Ruth Hubbard gives a wonderfully detailed picture of how the sexual segregation referred to by Willard operates:

> If a society puts half its children into short skirts and warns them not to move in ways that reveal their panties, while putting the other half into jeans and overalls and encouraging them to climb trees, play ball, and participate in other vigorous outdoor games; if later, during adolescence, the children who have been wearing trousers are urged to "eat like growing boys," while the children in skirts are warned to watch their weight and not get fat; if the half in jeans runs around in sneakers or boots, while the half in skirts totters about on spike heels, then these two groups of people will be biologically as well as socially different. Their muscles will be different, as will their reflexes, posture, arms, legs and feet, hand-eye coordination, and so on. (1990, 69)

Hubbard's quote is especially useful for the range of forces she refers to and the range of effects she documents. Catherine MacKinnon succinctly summarizes: "The differences attributed to sex are lines inequality draws, not the basis for those lines" (1990, 213).

In all these quotes is an argument for understanding the depth and range of sexism's impact: the effects of inequality of power touch every aspect of life, from the political to the biological. The more thoroughly sexual differentiation penetrates and structures our lives, the greater is its ability to create the sexes almost as separate species, beginning in infancy. Nonetheless, the differences created will be reinvented as natural and interpreted as evidence of female inferiority.

3. The differences inequality creates help maintain and justify inequality. Subordinated groups will be urged or required to adopt traits that in fact disadvantage them and will be used against them.

The revolutionary Mary Wollstonecraft is surely one of the finest explicators of this theme. In 1792 she writes: "I lament that women are systematically degraded by receiving the trivial attentions, which men think it manly to pay to the sex, when, in fact, they are insultingly supporting their own superiority. . . . How grossly do they insult us who thus advise us only to render ourselves gentle, domestic brutes!" (1988, 125, 89). The Grimké sisters, who became feminists in response to the hostility they confronted as frank abolitionist lecturers, both speak to this same theme in 1837. The criticism they faced is captured here, as is Angelina's response: "'All the generous promptings of chivalry, all the poetry of romantic gallantry, depend upon woman's retaining her place as dependent and defenceless, and making no claims, and maintaining no rights, but what are the gifts of honor, rectitude and love.' I cannot refrain from pronouncing this sentiment as beneath the dignity of any woman" (1968, 60–61).

Sarah shows the dynamics in different groups of women, as well as some common ground across difference. I quote her at some length:

> In the wealthy classes . . . there is a vast amount of secret suffering endured, from the forced submission of women to the opinions and whims of their husbands. . . . Our female slaves . . . are bought and sold in our slave markets, to gratify the brutal lust of those who bear the name of Christians. . . . Woman has more or less been made a *means* to promote the welfare of man, without due regard to her own happiness. . . . She has too well learned the lesson which MAN has labored to teach her. She has surrendered her dearest rights, and been satisfied with the privileges which man has assumed to grant her; she has been amused with the show of power, whilst man has absorbed all the reality into himself. . . . I believe the laws which deprive married women of their rights and privileges, have a tendency to lessen them in their own estimation as moral and responsible beings, and that their being made by civil law inferior to their husbands, has a debasing and mischievous effect upon them, teaching them practically the fatal lesson to look unto man for protection and indulgence. (2000, 190–200)

"Protection" and "indulgence" are unmasked as means to inequality, and the dangers of dependence are emphasized rather than sanitized or glorified. Negative self-evaluation is linked to legal status and public opinion. Women's status as means to others' ends holds across classes and seems for Sarah Grimké to capture the essence of sexual inequality—a form of human degradation. Women's playing by the rules maintains their subordination.

Finally, in 1844 Ann Richelieu Lamb explains the workings of created sexual differences in *Can Woman Regenerate Society?* "The little [a woman] has of either power or influence is crippled by the obstacles placed in her path. When she leads the way to pleasure or amusement, she is followed, and for a day, a short-lived day, is admired; . . . but to help in devising or practicing such schemes, as may be for the real benefit of mankind, becomes in her, a matter for ridicule, a subject for merriment, impertinence not to be endured! . . . We hear forever of the self-devotion of our sex. In nine cases out of ten such a feeling would be more aptly named by the designation of self-abasement or self-annihilation" (1982, 29). Survival in conditions of inequality can require the subordinated to acquire the personality and appearance demanded by the more dominant. Doing so also reinforces their subordination, however. This problem reappears in discussion of issues from dress and manners to mothering and rape. If sex is not a "role" one can step into and out of, the dilemma deepens; "self-abasement or self-annihilation" is what is being dictated.

4. Differences inequality creates do not speak only negatively about women or only positively about men.

Despite the emphasis on women's "inferiority," women evidence many strengths. Judith Sargent Murray, author of the wonderfully titled *Desultory Thoughts upon the Utility of Encouraging a Degree of Self-Complacency, Especially in Female Bosoms*, among many other plays, essays, and poems, makes strange that which seems familiar. Writing in 1790, she asserts, "But, suffer me to ask, in what the minds of females are so notoriously deficient or unequal" (1973, 18). Even acknowledging some "deficiencies" was seen by her as indicating nothing about women's inherent or potential intellectual abilities. In her hands, actions usually used against women become evidence of women's capabilities, without necessarily being exalted; for example, "the variety of fashions . . . which distinguish and adorn the female world" became evidence of "strength of inventive imagination" (18).

Many feminist thinkers emphasize that the goal is not for women to become what men have been. To accept men's lives as the norm or ideal is to reinforce patriarchal values. The idea that feminists want to be (like) men is an old, unimaginative drawing of dreams of equality. Wollstonecraft challenges it in 1792: "From every quarter have I heard exclamations against masculine women; but where are they to be found? If by this appellation men mean to inveigh against their ardor in hunting, shooting, and gaming, I shall most cordially join in the cry" (1988, 74). In *Woman's Mission* (1839), a book that went through thirteen editions, Sarah Lewis has to explain not women's but men's weaknesses:

Men are said to be more selfish than women. How can they help it? no pains are taken in their education to make them otherwise. That pugnacity which is so admired as a proof of *spirit,* is the very embodiment of the selfish principle—a fighting for their own rights—an assertion of their *own* superiority. They are taught at school to despise the weak, and practice the lesson at home in petty domestic torments to the weak of their circle—their sisters; receiving, at the same time, from those very sisters, a thousand little services, without consciousness and without gratitude. Is it astonishing that these boys should hereafter be selfish husbands and tyrannical fathers? (1982, 26)

Imagining a world in which women become like what men have been, in 1892 Anna Julia Cooper reevaluates both: "The world of thought under the predominant man-influence, unmollified and unrestrained by its complementary force, would become like Daniel's fourth beast: 'dreadful and terrible, and strong exceedingly.' . . . It smacks of the worship of the beast. . . . But, thank Heaven, side by side with the cold, mathematical, selfishly calculating, so-called practical and unsentimental instinct of the business man, there comes the sympathetic warmth and sunshine of good women . . . counteracting the selfishness of an acquisitive age" (1988, 53, 54, 131). Writing in 1912, Anna Garlin Spencer both points to many eminent women and, like Murray, draws unusual conclusions from some of women's "lesser" accomplishments. Teacher, journalist, and minister, she writes in *Women's Share in Social Culture:* "In view of these tremendous obstacles, it is fair to assume that when women in the past have achieved even a second or third place in the ranks of genius they have shown far more native ability than men have needed to reach the same eminence" (1968, 106). What we see here is a reframing of women's history. Recent feminist writing picks up on all of these themes. In 1978, Mary Daly reflects on the truth and limits of the claim Wollstonecraft earlier evaluated: "It may at first seem 'natural' for women to reason that one can break the spell by demonstrating that 'achievement' on male terms is natural to them. But after this is seen through, we encounter the problem of unmasking and moving beyond the mediocrity of such achievements without falling into opposing forms of mediocrity" (57). Adrienne Rich puts a twist on a subject earlier considered by Judith Sargent Murray: "[This does not] mean we should be training women students to 'think like men.' Men in general think badly: in disjuncture from their personal lives, claiming objectivity where the most irrational passions seethe. . . . It is not easy to think like a woman in a man's world. . . . To think like a woman in a man's world means thinking critically, refusing to accept the givens, making connections between facts and ideas which men have left unconnected. It means remembering that every mind resides in a body; remaining accountable to the female bodies in which we live; constantly retesting given hypotheses against lived experience" (1979, 244–45). Back at least to Pizan, "thinking like a woman" has had positive connotations.

Women have survived, against the odds, often while resisting patriarchal ideas and practices. In the words of essayist and poet Cherríe Moraga: "Loving you is like living in the war years. . . . Loving in the war years calls for this kind of risking without a home to call our own. . . . Refusing our enemy, fear. We're all we've got. You and I maintaining this war time morality where being queer and female is as rude as we can get" (1983, 29–30). It is one of the more persistent myths about feminism that feminists/women want to be men, a myth that reveals less about feminism than about antifeminism. Perhaps the more dominant always assume that outsiders want to resemble them. Deciding what is to be rejected and what to be sought forms the most fascinating part of feminist ethics and feminist science fiction and utopian literature. Neither "man-hating" nor a desire to be men captures the motives, the mood, the method, or the mentality of feminism.

5. So far is inequality from rendering women weak, powerless, and helpless, women are powerful enough to challenge their enforced subordination.

The closing of Abigail Adams's 1776 letter to John Adams is much more forceful than the more famous phrase from it, "Remember the ladies": "But you must remember that arbitrary power is like most other things which are very hard, very liable to be broken; and, notwithstanding all your wise laws and maxims, we have it in our power, not only to free ourselves, but to subdue our masters, and, without violence, throw both your natural and legal authority at our feet" (1973, 13). Jean-Jacques Rousseau's claim that women who gave up their "feminine" power would lose all influence over men meets this response from Mary Wollstonecraft in 1792: "I do not wish [women] to have power over men; but over themselves" (1988, 131). In 1832 lecturer, abolitionist, and essayist Maria W. Stewart also speaks to women's potential power: "O woman, woman! Upon you I call; for upon your exertions almost entirely depends whether the rising generation shall be any thing more than we have been or not" (1987, 55).

Sojourner Truth's incomparable 1851 speech speaks to the same subject: "If the first woman God ever made was strong enough to turn the world upside down all alone, these women together ought to be able to turn it back, and get it right side up again! And now they is asking to do it, the men better let them" (1997, 1). Both historically and recently, many have discussed women's past accomplishments as further proof of their power to effect change. Elizabeth Martinez is one example: "Some of us do not believe that in our culture, femininity has always meant: weak, passive, delicate looking...in other words, qualities that inflate the male ego. The woman of La Raza is traditionally a fighter and revolutionary. In the history of Mexico the nation closest to us, we find a long line of heroines—from the war of independence against Spain through the 1910 revolution and including the rebellions of the Yaqui Indians. The same holds true for other nations.... These are the traditions, this is the culture, that the revolutionary Chicana wants to revive" (2003, 43). "Victim feminism" has become something of a popular target—the idea that feminists portray all women as nothing but victims and all men as nothing but victimizers. The motive may simply be to deflect attention from crimes against women, but, either way, there is a great tradition in feminist theory of reckoning with women's power, deciding not whether she has it or should have it, but what forms it might take and what ends it should aim toward.

6. Equality is in the interest of all.

The idea that equality is somehow not in the interest of the whole community reveals that the calculus we perform generally excludes women's well-being and the consequences for others of women's well-being. Feminists have long emphasized that sexual equality is a social good.

Wollstonecraft characteristically puts the emphasis on progress: "I wish to see woman placed in a station in which she would advance, instead of retarding, the progress of those glorious principles that give a substance to morality.... The more equality there is established among men, the more virtue and happiness will reign in society" (1988, 3, 16). This connection of equality with progress is not unique to Wollstonecraft. Charlotte Perkins Gilman and Frances Wright, among others, also emphasize it. As the Owenite theorist and activist Wright wrote in 1829: "Until women assume the place in society which good sense and good feeling alike assign to them, human improvement must advance but feebly. It is in vain that we would circumscribe the power of one half of our race, and that half by far the most important and influential. If they exert it not for good, they will for evil; if they advance not knowledge, they will perpetuate ignorance. . . . Surely, then, if they knew their interests, they would desire the improvement of those who, if they do no advantage, will injure them" (1973, 22, 23). In 1892 Anna Julia Cooper, like Wright, stresses the pivotal role of women: "The position of woman in society determines the vital elements of its regeneration and progress" (1988, 21). And in 1926 Suzanne LaFollette, who in her critique of the state is reminiscent of Emma Goldman, pays attention to the calculus itself: "To assume that [society's] 'interests' may be promoted by the enslavement of one-half its members, is unreasonable. One may be permitted the doubtful assumption that this enslavement promotes the welfare of the other half of Society, but it is obvious that it can not promote the welfare of the whole" (1973, 543). LaFollette most succinctly argues the somewhat obvious point that women's subordination cannot affect positively a whole community made up in part of those disadvantaged women. All these authors point out how the subordination of one part of society will drag down the whole, including the dominant.

7. In particular, women's equality will benefit men.

The idea that sexual equality works against the interests of men is particularly revealing. Equality is easily understood as being in the interests of those who are subordinated—it constitutes a kind of promotion. But that equality should be against the interests of certain individuals reveals their favored status, the inequality we prefer in general to deny.

In 1706 Mary Astell writes: "Men never mistake their true Interest more than when they endeavour to keep Women in Ignorance" (1986b, 116). Frances Wright, in 1829, phrases it in a question: "Fathers and husbands! Do ye not also understand this fact? Do ye not see how, in the mental bondage of your wives and fair companions, ye yourselves are bound?" (1973, 115).

From another angle, Gertrude Bustill Mossell (1855–1948), Quaker, journalist, and author of *The Work of the Afro-American Woman* (1894) writes, in her critique of marriage: "Many wonder that so many people separate, my wonder is that so many remain together. Born in different places, reared differently, with different views, at every point, what wonder strife ensure" (Guy-Sheftall 1995, 56). Better relations between equal companions benefit both parties. Sexism, inequality, divides and alienates on both social and individual levels.

Anna Julia Cooper compares the question asked of women in circumstances of inequality with one for men posed by equality: "The question is
not now with the woman 'How shall I so cramp, stunt, simplify and nul-
lify myself as to make me eligible to the honor of being swallowed up into
some little man?' but the problem . . . now rests with the man as to how he
can so develop his God-given powers as to reach the ideal of a generation of
women who demand the noblest, grandest and best achievements of which
he is capable. . . . The men should thank us for requiring of them the richest
fruits which they can grow" (1988, 70–71). There is surely a thread connecting Astell's claim that women's ignorance injures men and Cooper's argument that educated women elevate men. But the benefits are not only to
men as separate individuals; rather, all these thinkers find in sexual equality
real hope for constructive relations between female and male partners.

Feminism has generally been seen as a potential "win" for women and
a "loss" for men; how else are we to understand why many simply assume
that men would be against equality? The assumption itself is evidence that
men possess more power than women, for only then could equality be a
"loss." Feminism entails more than redistribution of certain goods, then; it
requires a new scheme of values that calculates them differently.

8. Women's cause is linked with other political battles.

Inequality in one form or arena reinforces inequality in another. In 1792
Wollstonecraft writes, "One kind of despotism supports another" (1988,
150). The opposite is also true. "Tyrants would have cause to tremble," she
continues, "if reason were to become the rule of duty in any of the relations
of life, for the light might spread till perfect day appeared" (150). Anna Julia
Cooper writes, one hundred years later: "Woman's cause is the cause of the
weak; and when all the weak shall have received their due consideration,
then woman will have her 'rights'" (1988, 117). Cooper claims that women's
equality depends upon the equality of all subordinated groups.

Exclusion thus runs counter to the goals and the heart of feminism.
Cooper continues: "The cause of freedom is not the cause of a race or a sect,
a party or a class,—it is the cause of human kind, the very birthright of
humanity. . . . The Woman's Movement, is essentially such an embodiment,
if its pioneers could only realize it, of the universal good. And specially
important is it that there be no confusion of ideas among its leaders as to
its scope and universality" (121). Cooper alludes to a gap between political

theory and practice here, one that feminists today still struggle with, that still costs dearly. Her emphasis on feminism's "scope" is especially note-worthy and is counter to characterizations of feminism as another "special interest."

Audre Lorde, in 1984, makes a similar point by focusing on some of the costs: "Do you ever really read the work of Black women? . . . When patriarchy dismisses us, it encourages our murderers. When radical lesbian feminist theory dismisses us, it encourages it own demise" (68–69). Lorde reminds us, as perhaps in the present volume the earlier chapter on Pizan did, that feminists are apt to fall into some of the same patterns as anti-feminists—the consequences can be equally dire, but for feminists are also self-defeating. As Andrea Dworkin pithily summarizes it, "Nothing in this system is unrelated to anything else" (1988, 148).

9. Inequality will be veiled, minimized, excused, and denied.

In 1837, Harriet Martineau, prolific author of works on economics, politics, religion, and history, writes: "While woman's intellect is confined, her morals crushed, her health ruined, her weaknesses encouraged, and her strength punished, she is told that her lot is cast in the paradise of women: and there is no country in the world where there is so much boasting of the 'chival-rous' treatment she enjoys. . . . In short, indulgence is given her as a substi-tute for justice" (1973, 125). Martineau beautifully draws out the contrast between women's reality and patriarchy's portrayal of it. The distance be-tween the two is remarkable, though often unremarked upon. Martineau's conclusion, calling the tactic "indulgence," helps to explain how it works. In 1855, Lucy Stone, cofounder of the American Woman Suffrage Association and editor of *Woman's Journal,* adds the following: "We are told that woman has all the rights she wants; and even women, I am ashamed to say, tell us so. They mistake the politeness of men for rights—seats while men stand in this hall to-night, and their adulation; but these are mere courtesies. We want rights" (1968, 72). Stone calls "courtesies" what Martineau names "in-dulgence," but both contrast it with equality: "justice" and "rights." Stone, like Lorde above, notes women's susceptibility to these self-defeating ideas and practices.

Finally, Carrie Chapman Catt, a founder of the League of Women Voters and the Women's Peace Party, writes, in 1902: "He has worshipped her ideal through the age of chivalry as though she were a goddess, but he had governed her as though she were an idiot" (1968, 209). Catt sees this contrast as one aspect of the veiling of inequality. It seems as though there is a tremendous will to believe that the sexes are being treated as equals. Any evidence to the contrary is, at most, called an exception to an otherwise just state of affairs. This makes it terribly easy to mask domination and to blame the subordinated for making inequality an issue, as is explored in the theme that follows.

10. Calls for equality will meet resistance.

Frederick Douglass explains, in 1848: "We are not insensible that the bare mention of this truly important subject in any other than terms of contemptuous ridicule and scornful disfavor, is likely to excite against us the fury of bigotry and the folly of prejudice. A discussion of the rights of animals would be regarded with far more complacency by many of what are called the wise and the good of our land, than would be a discussion of the rights of women" (1976, 50). William Lloyd Garrison notes the same problem, in 1853: "How has this Woman's Rights movement been treated in this country, on the right hand and on the left? This nation ridicules and derides this movement, and spits upon it, as fit only to be cast out and trampled underfoot. This is not ignorance. They know all about the truth. It is the natural outbreak of tyranny" (1996, 72). Garrison and Douglass agree in their characterization of how women's rights are generally viewed—it is not inequality we find contemptuous, but a movement for equality and its advocates. Garrison points out that public opinion on this does not follow the usual pattern between the right and left. He also stresses that its cause is *not* ignorance, the only explanation that is comfortable for those unwilling to cast blame on anyone, but tyranny.

Florynce Kennedy explains that resistance may be justified, sometimes ridiculously, as response to a perceived threat. For example, "This magnifying of hard-won advancement makes it seems that a weak gnarled tree that pushes through the concrete in Brooklyn is a threat to miles of centuries-old forests which have flourished in fertile lands where the best of expert care has been lavished" (1995, 103). In 1983 Andrea Dworkin writes of the "threats" feminism does represent: "We frequently find ourselves in these dangerous and difficult situations because we are challenging not only power—and power is serious, power is important—but notions of reality with which people have become comfortable even though they protest them" (1988, 143).

Resistance, misrepresentation, backlash, and mystification are what we should expect, as noted in the earlier chapter on Seneca Falls in this volume. It is (unfortunately in terms of where we would rather direct our energy) a "normal" response against the cessation of privilege and against the unfamiliar, if the familiar structures life as deeply as the sexual division of labor does. We have to listen to stories of what enables people to challenge and resist inequality and embrace change. Again, our history shows that some people are always advocating for equality.

Frances Wright, who worked on issues from dress and suffrage to slavery and socialism, says, in 1829: "It is with delight that I have distinguished, at each successive meeting, the increasing ranks of my own sex. Were the vital principle of human equality universally acknowledged, it would be to my fellow beings without regard to nation, class, sect, or sex, that I should delight to address myself. But until equality prevail in condition, opportunity, and instruction, it is every where to the least favored in these advantages, that I most especially and anxiously incline" (1973, 20). Few like to be reminded of inequality. Not to acknowledge it, however, is to perpetuate it. We have to hold on to our visions. Andrea Dworkin, 1983: "There is nothing that feminists want more than to become irrelevant. We want the end of the exploitation of women. . . . There is one thing that is not practical, and it's the thing I believe in most, and that is the importance of vision in the midst of what has to be done, never forgetting for one minute the world that you really want to live in and how you want to live in it and what it means to you and how much you care about it—what you want for yourselves and what you want for the people that you love. . . . Change is not impossible. It is not impossible" (1988, 152).

CONCLUDING THOUGHTS

I find myself wanting to go on, to discuss more ideas that reappear over the centuries. A commitment to equality is compatible with recognition of diversity. Whatever sexual differences a political community decides to emphasize, they do not preclude the possibility of sexual equality. Every historical text I pick up offers either more quotes or more concepts.

The heritage found in the canon is not our only one. Substantively, that tradition has not wrestled with these ideas from the history of feminist theory. Such a gap makes the canonical teachings less convincing, less authoritative, and less imaginative.

Ultimately, for many authors, whatever differences may be said to exist between the sexes, like differences within each sex, they pale because of the deepest common ground. As Margaret Fuller wrote, "What Woman needs is not as a woman to act or rule, but as a nature to grow, as an intellect to discern, as a soul to live freely and unimpeded, to unfurl such powers as were given her when we left our common home. . . . Woman is not only a part of Man, bone of his bone, and flesh of his flesh, born that men might not be lonely—but that women are in themselves possessors of and possessed by immortal souls" (1971, 38, 56).

I close with a quote by Ann Lane, who has written about two different approaches to the history of feminist theory:

> Mary Beard is read today, I think, primarily by feminist historians, and she is read in the same way that we read Mary Astell, Mary Woll-stonecraft, and Margaret Fuller, valued as a retrieved forebear. We read in the past to understand our intellectual, ideological, political, and historical roots. We read the words of our foremothers to be inspired, not to be taught, as obeisance to our neglected ancestors, not to study from their texts. We are grateful to Mary Beard because she is part of our history. And so we read the work of our forebears only partially and therefore improperly. We still do not examine the work of Mary Ritter Beard to address the issues she raised. She is still not understood for what she has to say about future directions for research; we still examine her ideas not to discover the way we might proceed, only to understand the path we have thus far come. (1988, xii)

When we have been reading them at all, we have been reading our foremothers to learn *of* them, not to learn *from* them. That profound difference affects our understanding of those authors and, potentially, our understanding of the world. They *should* inspire us, but we sell them short when we are moved only by their existence, and not also by their ideas.

REFERENCES

Ackelsberg, Martha A., and Mary Lyndon Shanley. 1996. "Privacy, Publicity, and Power: A Feminist Rethinking of the Public-Private Distinction." In *Revisioning the Political: Feminist Reconstructions of Traditional Concepts in Western Political Theory,* ed. Nancy J. Hirschmann and Christine Di Stefano. Boulder, Colo.: Westview.

Adams, Abigail. 1973. "Abigail Adams vs. John Adams." [1776.] In *The Feminist Papers: Adams to de Beauvoir,* ed. Alice Rossi, 7–15. Boston: Northeastern University Press.

Adler, Mortimer. 1997. "Selecting Works for the 1990 Edition of the Great Books of the Western World." http://books.mirror.org/gb.sel1990.html (accessed December 10, 2007).

Alcoff, Linda. 2003. "Gadamer's Feminist Epistemology." In *Feminist Interpretations of Hans-Georg Gadamer,* ed. Lorraine Code. University Park: Pennsylvania State University Press.

Alexander, Archibald Browning Drysdale. 1922. *A Short History of Philosophy.* Glasgow: Maclehose, Jackson.

Anderson, Bonnie S. 1998. "The Lid Comes Off: International Radical Feminism and the Revolutions of 1848." *NWSA Journal* 10, no. 2: 1–12.

———. 2000. *Joyous Greetings: The First International Women's Movement, 1830–1860.* Oxford: Oxford University Press.

Anzaldúa, Gloria. 1990. *Making Face, Making Soul: Creative and Critical Perspectives by Women of Color.* San Francisco: Aunt Lute Foundation Books.

Aristotle. 1975. *Politics.* Ed. and trans. Ernest Barker. New York: Oxford University Press.

Astell, Mary. 1986a. *The Christian religion as profess'd by a daughter of the Church of England.* [1705.] In *The First English Feminist: "Reflections upon Marriage" and Other Writings by Mary Astell,* ed. Bridget Hill. New York: St. Martin's Press.

———. 1986b. *Reflections upon Marriage.* [1706.] In *The First English Feminist: "Reflections upon Marriage" and Other Writings by Mary Astell,* ed. Bridget Hill. New York: St. Martin's.

———. 1986c. *A Serious Proposal to the Ladies for the Advancement of Their True and Greatest Interest.* [1696.] In *The First English Feminist: "Reflections upon Marriage" and Other Writings by Mary Astell,* ed. Bridget Hill. New York: St. Martin's Press.

———. 1996a. *An impartial enquiry into the causes of rebellion and civil war in this kingdom.* [1704.] In *Astell: Political Writings,* ed. Patricia Springborg. Cambridge: Cambridge University Press.

———. 1996b. *Some Reflections upon Marriage.* [1706.] In *Astell: Political Writings,* ed. Patricia Springborg. Cambridge: Cambridge University Press.

Atherton, Margaret, ed. 1994. *Women Philosophers of the Early Modern Period.* Indianapolis: Hackett.

Badran, Margot, and Miriam Cooke, eds. 1990. *Opening the Gates: A Century of Arab Feminist Writing.* Bloomington: Indiana University Press.

Barker, Ernest. 1975. *The "Politics" of Aristotle.* Ed. and trans. Ernest Barker. New York: Oxford University Press.

Bauer, Nancy. 2001. *Simone de Beauvoir, Philosophy, and Feminism.* New York: Columbia University Press.

Beauvoir, Simone de. 1989. *The Second Sex.* [1949.] New York: Vintage Books.

Becker, Carl L. 1958. *The Declaration of Independence: A Study in the History of Political Ideas.* New York: Vintage Books.

Bederman, Gail. 2005. "Revisiting Nashoba: Slavery, Utopia, and Frances Wright in America, 1818–1826." *American Literary History* 17, no. 3: 438–59.

Benn, Stanley. 1967. "Moral and Social Equality." In *The Encyclopedia of Philosophy,* ed. Paul Edwards, 3:38–42. New York: Macmillan.

Bernhard, Virginia, and Elizabeth Fox-Genovese, eds. 1995. *The Birth of American Feminism: The Seneca Falls Woman's Convention of 1848.* St. James, N.Y.: Brandywine Press.

Black, Naomi. 1983. "Virginia Woolf: The Life of Natural Happiness." In *Feminist Theorists: Three Centuries of Key Women Thinkers,* ed. Dale Spender. New York: Pantheon.

Bloom, Allan. 1968. "Interpretive Essay." In *The "Republic" of Plato,* trans. Allan Bloom. New York: Basic Books.

Bluestone, Natalie. 1987. *Women and the Ideal Society: Plato's "Republic" and Modern Myths of Gender.* Amherst: University of Massachusetts Press.

Blumenfeld-Kosinski, Renate. 1997a. "Christine de Pizan and the Misogynistic Tradition." In *The Selected Writings of Christine de Pizan,* ed. Renate Blumenfeld-Kosinski, 297–311. New York: Norton.

———, ed. 1997b. *The Selected Writings of Christine de Pizan.* New York: Norton.

Bordo, Susan. 1993. *Unbearable Weight: Feminism, Western Culture, and the Body.* Berkeley and Los Angeles: University of California Press.

Bowle, John. 1961. *Western Political Thought.* London: Methuen.

Brabant, Margaret. 1992. *Politics, Gender, and Genre: The Political Theory of Christine de Pizan.* Boulder, Colo.: Westview.

Brodribb, Somer. 1992. *Nothing Mat(t)ers: A Feminist Critique of Postmodernism.* North Melbourne, Australia: Spinifex Press.

Brownlee, Kevin. 1997. "Authority in Ditié de Jehanne d'Arc." In *The Selected Writings of Christine de Pizan,* ed. Renate Blumenfeld-Kosinski. New York: Norton.

Cahill, Susan Neunzig, ed. 1997. *Wise Women: Over Two Thousand Years of Spiritual Writing by Women.* New York: Norton.

Cahn, Steven M., ed. 1997. *Classics of Modern Political Theory: Machiavelli to Mill.* New York: Oxford University Press.

Canovan, Margaret. 1974. *The Political Thought of Hannah Arendt.* New York: Harcourt Brace Jovanovich.

———. 1994. *Hannah Arendt: A Reinterpretation of Her Political Thought.* Cambridge: Cambridge University Press.

Carroll, Berenice. 1990. "The Politics of 'Originality': Women and the Class System of the Intellect." *Journal of Women's History* 2, no. 2: 136–63.

———. 2000. "Notes." In *Women's Political and Social Thought,* ed. Hilda Smith and Berenice Carroll. Bloomington: Indiana University Press.

Catt, Carrie Chapman. 1968. "President's Annual Address." [1902.] In *Up from the Pedestal: Selected Writings in the History of American Feminism,* ed. Aileen S. Kraditor, 206–11. Chicago: Quadrangle Books.

Ceplair, Larry, ed. 1991. *Charlotte Perkins Gilman: A Nonfiction Reader.* New York: Columbia University Press.

Chevigny, Bell Gale. 1976. *The Woman and the Myth: Margaret Fuller's Life and Writings.* Old Westbury, N.Y.: Feminist Press.

Clark, Gordon H. 1957. *Thales to Dewey: A History of Philosophy.* Boston: Houghton Mifflin.

Clark, Lorenne M. G., and Lynda Lange. 1979. *The Sexism of Social and Political Theory: Women and Reproduction from Plato to Nietzsche.* Toronto: University of Toronto Press.

Clark, Stephen R. L. 1975. *Aristotle's Man: Speculations upon Aristotelian Anthropology.* New York: Oxford University Press.

Clough, Patricia Ticineto. 1994. *Feminist Thought.* Oxford: Blackwell.

Collins, James Daniel. 1954. *A History of Modern European Philosophy.* Milwaukee, Wis.: Bruce.

Collins, Patricia Hill. 1990. *Black Feminist Thought: Knowledge, Consciousness, and the Politics of Empowerment.* Boston: Unwin Hyman.

Cooper, Anna Julia. 1945. "Equality of Races and the Democratic Movement." Cooper Papers, Box 23–5, Folder 62, Howard University.

———. 1988. *A Voice From the South.* [1892.] New York: Oxford University Press.

———. n.d. "Thy Neighbor as Thyself." Cooper Papers, Howard University.

Cruz, Sor Juana Inés de la. 1987. *Reply to Sor Philothea.* In *A Woman of Genius: The Intellectual Autobiography of Sor Juana Inés de la Cruz,* trans. Margaret Sayers Peden. Salisbury, Conn.: Lime Rock Press.

Curley, Edwin. 1994. Introduction to *Leviathan,* by Thomas Hobbes. Indianapolis: Hackett.

Dalby, Liza. 2001. "The Pillow Book of Sei Shōnagon." lizadalby.com.pillowbkpage.htm (accessed April 22, 2005).

Daly, Mary. 1978. *Gyn/Ecology: The Metaethics of Radical Feminism.* Boston: Beacon Press.

Daugherty, Heather. 1999. "The Life of Sei Shōnagon." www.stark.kent.edu/~jmoneysmith/gbi/ourwcb/daugherty (accessed 2001).

Davis, Paulina. 2007. "Proceedings of the 1850 National Woman's Rights Convention." http://www.wwhp.org/Resources.

Delacour, Jonathon. 2002. "Ladies in Rivalry." http://weblog.delacour.net/archives/2002/03/ladies_in_rivalry.php (accessed April 22, 2005).

Dewey, John. 1916. *Democracy and Education.* New York: Free Press.

Diamond, Irene, and Gloria Orenstein, eds. 1990. *Reweaving the World: The Emergence of Ecofeminism.* San Francisco: Sierra Club Books.

Dietz, Mary. 1987. "Context Is All: Feminism and Theories of Citizenship." *Daedalus* 116 (Fall): 1–24.

Disse, Dorothy. 2005. "Other Women's Voices: Translations of Women's Writing Before 1700." http://home.infionline.net/~ddisse/shonagon.html (accessed April 22, 2005).

Donovan, Josephine. 1985. *Feminist Theory: The Intellectual Traditions of American Feminism.* New York: Frederick Ungar.

Douglass, Frederick. 1976. "The Rights of Women." [1848.] In *Frederick Douglass on Women's Rights,* ed. Philip S. Foner, 49–51. New York: Da Capo Press.

Duran, Jane. 2000. "Mary Astell: A Pre-Humean Christian Empiricist and Feminist." In *Presenting Women Philosophers,* ed. Cecile Tougas and Sara Ebenreck. Philadelphia: Temple University Press.

———. 2006. *Eight Women Philosophers: Theory, Politics, and Feminism.* Urbana: University of Illinois Press.

Dworkin, Andrea. 1974. *Woman Hating.* New York: E. P. Dutton.

———. 1988. "Feminism: An Agenda." In *Letters from a War Zone: Writings, 1976–1989.* New York: E. P. Dutton.

Dykeman, Therese Boos, ed. 1999. *The Neglected Canon: Nine Women Philosophers, First to the Twentieth Century.* Dordrecht: Kluwer Academic.

Ebenstein, William. 1969. *Great Political Thinkers: Plato to the Present.* 4th ed. New York: Holt, Rinehart and Winston.

Eisenstein, Zillah. 1981. *The Radical Future of Liberal Feminism.* New York: Longman.

Ellert, F. C. 1958. Introduction to *Oppression and Liberty,* by Simone Weil, trans. Arthur Wills and John Petrie. Amherst: University of Massachusetts Press.

Elshtain, Jean Bethke. 1981. *Public Man, Private Woman: Women in Social and Political Thought.* Princeton: Princeton University Press.

———. 2002a. *Jane Addams and the Dream of American Democracy: A Life.* New York: Basic Books.

———. 2002b. *The Jane Addams Reader.* New York: Basic Books.

Emma Goldman Papers Project. sunsite.berkeley.edu/Goldman/project.html (accessed December 10, 2007).

l'Enclos, Ninon. 1903. "To the Modern Leontium." http://www.aelliott.com/reading/ninon/letter_leontium/ (accessed March 10, 2008).

Ettinger, Elzbieta. 1986. *Rosa Luxemburg: A Life.* Boston: Beacon Press.

Falco, Maria, ed. 1996. *Feminist Interpretations of Mary Wollstonecraft.* University Park: Pennsylvania State University Press.

First, Ruth, and Ann Scott. 1980. *Olive Schreiner.* New Brunswick: Rutgers University Press.

Foner, Philip S. 1976. *We, the Other People: Alternative Declarations of Independence by Labor Groups, Farmers, Woman's Rights Advocates, Socialists, and Blacks, 1829–1975.* Urbana: University of Illinois Press.

Forhan, Kate Langdon. 2002. *The Political Theory of Christine de Pizan.* Surrey, U.K.: Ashgate.

Foster, Michael B. 1941. *Masters of Political Thought.* Vol. 1. Boston: Houghton Mifflin.

Frye, Marilyn. 1983. *The Politics of Reality: Essays in Feminist Theory.* Freedom, Calif.: Crossing Press.

———. 1992. "The Possibility of Feminist Theory." In *Willful Virgin: Essays in Feminism,* 59–75. Freedom, Calif.: Crossing Press.

Fukumori, Naomi. 1997. "Sei Shonagon's *Makura no soshi:* A Re-visionary History." *Journal of the Association of Teachers of Japanese* 31, no. 1:1–44.

———. 2003. "Observations by a Scholar of Japanese Literature: Encyclopedia of an Ordinary Life as an Encyclopedia of Okashi." www.encyclopediaofanordinarylife.com/pages/reviews>full.php?id=12_0_4_0_C (accessed April 22, 2005).

Fuller, Margaret. 1971. *Woman in the Nineteenth Century.* [1845.] New York: Norton.

Gage, Matilda Joslyn. 1980. *Woman, Church, and State: The Original Exposé of Male Collaboration Against the Female Sex.* [1893.] Watertown, Mass.: Persephone Press.

———. "Seneca Falls Woman's Rights Convention." Matilda Goslyn Gage Web site. http://www.pinn.net/~sunshine/gage/mjg.html.

Gardiner, Patrick. 1969. *Nineteenth-Century Philosophy.* New York: Free Press.

Gardner, Catherine Villanueva. 2000. *Rediscovering Women Philosophers: Philosophical Genre and the Boundaries of Philosophy.* Boulder, Colo.: Westview Press.

Garrison, William Lloyd. 1996. "Men Are Responsible for Women's Oppression." In *The Women's Rights Movement: Opposing Viewpoints,* ed. Brenda Stalcup, 70–74. San Diego, Calif.: Greenhaven Press.

Gates, Henry Louis, Jr. 1988. "Foreword: In Her Own Write." In *A Voice From the South,* by Anna Julia Cooper, vii–xxii. New York: Oxford University Press.

Gilman, Charlotte Perkins. 1979. *Herland.* New York: Pantheon Books.

———. 1998. *Herland.* Mineola, N.Y.: Dover.

———. 2003. *Concerning Children.* Lanham, Md.: Altamira Press.

Glassgold, Peter, ed. 2001. *Anarchy! An Anthology of Emma Goldman's "Mother Earth."* Washington, D.C.: Counterpoint.

globaled. 2000. "The Pillow Book." www.globaled.org/spot_JP/ciii.html (accessed 2001).

Godwin, William. 1987. *Memoirs of the Author of "The Rights of Woman."* New York: Penguin.

Goldman, Emma. 1969. *Anarchism and Other Essays.* New York: Dover.

———. 1972. *Red Emma Speaks: Selected Writings and Speeches.* Comp. and ed. Alix Kates Shulman. New York: Vintage Books.

Gottlieb, Beatrice. 1997. "The Problem of Feminism in the Fifteenth Century." In *The Selected Writings of Christine de Pizan,* ed. Renate Blumenfeld-Kosinski, 274–97. New York: Norton.

Gray, Alice, Steve Stephens, and John Van Diest. 1999. *Lists to Live By: For Everything That Really Matters.* Sisters, Ore.: Multnomah.

Green, Karen. 1995. *The Woman of Reason: Feminism, Humanism, and Political Thought.* New York: Continuum.

Greenaway, Peter. 2005. "105 Years of Illustrated Text." *Zoetrope* 5, no. 1. www.all-story.com/issues.cgi?action=show_story&story_id=99&part=all.

Greer, David. 2000. "The Lists of a Lady-in-Waiting: A Portrait of the Author of *The Pillow Book.*" www.kampo.co.jp/kyoto-journal/kjselections/kjshonagon (accessed January 6, 2002).

Griffin, Susan. 1978. *Woman and Nature: The Roaring Inside Her.* New York: Harper and Row.

———. 1981. *Pornography and Silence: Culture's Revenge Against Nature.* New York: Harper and Row.

Grimké, Angelina. 1968. "Letters to Catherine E. Beecher." [1838.] In *Up from the Pedestal: Selected Writings in the History of American Feminism,* ed. Aileen S. Kraditor, 58–66. Chicago: Quadrangle Books.

Grimké, Sarah. 2000. "Letters on the Equality of the Sexes, and the Condition of Woman." [1838.] In *Women's Political and Social Thought,* ed. Hilda Smith and Berenice Carroll, 189–204. Bloomington: Indiana University Press.

Grimshaw, Jean. 1986. *Philosophy and Feminist Thinking.* Minneapolis: University of Minnesota Press.

Gross, Elizabeth. 1987. "What Is Feminist Theory?" In *Feminist Challenges: Social and Political Theory,* ed. Carole Pateman and Elizabeth Gross, 190–204. Boston: Northeastern University Press.

Gunther-Canada, Wendy. 2001. *Rebel Writer: Mary Wollstonecraft and Enlightenment Politics.* DeKalb: Northern Illinois University Press.

Guy-Sheftall, Beverly, ed. 1995. *Words of Fire: An Anthology of African-American Feminist Thought.* New York: New Press.

Haaland, Bonnie. 1993. *Emma Goldman: Sexuality and the Impurity of the State.* Montreal: Black Rose Books.

Hamington, Maurice. 2007. "Two Leaders, Two Utopias: Jane Addams and Dorothy Day." *NWSA Journal* 19: 159–86.

Hamlyn, D. W. 1987. *A History of Western Philosophy.* New York: Viking Press.

Haraway, Donna. 1990. "A Manifesto for Cyborgs: Science, Technology, and Socialist Feminism." *Socialist Review* 80 (March/April): 64–107.

Harmon, M. J. 1964. *Political Thought: From Plato to the Present.* New York: McGraw-Hill.

Harris, Sharon M., ed. 1995. *Selected Writings of Judith Sargent Murray.* Oxford: Oxford University Press.

Hart, Richard E. 2004. "Susan K. Langer, 1895–1985." In *The Blackwell Guide to American Philosophy,* ed. Armen T. Marsoobian and John Ryder. Malden, Mass.: Blackwell.

Hartsock, Nancy C. M. 1983. *Money, Sex, and Power: Toward a Feminist Historical Materialism.* New York: Longman.

———. 2003. "The Feminist Standpoint: Toward a Specifically Feminist Historical Materialism." In *Feminist Theory Reader: Local and Global Perspectives,* ed. Carole McCann and Seung-Kyung Kim. New York: Routledge.

Hays, Mary. 1988. "Memoirs of Mary Wollstonecraft." [1797–98.] In *A Vindication of the Rights of Woman,* 2nd ed., ed. Carol H. Poston, 228–29. New York: Norton.

Held, Virginia. 1987. "Non-contractual Society: A Feminist View." *Canadian Journal of Philosophy,* supp. no. 13: 111–37.

Hewitt, Nancy A. 1986. "Feminist Friends: Agrarian Quakers and the Emergence of Woman's Rights in America." *Feminist Studies* 12, no. 1: 27–49.

Hill, Bridget, ed. 1986. *The First English Feminist: "Reflections upon Marriage" and Other Writings by Mary Astell.* New York: St. Martin's Press.

Hirschmann, Nancy J. 1992. *Rethinking Obligation: A Feminist Method for Political Theory.* Ithaca: Cornell University Press.

Hirschmann, Nancy, and Christine Di Stefano, eds. 1996. *Revisioning the Political: Feminist Reconstructions of Traditional Concepts in Western Political Theory.* Boulder, Colo.: Westview Press.

Hobbes, Thomas. 1994. *Leviathan.* Indianapolis: Hackett.

Hoff, Joan. 1991. *Law, Gender, and Injustice: A Legal History of U.S. Women.* New York: New York University Press.

Holmes, Richard. 1987. Introduction to *Mary Wollstonecraft and William Godwin: A Short Residence in Sweden and Memoirs of the Author of "The Rights of Woman."* New York: Penguin Books.

Hubbard, Ruth. 1990. "The Political Nature of 'Human Nature.'" In *Theoretical Perspectives on Sexual Difference,* ed. Deborah L. Rhode, 63–73. New Haven: Yale University Press.

Hutchinson, Louise D. 1982. *Anna Julia Cooper: A Voice From the South.* Washington, D.C.: Smithsonian Press.

Jacobs, Jo Ellen, ed. 1998. *The Complete Works of Harriet Taylor Mill.* Bloomington: Indiana University Press.

Jaggar, Alison. 1983. *Feminist Politics and Human Nature.* Lanham, Md.: Rowman and Littlefield.

———, ed. 1994. *Living with Contradictions.* Boulder, Colo.: Westview.

James, Susan, ed. 2003. *Margaret Cavendish: Political Writings.* Cambridge: Cambridge University Press.

Janeway, Elizabeth. 1980. *Powers of the Weak.* New York: Alfred A. Knopf.

Johnson, E. Pauline. 1893. "A Red Girl's Reasoning." *Dominion Magazine* 2, no. 1: 19–28.

Johnston, David. 1997. "Theory and Transformation: The Politics of Enlightenment." In *Leviathan,* ed. Richard E. Glathman and David Johnston, with interpretations. New York: Norton.

Jones, Howard Mumford. 1953. *The Pursuit of Happiness.* Cambridge: Harvard University Press.

Jones, Kathleen B. 1993. *Compassionate Authority: Democracy and Representation.* New York: Routledge.

Jones, W. T., ed. 1959. *Masters of Political Thought.* Vol. 3. Boston: Houghton Mifflin.

Karcher, Carolyn L., ed. 1997. *A Lydia Maria Child Reader.* Durham: Duke University Press.

Kennedy, Florynce. 1995. "A Comparative Study: Accentuating the Similarities of the Societal Position of Women and Negroes." In *Words of Fire: An Anthology of African-American Feminist Thought,* ed. Beverly Guy-Sheftall, 102–6. New York: New Press.

Kerber, Linda K. 1987. "From the Declaration of Independence to the Declaration of Sentiments: The Legal Status of Women in the Early Republic." In *Women, the Law, and the Constitution,* ed. Kermit Hall, 115–24. New York: Garland.

Kersey, Ethel M. 1989. *Women Philosophers: A Bio-critical Source Book.* Oxford, U.K.: Greenwood Press.

Kingdom, Elizabeth. 1991. "Formal Declarations of Rights." In *What's Wrong with Rights,* 132–47. Edinburgh: Edinburgh University Press.

Kinnaird, Joan. 1983. "Mary Astell: Inspired by Ideas." In *Feminist Theorists: Three Centuries of Key Women Thinkers,* ed. Dale Spender, 28–39. New York: Random House.

Kleinberg, Susan J. 1975. Introduction to *Life and Writings of Amelia Bloomer.* New York: Schocken Books.

Kraditor, Aileen S., ed. 1968. *Up from the Pedestal: Selected Writings in the History of American Feminism.* Chicago: Quadrangle Books.

LaFollette, Suzanne. 1973. "Concerning Women." In *The Feminist Papers: From Adams to de Beauvoir,* ed. Alice Rossi, 541–65. Boston: Northeastern University Press.

Lamb, Ann Richelieu. 1982. *Can Woman Regenerate Society?* [1844.] In *Strong-Minded Women and Other Lost Voices from Nineteenth-Century England,* ed. Janet Murray, 28–31. New York: Pantheon.

Lane, Ann J. 1988. *Mary Ritter Beard: A Sourcebook.* Boston: Northeastern University Press.

———. 1990. *To "Herland" and Beyond: The Life and Work of Charlotte Perkins Gilman.* New York: Pantheon.

Le Doeuff, Michele. 1989. *Hipparchia's Choice: An Essay Concerning Women, Philosophy, etc.* Cambridge, Mass.: Basil Blackwell.

Lemert, Charles, and Esme Bhan, eds. 1998. *The Voice of Anna Julia Cooper: Including "A Voice From the South" and Other Important Essays, Papers, and Letters.* Lanham, Md.: Rowman and Littlefield.

Lerner, Gerda. 1998. *The Feminist Thought of Sarah Grimké.* Oxford: Oxford University Press.

———. 2000. "Why Have There Been So Few Women Philosophers?" In *Presenting Women Philosophers,* ed. Cecile T. Tougas and Sara Ebenreck, 5–14. Philadelphia: Temple University Press.

Lewis, Sarah. 1982. *Woman's Mission.* [1839.] In *Strong-Minded Women and Other Lost Voices from Nineteenth-Century England,* ed. Janet Murray, 23–39. New York: Pantheon.

Liberty! Teacher's Guide. 2006. www.pbs.org/ktca/liberty/tguide_2.html.

Lilley, Kate. 1992. Introduction to *Margaret Cavendish: "The Blazing World" and Other Writings.* New York: Penguin.

Lindgren, J. Ralph, and Nadine Taub. 1993. *The Law of Sex Discrimination.* 2nd ed. Minneapolis/St. Paul: West.

Link, Frederick M. 1967. Introduction to *The Rover,* by Aphra Behn. Lincoln: University of Nebraska Press.

Lloyd, Genevieve. 1984. *The Man of Reason: "Male" and "Female" in Western Philosophy.* Minneapolis: University of Minnesota Press.

Lodge, Rupert C. 1949. *The Great Thinkers.* London: Routledge and Kegan Paul.

Lorde, Audre. 1984. "An Open Letter to Mary Daly." In *Sister Outsider.* Freedom, Calif.: Crossing Press.

Lowell, Amy. 1920. Introduction to *Diaries of Court Ladies of Old Japan,* trans. Annie Shepley Omori and Kochi Doi. Boston: Houghton Mifflin.

Lugones, Maria C., and Elizabeth Spelman. 1986. "Have We Got a Theory for You! Feminist Theory, Cultural Imperialism and the Demand for 'The Woman's Voice.'" In *Women and Values: Readings in Recent Feminist Philosophy,* ed. Marilyn Pearsall, 19–31. Belmont, Calif.: Wadsworth.

MacIntyre, Alasdair. *After Virtue.* Notre Dame: University of Notre Dame Press.

Mackenzie, Catriona. 1993. "Reason and Sensibility: The Ideal of Women's Self-Governance in the Writings of Mary Wollstonecraft." *Hypatia* 8 (Fall): 181–203.

MacKinnon, Catharine A. 1979. *Sexual Harassment of Working Women.* New Haven: Yale University Press.

———. 1990. "Legal Perspectives on Sexual Difference." In *Theoretical Perspectives on Sexual Difference,* ed. Deborah L. Rhode, 213–25. New Haven: Yale University Press.

Macpherson, C. B. 1962. *The Political Theory of Possessive Individualism: Hobbes to Locke.* Oxford: Clarendon Press.

———. 1968. Introduction to *Leviathan,* by Thomas Hobbes. London: Penguin Books.

Malebranche, Nicolas. 1678. *De la recherche de la verité: Ou l'on traitte de la nature de l'esprit de l'homme, & de l'usage qu'il en doit faire pour éviter l'erreur dans les sciences.* Paris.

Mansbridge, Jane. 1983. *Beyond Adversary Democracy.* Chicago: University of Chicago Press.

March, Artemis. 1982. "Female Invisibility in Androcentric Sociological Theory." *Insurgent Sociologist* 11, no. 2: 99–107.

Marso, Lori Jo. 1999. *(Un)Manly Citizens: Jean-Jacques Rousseau's and Germaine de Stael's Subversive Women.* Baltimore: Johns Hopkins University Press.

———. 2006. *Feminist Thinkers and the Demands of Femininity: The Lives and Work of Intellectual Women.* New York: Routledge.

Marso, Lori Jo, and Patricia Moynagh, eds. 2006. *Simone de Beauvoir's Political Thinking.* New York: Routledge.

Martineau, Harriet. 1973. *Society in America.* [1837.] In *The Feminist Papers: From Adams to de Beauvoir,* ed. Alice Rossi, 125–43. Boston: Northeastern University Press.

Martinez, Elizabeth. 2003. "La Chicana." In *Feminist Theory Reader: Local and Global Perspectives,* ed. Carole R. McCann and Seung-Kyung Kim. New York: Routledge.

McCann, Carole, and Seung-Kyung Kim, eds. 2002. *Feminist Theory Reader: Local and Global Perspectives.* New York: Routledge.

McFarland, Dorothy Tuck, and Wilhelmina Van Ness. 1987. *Simone Weil: Formative Writings, 1929–1941.* London: Routledge and Kegan Paul.

McKivigan, John R., and Stanley Harrold. 2003. "Antislavery Violence: Sectional, Racial, and Cultural Conflict in Antebellum America." www.cw-book-news.com/excerpts/antislave.html.

Meyer, Alfred G. 1985. *The Feminism and Socialism of Lily Braun.* Bloomington: Indiana University Press.

Mill, Harriet Taylor. 1998. *The Complete Works of Harriet Taylor Mill.* Ed. Jo Ellen Jacobs. Bloomington: Indiana University Press.

Mill, John Stuart. 1978. *On Liberty.* Indianapolis: Hackett.

———. 1988. *The Subjection of Women.* [1869.] Indianapolis: Hackett.

———. 1989. *On Liberty.* In *J. S. Mill: "On Liberty" and Other Writings,* ed. Stefan Collini. New York: Cambridge University Press.

Miller, Alice Duer. 1968. *Are Women People? A Book of Rhymes for Suffrage Times.* In *Up from the Pedestal: Selected Writings in the History of American Feminism,* ed. Aileen Kraditor. Chicago: Quadrangle Books.

Millet, Kate. 1969. *Sexual Politics.* New York: Avon Books.

Mills, Charles W. 1997. *The Racial Contract.* Ithaca: Cornell University Press.

Minh-ha, Trinh T. 1989. *Woman, Native, Other: Writing Postcoloniality and Feminism.* Bloomington: Indiana University Press.

Miyake, Lynne K. 2002. "Teaching *The Pillow Book.*" www.isop.ucla.edu/eas/japan/lessons/pillowbook-lesson.htm (accessed 2005).

Moraga, Cherríe. 1983. *Loving in the War Years.* Boston: South End Press.

Morgan, Edmund. 1976. *The Meaning of Independence: John Adams, George Washington, and Thomas Jefferson.* New York: Norton.

Morgan, Michael. 2006. *Classics of Moral and Political Theory.* Indianapolis: Hackett.

Morris, Ivan. 1991. Introduction to *The Pillow Book of Sei Shōnagon.* New York: Columbia University Press.

Morris, Mark. 1980. "Sei Shonagon's Poetic Catalogues." *Harvard Journal of Asiatic Studies* 40, no. 1: 5–54.

Mossell, Gertrude Bustille. 1995. "The Opposite Point of View." [1894.] In *Words of Fire: An Anthology of African-American Feminist Thought,* ed. Beverly Guy-Sheftall, 56–59. New York: New Press.

Murray, Janet Horowitz, ed. 1982. *Strong-Minded Women and Other Lost Voices from Nineteenth-Century England.* New York: Pantheon.

Murray, Judith Sargent. 1973. "On the Equality of the Sexes." [1790.] In *The Feminist Papers: From Adams to de Beauvoir,* ed. Alice Rossi, 18–24. Boston: Northeastern University Press.

———. 2006. "Unitarian Universalist Women's Heritage Society." www.uuwhs.org/murray.php.

Nye, Andrea. 1988. *Feminist Theory and the Philosophies of Man.* New York: Routledge.

———. 1994. *Philosophia: The Thought of Rosa Luxemburg, Simone Weil, and Hannah Arendt.* New York: Routledge.

O'Brien, Mary. 1983. *The Politics of Reproduction.* Boston: Routledge and Kegan Paul.

Okin, Susan Moller. 1979. *Women in Western Political Thought.* Princeton: Princeton University Press.

———. 1989. *Justice, Gender, and the Family.* New York: Basic Books.

Olson, Alix. 2004. "womyn before." In *Independence Meal: The Ingredients.* N.p.: New London Press.

O'Neill, Daniel I. 2007. *The Burke-Wollstonecraft Debate: Savagery, Civilization, and Democracy.* University Park: Pennsylvania State University Press.

O'Neill, William L. 1972. Introduction to *Charlotte Perkin's Gilman's "The Home: Its Work and Influence."* Urbana: University of Illinois.

Paris, David. 2004. "The Pillow Book." National Clearinghouse for U.S.-Japan Studies. www.indiana.edu~/japan/LP/LS57.html (accessed April 25, 2005).

Pateman, Carole. 1979. *The Problem of Political Obligation: A Critical Analysis of Liberal Theory.* New York: John Wiley and Sons.

———. 1988. *The Sexual Contract.* Stanford: Stanford University Press.

———. 1989. *The Disorder of Women: Democracy, Feminism, and Political Theory.* Stanford: Stanford University Press.

———. 1998. "Women's Writing, Women's Standing: Theory and Politics in the Early Modern Period." In *Women Writers and the Early Modern British Political Tradition,* ed. Hilda Smith. Cambridge: Cambridge University Press.

Peden, Margaret Sayers, trans. 1987. *A Woman of Genius: The Intellectual Autobiography of Sor Juana Inés de la Cruz,* by Sor Juana Inés de la Cruz. Salisbury, Conn.: Lime Rock Press.

Perry, Ruth. 1986. *The Celebrated Mary Astell: An Early English Feminist.* Chicago: University of Chicago Press.

———. 1990. "Mary Astell and the Feminist Critique of Possessive Individualism." *Eighteenth-Century Studies* 23, no. 4: 444–57.

Peters, R. S. 1962. Introduction to *Leviathan,* by Thomas Hobbes. New York: Macmillan.

Phelan, Shane. 1991. *Identity Politics: Lesbian Feminism and the Limits of Community.* Philadelphia: Temple University Press.

Phillippy, Patricia. 1997. "Establishing Authority: Boccaccio's *De Claris Mulieribus* and Christine de Pizan's *Le livre de la cité des dames.*" In *The Selected Writings of Christine de Pizan,* ed. Renate Blumenfeld-Kosinski. New York: Norton.

Pitkin, Hannah. 1984. *Fortune Is a Woman: Gender and Politics in the Thought of Niccolò Machiavelli.* Berkeley and Los Angeles: University of California Press.

Pizan, Christine de. 1982. *The Book of the City of Ladies.* Trans. Earl Jeffrey Richards. New York: Persea Books.

———. 1997. *The Selected Writings of Christine de Pizan.* Ed. Renate Blumenfeld-Kosinski. New York: Norton.

———. 1999. *The Book of the City of Ladies.* Trans. Rosalind Brown-Grant. New York: Penguin Books.

Plato. 1974. *Plato's "Republic."* Trans. G. M. A. Grube. Indianapolis: Hackett.

Plattel, Martin. 1972. *Utopian and Critical Thinking.* New York: Humanities Press.

Porter, Jene M., ed. 1997. *Classics in Political Philosophy.* 2nd ed. Scarborough, Ontario: Prentice Hall.

Poston, Carol, ed. 1988. *A Vindication of the Rights of Woman.* New York: Norton.

Proceedings, 1850 Women's Rights Convention. http://www.assumption.edu/whw/old/Proceedings%20of%20the%20Woman%27s.htm%20 (accessed June 19, 2006).

Quilligan, Maureen. 1991. *The Allegory of Female Authority: Christine de Pizan's "Cité des Dames."* Ithaca: Cornell University Press.

Rhode, Deborah. 1990. *Theoretical Perspectives on Sexual Difference.* New Haven: Yale University Press.

Rich, Adrienne. 1976. *Of Woman Born: Motherhood as Experience and Institution.* New York: Norton.

———. 1979. *On Lies, Secrets, and Silence: Selected Prose, 1966–1978.* New York: Norton.

Richardson, Marilyn, ed. 1987. *Maria W. Stewart: America's First Black Woman Political Writer: Essays and Speeches.* Bloomington: Indiana University Press.

Rosenthal, Bernard. 1971. Introduction to *Woman in the Nineteenth Century,* by Margaret Fuller. New York: Norton.

Rossi, Alice. 1973. *The Feminist Papers: From Adams to de Beauvoir.* Boston: Northeastern University Press.

Rousseau, Jean-Jacques. 1968. *La Nouvelle Héloise: Julie, or The New Eloise.* Trans. Judith McDowell. University Park: Pennsylvania State University Press.

———. 1979. *Emile; or, On Education.* New York: Basic Books.

Ruddick, Sara. 1980. "Maternal Thinking." *Feminist Studies* 6: 342–67.

———. 1986. "Maternal Thinking." In *Women and Values: Readings in Recent Feminist Philosophy,* ed. Marilyn Pearsall, 340–51. Belmont, Calif.: Wadsworth.

———. 1993. "Maternal Thinking." In *Women and Values: Readings in Recent Feminist Philosophy,* 2nd ed., ed. Marilyn Pearsall, 368–79. Belmont, Calif.: Wadsworth.

Runes, Dagobert D., ed. 1959. *Treasury of World Philosophy.* Paterson, N.J.: Littlefield, Adams.

Russell, Bertrand. 1946. *A History of Western Philosophy.* London: Routledge.

Ryan, Joseph E. 1995. "Prelude to Seneca Falls: An Analysis of Elizabeth Cady Stanton." *New England Journal of History* 52 (Spring): 21–27.

Sandel, Michael. 1982. *Liberalism and the Limits of Justice.* Cambridge: Cambridge University Press.

Sapiro, Virginia. 1992. *A Vindication of Political Virtue: The Political Theory of Mary Wollstonecraft.* Chicago: University of Chicago Press.

Saxonhouse, Arlene W. 1985. *Women in the History of Political Thought: Ancient Greece to Machiavelli.* Westport, Conn.: Praeger.

Schneir, Miriam, ed. 1972. *Feminism: The Essential Historical Writings.* New York: Random House.

Scott, James. 1990. *Domination and the Arts of Resistance: Hidden Transcripts.* New Haven: Yale University Press.

Seaglove, Ilene, and Paul Bob Velick. 2000. *List Your Life: Listing the Risks You Can Take to Enhance Your Life.* New York: MJF Books.

Shockley, Ann. 1989. *Afro-American Women Writers, 1746–1933: An Anthology and Critical Guide.* New Haven, Conn.: Meridian Books.

Shōnagon, Sei. 1991. *The Pillow Book of Sei Shōnagon.* Trans. Ivan Morris. New York: Columbia University Press.

Sigerman, Harriet. 1994. *An Unfinished Battle: American Women, 1848–1865.* Oxford: Oxford University Press.

Simons, Margaret. 1999. *Beauvoir and the Second Sex: Feminism, Race, and the Origins of Existentialism.* Lanham, Md.: Rowman and Littlefield.

Smith, Hilda. 1982. *Reason's Disciples: Seventeenth-Century English Feminists.* Urbana: University of Illinois Press.

Smith, Hilda, and Berenice Carroll, eds. 2000. *Women's Political and Social Thought.* Bloomington: Indiana University Press.

Snitow, Ann. 1990. "A Gender Diary." In *Conflicts in Feminism,* ed. Marianne Hirsch and Evelyn Fox Keller. New York: Routledge.

Spelman, Elizabeth. 1988. *Inessential Woman: Problems of Exclusion in Feminist Thought.* Boston: Beacon Press.

Spencer, Anna Garlin. 1968. *Woman's Share in Social Culture.* [1912.] In *Up from the Pedestal,* ed. Aileen Kraditor, 98–107. Chicago: Quadrangle Books.

Spender, Dale. 1982. *Women of Ideas and What Men Have Done to Them.* London: Routledge.

———, ed. 1983. *Feminist Theorists: Three Centuries of Key Women Thinkers.* New York: Pantheon Books.

Springborg, Patricia. 1995. "Mary Astell (1666–1731), Critic of Locke." *American Political Science Review* 89 (September): 621–33.

————. 1996. Introduction to *Astell: Political Writings*, ed. Patricia Springborg. Cambridge: Cambridge University Press.

————. 2006. *Mary Astell: Theorist of Freedom from Domination*. Cambridge: Cambridge University Press.

Stanton, Elizabeth Cady. 1848. "Address: First Women's Rights Convention." www.libertynet.org/edcivic/stanton.html.

Steinberger, Peter, ed. 2000. *Readings in Classical Political Thought*. Indianapolis: Hackett.

Stephano, Christine de. 1983. "Masculinity as Ideology in Political Theory: Hobbesian Man Considered." *Women's Studies International Forum* 6: 633–44.

Stewart, Maria. 1987. *Maria W. Stewart: America's First Black Woman Political Writer*. [1832.] Bloomington: Indiana University Press.

Stone, Lucy. 1968. "Speech." [1855.] In *Up from the Pedestal*, ed. Aileen Kraditor, 71–73. Chicago: Quadrangle Books.

Stone-Mediatore, Shari. 2000. "Hannah Arendt and Susan Griffin: Toward a Feminist Metahistory." In *Presenting Women Philosophers*, ed. Cecile Tougas and Sara Ebenreck. Philadelphia: Temple University Press.

————. 2007. "Challenging Academic Norms: An Epistemology for Feminist and Multicultural Classrooms." *NWSA Journal* 19 (Fall): 55–78.

Stuurman, Siep. 2000. "The Canon of the History of Political Thought: Its Critique and a Proposed Alternative." *History and Theory* 29, no. 2: 147–66.

Sullivan, Gary. 2003. "Everything That I Have Seen and Felt Is Included; or, *The Pillow Book* as the Ultimate Anti-formalist Gesture." http://garysullivan.blogspot.com/2003_05_25_garysullivan_archive.html (accessed April 22, 2005).

Sunstein, Emily W. 1975. *A Different Face: The Life of Mary Wollstonecraft*. Boston: Little, Brown.

Tanaka, Yuko. 1993. "Ren: The Mechanism of Linking in Japanese Culture." www.lian.com/TANAKA/englishpapers/renhis.htm (accessed April 25, 2005).

Taylor, Charles. 1994. "The Politics of Recognition." In *Multiculturalism*, ed. Amy Gutmann, 25–73. Princeton: Princeton University Press.

Thiele, Beverly. 1986. "Vanishing Acts in Social and Political Thought: Tricks of the Trade." In *Feminist Challenges: Social and Political Theory*, ed. Carole Pateman and Elizabeth Gross. Boston: Northeastern University Press.

Thiele, Leslie Paul. 2003. *Thinking Politics: Perspectives in Ancient, Modern, and Postmodern Political Theory*. 2nd ed. New York: Chatham House.

Thomas, M. Carey. 1968. "Present Tendencies in Women's College and University Education." In *Up From the Pedestal: Selected Writings in the History of American Feminism*, ed. Aileen S. Kraditor. Chicago: Quadrangle Books.

Tinder, Glenn. 2003. *Political Thinking: The Perennial Questions*. New York: Longman.

Todd, Janet. 1989. Introduction to *A Wollstonecraft Anthology*. New York: Columbia University Press.

Tomalin, Claire. 1974. *The Life and Death of Mary Wollstonecraft*. New York: Harcourt Brace Jovanovich.

Tong, Rosemarie. 1989. *Feminist Thought*. Boulder, Colo.: Westview.

Tougas, Cecile T., and Sara Ebenreck, eds. 2000. *Presenting Women Philosophers*. Philadelphia: Temple University Press.

Tronto, Joan. 1993. *Moral Boundaries: A Political Argument for an Ethic of Care*. New York: Routledge.

Truth, Sojourner. 1997. "Ain't I a Woman?" http://www.fordham.edu/halsall/mod/sotruth-woman.html (accessed November 9, 2008).

————. 2007. "Ain't I a Woman?" [1851.] http://afroamhistory.about.com/library/blsojourner_truth_index.htm (accessed December 26, 2007).

Tuana, Nancy. 1992. *Woman and the History of Philosophy.* New York: Paragon House.

————. 2004. "The Forgetting of Gender." In *Teaching New Histories of Philosophy: Proceedings of a Conference,* ed. J. B. Schneewind, 61–85. Princeton: University Center for Human Values.

Tulloch, Gail. 1989. *Mill and Sexual Equality.* London: Harvester Wheatsheaf.

Von Fritz, Kurt, and Ernst Kapp. 1950. *Aristotle's "Constitution of Athens" and Related Texts.* New York: Hafner.

Washburn. 2001. "Sei Shōnagon." www.washburn.edu/reference/bridge24/Shonagon.html (accessed September 24, 2004).

Washington, Mary Helen. 1988. Introduction to *A Voice from the South.* New York: Oxford University Press.

Waters, Kristin. 2000. *Women and Men Political Theorists: Enlightened Conversations.* Oxford: Basil Blackwell.

Weiss, Penny A. 1993. *Gendered Community: Rousseau, Sex, and Politics.* New York: New York University Press.

————. 1996. "The Gendered Fate of Political Theorists." In *Feminist Interpretations of Mary Wollstonecraft,* ed. Maria Falco. University Park: Pennsylvania State University Press.

————. 1998. *Conversations with Feminism: Political Theory and Practice.* Lanham, Md.: Rowman and Littlefield.

Weiss, Penny A., and Marilyn Friedman, eds. 1995. *Feminism and Community.* Philadelphia: Temple University Press.

Weiss, Penny A., and Loretta Kensinger, eds. 2007. *Feminist Interpretations of Emma Goldman.* University Park: Pennsylvania State University Press.

Wellman, Judith. 2004. *The Road to Seneca Falls: Elizabeth Cady Stanton and the First Woman's Rights Convention.* Urbana: University of Illinois.

Wikipedia. 2005. "Sei Shōnagon." http://en.wikipedia.org/wiki/Sei_Shonagon (accessed April 22, 2005).

————. 2006. "United States Declaration of Independence." http://en.wikipedia.org/wiki/United_States_Declaration_of_Independence.

Willard, Emma. 1968. "Address to the Public." In *Up From the Pedestal: Selected Writings in the History of American Feminism,* ed. Aileen S. Kraditor, 79–82. Chicago: Quadrangle Books.

Wills, Garry. 1978. *Inventing America: Jefferson's Declaration of Independence.* New York: Vintage Books.

Witt, Charlotte. 2003. "How Feminism is Re-writing the Philosophical Canon." www.uh.edu/~cfreelan/SWIP/Witt.html (accessed March 10, 2008).

Wollstonecraft, Mary. 1972. *Original Stories from Real Life: With Conversations, Calculated to Regulate the Affections, and Form the Mind to Truth and Goodness.* [1791.] London: Folcraft Library Editions.

————. 1975. *Maria; or, The Wrongs of Woman.* New York: Norton.

————. 1988. *A Vindication of the Rights of Woman.* 2nd ed. Ed. Carol H. Poston. New York: Norton.

————. 1995a. *Thoughts on the Education of Daughters.* [1787.] Bristol: Thoemmes Press.

————. 1995b. *A Vindication of the Rights of Men.* In *A Vindication of the Rights of Men with A Vindication of the Rights of Women and Hints,* ed. Sylvana Tomaselli. Cambridge: Cambridge University Press.

———. 1997. *A Wollstonecraft Anthology.* Ed. Janet Todd. Bloomington: Indiana University Press.

Woolf, Virginia. 1938. *Three Guineas.* New York: Harcourt Brace Jovanovich.

Wright, Frances. 1973. "Of Free Inquiry." [1829.] In *The Feminist Papers: From Adams to Beauvoir,* ed. Alice Rossi, 108–17. Boston: Northeastern University Press.

INDEX

CPSIA information can be obtained at www.ICGtesting.com
Printed in the USA
LVOW040142050113

314348LV00002B/4/P